Lewis Foreman Day

Windows

A Book about stained and painted Glass

Lewis Foreman Day

Windows
A Book about stained and painted Glass

ISBN/EAN: 9783743310810

Manufactured in Europe, USA, Canada, Australia, Japa

Cover: Foto ©Thomas Meinert / pixelio.de

Manufactured and distributed by brebook publishing software (www.brebook.com)

Lewis Foreman Day

Windows

by LEWIS F. DAY
author of Nature
in Ornament &
other Text-books
of Design.

1897 LONDON
B.T. BATSFORD 94 High Holborn, W.C.

TO THOSE WHO KNOW NOTHING OF STAINED GLASS; TO THOSE WHO KNOW SOMETHING, AND WANT TO KNOW MORE; TO THOSE WHO KNOW ALL ABOUT IT, AND YET CARE TO KNOW WHAT ANOTHER MAY HAVE TO SAY UPON THE SUBJECT:—I DEDICATE THIS BOOK.

PREFACE.

A STAINED glass window is itself the best possible illustration of the difference it makes whether we look at a thing from this side or from that. Gœthe used this particular image in one of his little parables, comparing poems to painted windows, dark and dull from the market-place, bright with colour and alive with meaning only when we have crossed the threshold of the church.

I may claim to have entered the sanctuary, and not irreverently. My earliest training in design was in the workshops of artists in stained glass. For many years I worked exclusively at glass design, and for over a quarter of a century I have spent great part of my leisure in hunting glass all Europe over.

This book has grown out of my experience. It makes no claim to learnedness. It tells only what the windows have told me, or what I understood them to say. I have gone to glass to get pleasure out of it, to learn something from it, to find out the way it was done, and why it was done so, and what might yet perhaps be done. Anything apart from that did not so much interest me. Those, therefore, who desire minuter and more precise historic information must consult the works of Winston, Mr. Westlake, and the many continental authorities, with whose learned writings this more practical, and, in a sense, popular, volume does not enter into any sort of competition.

My point of view is that of art and workmanship, or, more precisely speaking, workmanship and art, workmanship being naturally the beginning and root of art. We are workmen first and artists afterwards—perhaps.

What I have tried to do is this: In the first place (Book I.),

I set out to trace the course of *workmanship*, to follow the technique of the workman from the twelfth century to the seventeenth, from mosaic to painting, from archaism to pictorial accomplishment ; and to indicate at what cost of perhaps more decorative qualities the later masterpieces of glass painting were bought.

In the second place (Book II.), I have endeavoured to show the course of *design* in glass, from the earliest Mediæval window to the latest glass picture of the Renaissance.

Finally (Book III.), I have set apart for separate discussion questions not in the direct line either of design or workmanship, or which, if taken by the way, would have hindered the narrative and confused the issue.

The rather lengthy chapter on "*Style*" is addressed to that large number of persons who, knowing as yet nothing about the subject, may want *data* by which to form some idea as to the period of a window when they see it : the postscript more nearly concerns the designer and the worker in glass.

In all this I have tried to put personality as much as possible aside, and to tell my story faithfully and without conscious bias. But I make no claim to impartiality, as the judge upon the bench understands it. We take up art or law according to our temperament. I can pretend to judge only as one interested, to be impartial only as an artist may.

LEWIS F. DAY.

13, MECKLENBURGH SQUARE, LONDON.
January 29th, 1897.

NOTE IN REFERENCE TO ILLUSTRATIONS.

Theoretically the illustrations to a book about windows should be in colour. Practically coloured illustrations of stained glass are out of the question, as all who appreciate its quality well know. It may be possible, although it has hardly proved so as yet, to print adequate representations of coloured windows, but only at a cost which would defeat the end here in view.

The EFFECT of glass is best suggested by process renderings of photographs from actual windows or from very careful water-colour drawings, such as those very kindly placed at my disposal by Mr. T. M. Rooke (pages 128, 159, 337) and Mr. John R. Clayton (pages 51, 74, 98, 186, 207, 252, 286, 304, 342), an artist whose studio has been the nursery of a whole generation of glass designers.

Details of DESIGN are often better seen in the reproductions of tracings or slight pen-drawings, little more than diagrams it may be, but done to illustrate a point. That is the intention throughout, to illustrate what is said, not simply to beautify the book.

The direction of the pen-lines gives, wherever it was possible, a key to the colour scheme. Red, that is to say, is represented by vertical lines, blue by horizontal, yellow by dots, and so on, according to heraldic custom.

TABLE OF CONTENTS.

BOOK I.

THE COURSE OF CRAFTSMANSHIP.

CHAP.		PAGE
I.	THE BEGINNINGS OF GLASS	1
II.	THE MAKING OF A WINDOW	5
III.	GLAZING	15
IV.	EARLY MOSAIC WINDOWS	32
V.	PAINTED MOSAIC	43
VI.	GLASS PAINTING (MEDIÆVAL)	59
VII.	GLASS PAINTING (RENAISSANCE)	67
VIII.	ENAMEL PAINTING	77
IX.	THE NEEDLE-POINT IN GLASS PAINTING	87
X.	THE RESOURCES OF THE GLASS WORKER (A RECAPITULATION)	95

BOOK II.

THE COURSE OF DESIGN.

XI.	THE DESIGN OF EARLY GLASS	111
XII.	MEDALLION WINDOWS	123
XIII.	EARLY GRISAILLE	137
XIV.	WINDOWS OF MANY LIGHTS	151
XV.	MIDDLE GOTHIC DETAIL	162
XVI.	LATE GOTHIC WINDOWS	178
XVII.	SIXTEENTH CENTURY WINDOWS	201
XVIII.	LATER RENAISSANCE WINDOWS	220
XIX.	PICTURE WINDOWS	236
XX.	LANDSCAPE IN GLASS	251
XXI.	ITALIAN GLASS	260

CONTENTS.

Chap.		Page
XXII.	Tracery Lights and Rose Windows	272
XXIII.	Quarry Windows	283
XXIV.	Domestic Glass	296
XXV.	The Use of the Canopy	311
XXVI.	A Plea for Ornament	317

BOOK III.

BY THE WAY.

XXVII.	The Characteristics of Style	322
XXVIII.	Style in Modern Glass (a Postscript)	354
XXIX.	Jesse Windows, and other Exceptions in Design	360
XXX.	Story Windows	371
XXXI.	How to see Windows	380
XXXII.	Windows worth Seeing	385
XXXIII.	A Word on Restoration	404

WINDOWS, A BOOK ABOUT STAINED GLASS

BOOK I.

CHAPTER I.

THE BEGINNINGS OF GLASS.

THE point of view from which the subject of stained glass is approached in these chapters relieves me, happily, from the very difficult task of determining the date or the whereabouts of the remote origin of coloured windows, and the still remoter beginnings of glass itself. The briefest summary of scarcely disputable facts bearing upon the evolution of the art of window making, is here enough. We need not vex our minds with speculation.

White glass (and that of extreme purity) would seem to have been known to the Chinese as long ago as 2300 B.C., for they were then already using astronomical instruments, of which the lenses were presumably of glass. Of coloured glass there is yet earlier record. Egyptologists tell us that at least five if not six thousand years ago the Egyptians made jewels of glass. Indeed, it is more than probable that this was the earliest use to which stained glass was put, and that the very *raison d'être* of glass making was a species of forgery. In some of the most ancient tombs have been found scarabs of glass in deliberate imitation of rubies and emeralds, sapphires and other precious stones. The glass beads found broadcast in three quarters of the globe were quite possibly passed off by Phœnician traders upon the confiding barbarian as jewels of great price. At all events, glass beads, according to Sir John Lubbock, were in use in the bronze age; and, if we may trust the evidence of etymology, "bedes" are perhaps as ancient as praying.

Apart from trickery and fraud, to imitate seems to be a foible of humanity. The Greeks and their Roman successors made glass in imitation of agate and onyx and all kinds of precious marbles. They devised also coloured glass coated with white glass, which could be cut cameo fashion—a kind of glass much used, though in a different way, in later Mediæval windows.

The Venetians carried further the pretty Greek invention of embedding vitreous threads of milky white or colour in clear glass, the most beautiful form of which is that known as *latticelli*, or *reticelli* (reticulated or lace glass), from the elaborate twisting and interlacing of the threads; but nothing certain seems to be known about Venetian glass until the end of the eleventh century, although by the thirteenth the neighbouring island of Murano was famous for its production. The Venetians found a new stone to imitate, aventurine, and they imitated it marvellously.

So far, however, glass was used in the first instance for jewellery, and in the second for vessels of various kinds. Its use in architecture was confined mainly to mosaic, originally, no doubt, to supply the place of brighter tints not forthcoming in marble.

Of the use of glass in windows there is not very ancient mention. The climate of Greece or Egypt, and the way of life there, gave scant occasion for it. But at Herculaneum and Pompeii, there have been found fair sized slabs of window glass, not of very perfect manufacture, apparently cast, and probably at no time very translucent. Remains also of what was presumably window glass have been found among the ruins of Roman villas in England. In the basilicas of Christian Rome the arched window openings were sometimes filled with slabs of marble, in which were piercings to receive glass (which may or may not have been coloured), foreshadowing, so to speak, the plate tracery of Early Gothic builders. According to M. Lévy, the windows of Early Mediæval Flemish churches were often filled in this Roman way with plaques of stone pierced with circular openings to receive glass.

Another Roman practice was to set panes of glass in bronze or copper framing, and even in lead. Here we have the beginning of the practice identified with Mediæval glaziers.

There is no reason to suppose that the ancients practised glass painting as we understand it. Discs of Greek glass have been found which are indeed painted, but not (I imagine) with colour fused with the material; and certainly these were not used for windows.

The very early Christians were not in a position to indulge in, or even to desire, luxuries such as stained glass windows, but St. Jerome and St. Chrysostom make allusion to them. It is pretty certain that these must have been simple mosaics in stained glass, unpainted: one reads that between the lines of the records that have come down to us.

Stained and painted glass, such as we find in the earliest existing Mediæval windows, may possibly date back to the reign of Charlemagne (800), but it may safely be said not to occur earlier than the Holy Roman Empire. A couple of hundred years later mention of it begins to occur rather frequently in Church records; and there is one particular account of the furnishing of the chapel of the first Benedictine Monastery at Monte Cassino with a whole series of windows in 1066—which fixes the date of the Norman Conquest as a period at which stained glass windows can no longer have been uncommon. The Cistercian interdict, restricting the order to the use of white glass (1134), argues something like ecclesiastical over-indulgence in rich windows before the middle of the next century.

Fragments, more or less plentiful, of the very earliest glass may still remain embedded in windows of a later period (the material was too precious not to have been carefully preserved); but archæologists appear to be agreed that no complete window of the ninth or tenth century has been preserved, and that even of the eleventh there is nothing that can quite certainly be identified. After that doctors begin to differ. But the general consensus of opinion is, that there is comparatively little that can be incontrovertibly set down even to the twelfth century. The great mass of Early Gothic Glass belongs indubitably to the thirteenth century; and when one speaks of Early Glass it is usually thirteenth century work which is meant.

The remote origin of glass, then, remains for ever lost in the mist of legendary days. There is even a fable to the effect that it dates from the building of the Tower of Babel, when God's fire from heaven vitrified the bricks employed by its too presumptuous builders.

Coloured glass comes to us from the East; that much it is safe to conclude. From ancient Egypt, probably, the art of the glass-worker found its way to Phœnicia, thence to Greece and Rome, and so to Byzantium, Venice, and eventually France, where stained glass windows, as we know them, first occur.

It is probably to the French that Europe owes the introduction of coloured windows, a colony of Venetian glass-workers having, they say, settled at Limoges in the year 979.

Some of the earliest French glass is to be found at Chartres, Le-Mans, Angers, Reims, and Châlons-sûr-Marne; and at the *Musée des Arts Décoratifs*, at Paris, there are some fragments of twelfth century work which may be more conveniently examined than the work *in situ*. The oldest to which one can assign a definite date is that at St. Denis (1108) but its value is almost nullified by expert restoration.

In Germany the oldest date is ascribed to some small windows at Augsburg, executed, it is said, by the monks of Tegernsee about the year 1000. There is also a certain amount of twelfth century work incorporated in the later windows at Strasbourg. The oldest remains of glass in England are, in all probability, certain fragments in the nave of York Minster. The more important windows at Canterbury, Salisbury, and Lincoln are of the thirteenth century.

CHAPTER II.

THE MAKING OF A WINDOW.

SINCE it is proposed to approach the subject of stained glass in the first place from the workmanlike and artistic, rather than the historical or antiquarian, point of view, it may be as well to begin by explaining precisely what a stained glass window is.

It is usual to confound "stained" with "painted" glass. Literally speaking, these are two quite distinct things. Stained glass is glass which is coloured, as the phrase goes, " in the pot;" that is to say, there is mixed with the molten white glass a metallic oxide which stains it green, yellow, blue, purple, and so on, as the case may be; for which reason this self-tinted glass is called "pot-metal." This is a term which will recur again and again. Once for all, "pot-metal" is glass in which the colour is *in* the glass and not painted *upon* it.

It goes without explanation that, each separate sheet of pot-metal glass being all of one colour, a vari-coloured window can only be produced in it by breaking up the sheets and putting them together in the form of a mosaic: in fact, that is how the earliest windows were executed, and they go by the name of mosaic glass. The glass is, however, not broken up into tesseræ, but shaped according to the forms of the design. In short, those portions of it which are white have to be cut out of a sheet of white glass, those which are blue out of a sheet of blue glass, those which are yellow out of a sheet of yellow, and so on; and it is these pieces of variously tinted glass, bound together by strips of lead, just as the tesseræ of a pavement or wall picture are held in place by cement, which constitute a stained glass window. The artist is as yet not concerned in painting, but in glazing—that is to say, putting together little bits of glass, just as an inlayer does, or as a mosaic worker puts together pieces of wood, or marble, or burnt clay, or even opaque glass.

There is illustrated opposite a piece of Old Burmese incrusted decoration, a mosaic of white and coloured glass bound together by strips of metal, which, were it but clear instead of silvered at the back, would be precisely the same thing as an early mosaic window, even to the completion of the face by means of paint—of which more presently. In painted glass, on the other hand, the colour is not in the glass but upon it, more or less firmly attached to it by the action of the fire. A metallic colour which has some affinity with glass, or which is ground up with finely powdered glass, is used as a pigment, precisely as ceramic colours are used in pottery painting. The painted glass is then put into a kiln and heated to the temperature at which it is on the point of melting, whilst the colour actually does melt into it. By this means it is possible to paint a coloured picture upon a single sheet of white glass, as has been proved at Sèvres.

Strictly speaking, then, stained and painted glass are the very opposite one to the other. But in practice the two processes of glazing and painting were never kept apart. The very earliest glass was no doubt pure mosaic. It was only in our own day that the achievement (scientific rather than artistic) of a painted window of any size, independent of glazier's work, was possible. Painting was at first always subsidiary to glazier's work; after that, for a time, glazier and painter worked hand in hand upon equal terms; eventually the painter took precedence, and the glazier became ever more and more subservient to him. But from the twelfth to the seventeenth century there is little of what we call, rather loosely, sometimes "stained" and sometimes "painted" glass, in which there is not both staining and painting—that is to say, stained glass is used, and there is painting upon it. The difference is that in the earlier work the painting is only used to help out the stained glass, and in the later the stained glass is introduced to help the painting.

That amounts, it may be thought, to much the same thing; and there does come a point where staining and painting fulfil each such an important part in the window that it is difficult to say which is the predominating partner in the concern. For the most part, however, there is no manner of doubt as to which practice was uppermost in the designer's mind, as to the idea with which he set out, painting or glazing; and it makes all the

1. INCRUSTED GLASS MOSAIC, BURMESE (B. M.).

difference in the work—the difference, for example, between a window of the thirteenth century and one of the sixteenth, a difference about which a child could scarcely make a mistake, once it had been pointed out to him.

Here perhaps it will be as well to describe, once for all, the making of a mosaic window, and the part taken in it by the glazier and the painter respectively. It will be easier then to discriminate between the two processes employed, and to discuss them each in relation to the other.

The actual construction of an early window is very much like the putting together of a puzzle. The puzzle of our childhood usually took the form of a map. It has occurred to me, therefore, to show how an artist working strictly after the manner of the thirteenth century—the period, that is to say, when painting was subsidiary to glazing—would set about putting into glass a map of modern Italy. In the first place, he would draw his map to the size required. This he would do with the utmost precision, firmly marking upon the paper (the mediæval artist would have drawn directly on his wooden bench) the boundary line of each separate patch of colour in his design. Then, according to the colour each separate province or division was to be, he would take a separate sheet of "pot-metal" and lay it over the drawing, so as to be able to trace upon the glass itself the outline of such province or division. That done, he would proceed to cut out or shape the various pieces of glass to the given forms. In the case of a simple and compact province, such as Rome, Tuscany, Umbria (overleaf), that would be easy enough. On the other hand, a more irregular shape, say the province of Naples, with its promontories, would present considerable difficulties—difficulties practically insuperable by the early glazier, to whom the diamond as a cutting instrument was unknown, and whose appliances for shaping were of the rudest and most rudimentary.

If with the point of a red-hot iron you describe upon a sheet of glass a line, and then, taking the material between your two hands, proceed to snap it across, the fracture will take approximately the direction of the line thus drawn. That is how the thirteenth century glazier went to work, subsequently with a notched iron instrument, or "grozing iron" as it was called, laboriously chipping away the edges until he had reduced each piece of glass to the precise shape he wanted.

It will be seen at once that the simpler the line and the easier its sweep the more likely the glass would be to break clean to the line, whereas in the case of a jagged or irregular line there would always be great danger that at any one sharp turn in it the fracture would take that convenient opportunity of going in the way it should not. For example, the south coast of Italy would be dangerous. You might draw the line of the sole of the foot, but when it came to breaking the glass the high heel would be sure to snap off (there is a little nick there designed as if for the purpose of bringing about that catastrophe), and similarly that over-delicate instep would certainly not bear the strain put upon it, and would be bound to give way. It should be mentioned that even were such pieces once safely cut (which would nowadays be possible) the glass would surely crack at those points the first time there was any pressure of wind upon the window, and so the prudent man would still forestall that event by designing his glass as it could conveniently be cut, without attempting any *tour de force*, and strengthening it at the weak points with a line of lead, as has been done in the glass map opposite. There is a jutting promontory on the coast of Africa, which, even if safely cut, would be sure to break sooner or later at the point indicated by the dotted line.

The scale of execution would determine whether each or any province could be cut out of a single sheet of glass, but the lines of latitude and longitude would give an opportunity of using often three or four pieces of glass to a province without introducing lines which formed no part of the design. That, however, would be contrary to early usage, which was never to make use of the leads as independent lines, but only as boundaries between two colours. There is a reason for this reticence. You will see that in the surface of the sea, where the latitudinal and longitudinal lines come in most usefully, it is necessary to use also other leads, which mean nothing but that a joint is there desirable. These constructional leads, when they merely break up a background, are quite unobjectionable—they even give an opportunity of getting variety in the colour of the ground—but when some of the leads are meant to assert themselves as drawing lines and some are not, the result is inevitably confused.

All that the glass gives us in our mosaic map is the local

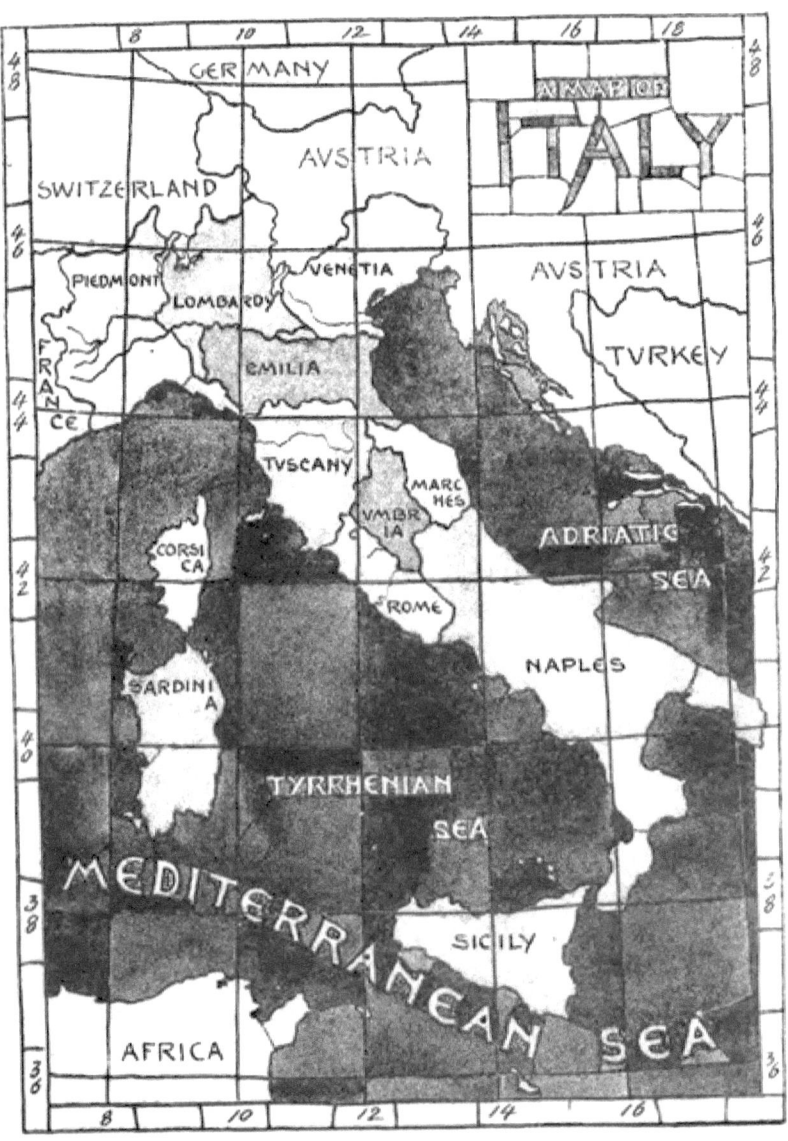

2. THE WAY A WINDOW IS GLAZED

colour of sea and land—the sea, let us say, dark blue, the countries, provinces, and islands each of its own distinctive tint. When it comes to giving their names, it would be possible indeed on a very large scale to cut the letters out of glass of darker colour, and glaze them in as shown in the title word "Italy." That would involve, as will be seen, a network of connecting lead lines. On a much smaller scale there would be nothing for it but to have recourse to the supplementary process, and paint them. The words Germany, Austria, Turkey, Naples, Sicily, and the rest would have to be simply painted in opaque colour upon the translucent glass.

But, once we have begun to use paint, there are intermediate ways between these two methods of inscription, either of which would be adopted according to the scale of the lettering. These are shown in the names of the seas. In the word "Mediterranean" each separate letter would be cut out of a piece of glass, corresponding as nearly as possible to its general outline or circumference, and its shape would be made perfect by "painting out"—that is to say, by obscuring with solid pigment that part of the glass (indicated by dots in the drawing) which was meant to retire into the background. Presuming this wording to be in a light colour and the background darkish, this amount of painting would, as a matter of fact, be quite lost in the dark colour. In the lesser descriptions "Tyrrhenian" and "Adriatic Sea," each separate word, instead of each letter, would be cut out of one piece of glass (or perhaps two in the longer words), and the background would be painted out as already described.

Paint would further be used to indicate the rivers, the mountains, the towns, or any other detail it was necessary to give, as well as to mark such indentations in the coastline as were too minute to be followed by the thick lead. As a matter of practice, it is usual to paint a marginal line of opaque colour round the glass representing just a little more than that portion eventually to be covered by the flange of the lead, so as to make sure that that will not by any chance cut off from view what may be an important feature in the design.

For example, the mere projection of a lead which too nearly approached the delicate profile of a small face might easily destroy its outline. The glazier's lead, it should be explained, is a wire of about a quarter of an inch diameter, deeply grooved on two sides for the insertion of the glass. Imagine the surfaces exposed to view on each face of the window to be flattened, and you have a section very much like the letter **H**, the uprights representing the flanges, and the cross-bar the "core," which holds them together and supports the glass mosaic.

The process of painting employed so far is of the simplest; it consists merely in obscuring the glass with solid paint. This is laid on with a long-haired pencil or "tracing brush." The paint itself may be mixed with oil or gum and water, or any medium which will temporarily attach it to the glass and disappear in the kiln; for the real fixing of the paint is done solely by the action of the fire. The pigment employed consists, that is to say, of per-oxides of iron and manganese ground up with a sufficient amount of powdered flint-glass or some equivalent silicate, which by the action of the fire is fused with the glass (reduced to very nearly red heat), and becomes practically part and parcel of it.

Whenever a glass painter speaks of painted glass that is what he means—viz., that the colour is thus indelibly burnt in. After the middle of the sixteenth century various metallic oxides were used to produce various more or less transparent pigments (enamel colours as they are called to distinguish them from the pot-metal colours), but in the thirteenth century transparent enamel colours were as yet unknown to the glass painter, and he confined himself to the solid deep brown pigment already spoken of—an enamel also, strictly speaking, but by no means to be confounded with the enamel colours of later centuries. Those were colours used for colour's sake; this is simply an opaque substance used solely on account of its capacity to stop out so much of the colour of pot-metal glass as may be necessary in order to define form and give the drawing of detail; and in effect the brown, when seen against the light, does not tell as colour at all but merely as so much blackness. The only colour in the window is the colour of the various component pieces of glass. Thus in the case of an early figure (page 33) the face would be cut out of a sheet of pinkish glass and the features painted upon it in brown lines; each garment would be cut out of the tint it was meant to be, and the folds of the drapery outlined upon the pot-metal. In like manner a tree would be cut out of green glass, its stem perhaps out of brown, and only the forms of the leaves, and their veining, if any, would be traced in paint. In the execution of the map there is no occasion for further painting than this simplest and fittest kind of work, little more than the glazier would himself have done had his means allowed him. And in the very earliest glass the painter was almost as sparing of paint as this: he did, however—it was inevitable that he should—use lines, whether in drawing the features of a face or the folds of drapery, which were not quite solid, and which consequently only deepened the colour of the pot-metal, and did not quite obscure it: he went so far even as to pass a smear of still thinner colour, a half tint or less, over portions of the glass which he wished to lower in tone. He began, in fact, however tentatively, to introduce shading. Happily he was careful always to use it only as a softening influence in his design, and never to sacrifice to it anything of the intrinsic beauty and briiliancy of his glass.

The glass duly painted and burnt, the puzzle would be put together again on the bench, and bands of lead, grooved at each side to admit and hold the glass, would be inserted between the two pieces. These would be soldered together at the joints where two leads met; a putty-like composition or "cement" would be rubbed into the interstices between lead and glass to stiffen it, and make it air- and water-tight: and, that done, the window was finished.

It would only remain (what would in practice have been done before cementing) to solder to the leads at intervals sundry loose ends of copper-wire, eventually to be twisted round the iron saddle bars let into the stone framework of the window to support it; it would then be ready to be fixed in its place.

In contradistinction to the mosaic method of execution adopted by the thirteenth century glazier, a glass painter of the eighteenth century, and perhaps of the seventeenth, would, even though there were no necessity for longitudinal and latitudinal lines, cut up his window into oblong pieces of convenient size, only, of course, parallel and at right angles to one another.

The sea he might or might not glaze in blue glass: here and there perhaps, but not necessarily at all, an occasional province might be leaded in with a piece of pot-metal; but for the most part he would use panes of white glass, and rely for the colour of the provinces upon enamel. He would have no need to separate his enamel colours by a line of lead, and where he wanted a dividing line he would just paint it in opaque brown. This method of glass painting forms an altogether separate division of the subject, not yet under discussion. It is referred to here only by way of contrast, and to emphasise the fact that, though we are in the habit of using the term stained glass rather loosely—though a stained glass window is almost invariably helped out to some extent by painting (unless it be what is technically known as "leaded glass" or "plain glazing"), and though a painted window is seldom altogether innocent of glass that is stained—there are, as a matter of fact, two methods of producing coloured windows, the mosaic and the enamelled; and that however customary it may be to eke out either method by the other more or less, windows divide themselves into two broad divisions, according as it is pot-metal or enamel upon which the artist relies for his effect.

Between these two widely different ideals there are all manners and all degrees of compromise, and methods were employed which, to describe at this point, would only complicate matters. It will be my purpose presently to describe in detail the steps by which mere glazing developed into painted glass, and how painting came to supersede glazing; to show in how far painting was a help to the glazier, and in how far it was to his hurt; to describe, in short, the progress of the glass painter's art, to better and to worse; and to distinguish, as far as may be, the principles which govern or should govern it.

3. ANCIENT ARAB WINDOW.

CHAPTER III.

GLAZING.

THE art of the glass painter was at first only the art of the glazier. To say that may seem like self-contradiction. But it is not so. On the contrary, it is almost literally the truth; and it is difficult to find words which would more vividly express the actual fact.

We are accustomed to think of a painter as using pigment always in some liquid form, and applying it to wood or plaster, canvas or paper, with a brush. Should he lay it on with a palette knife, as he sometimes does, it is painting still. If he could by any possibility put together his colours in mid-air without the aid of paper, canvas, or other solid substance, it would still be painting. This is very much what the worker in stained glass, by the help of strips of intervening lead, practically succeeded in doing.

As a painter places side by side dabs of paint, so the glazier put side by side little pieces of coloured glass. (Glass, you see, was the medium in which his colour was fixed, just as oil, varnish, wax, or gum is the vehicle in which the painter's pigment is ordinarily held in suspension.) He could execute in this way upon the bench or the sloped easel quite an elaborate pattern in coloured glass; and although, in order to hold the parts together in a window frame, he had perforce to resort to some sort of binding, in lead or what not, he may still reasonably be said, if not actually to have painted in glass, at all events to have worked in it. In fact, until about the twelfth century, there were no glass painters, but only glaziers. Nay, more, it is to glaziers that we owe the glory of the thirteenth century windows, in which, be it remembered, each separate touch of colour is represented by a separate piece of glass, and each separate piece of glass is bounded by a framework of lead connecting it with the neighbouring pieces, whilst the detail added by the painter goes for not very much.

No strictly defined, nor indeed any approximate, date

4. Arab Window Lattice, Geometric.

can safely be given at which the art of the glass-worker sprang into existence. Arts do not spring into existence; they grow, developing themselves in most cases very slowly. The art of working in stained glass can only have been the result of a species of evolution. The germ of it lay in the circumstance that glass was originally made in comparatively small pieces (there were no large sheets of glass a thousand years or more ago), and so it was necessary, in order to glaze any but the smallest window opening, that these small pieces should be in some way cemented together. It followed naturally, in days when art was a matter of every-day concern, the common flower of wayside craftsmanship, that the idea of putting these pieces together in more or less ornamental fashion, should occur to the workman, since they must be put together somehow; and so, almost as a matter of course, would be developed the mosaic of transparent glass, which was undoubtedly the form stained glass windows first took.

It has been suggested that in some of the earliest windows the glazing is meant to take the form of tesserae; but the examples instanced in support of that idea afford very little ground for supposing any such intention on the part of the first glass-workers. It may more reasonably be presumed that any resemblance there may be between early glass and earlier wall mosaic comes of working in the same way; like methods inevitably lead to like results.

It is by no means certain, even, that the first glaziers were directly inspired by mosaic, whether of marble or of opaque glass. They were probably much more immediately influenced by the work of the enameller.

That may appear at the first mention strange, considering what has been said about the absolute divergence between mosaic and enamelled glass. But it must be remembered that enamelling itself among the Lombard Franks, the Merovingians, and the Anglo-Saxons, was a very different thing from what the Limousin made it in the sixteenth century. It was, in fact, a quite different operation, the only point in common between the two being that they were executed in vitreous colour upon a metal ground. The enamel referred to as having probably influenced the early glazier is of the severer kinds familiar in Byzantine work, and known as *champlevé* and *cloisonné*. In the one, you know, the design is scooped out of the metal ground, in the other its outline is bent in flat wire and soldered to the ground. In either case the resulting cells are filled with coloured paste, which, under the action of the fire, vitrifies and becomes embodied with the metal. In *champlevé* enamel naturally the metal ground is usually a distinguishing feature. In *cloisonné* the ground as well as the pattern is, of course, in enamel; but in either case the outlines, and, indeed, all drawing lines, are in metal. In *cloisonné* enamel the metal "*cloisons*," as they are called, fulfil precisely the function of the leads in glass windows; and it would have been more convenient to have left altogether out of account the sister process, were it not that, in the painting of quite early glass, the strokes with which the lines of the drapery and suchlike are rendered, bear quite unmistakable likeness to the convention of the Byzantine worker in *champlevé*. For that matter, one sees also in very early altar-pieces painted on wood, where gold is used for marking the folds of drapery, the very obvious inspiration of Byzantine enamel—but that is rather by the way.

5. ARAB LATTICE, GEOMETRIC.

The popular idea of an early window is that of a picture, or series of pictures, very imperfectly rendered. It may much more justly be likened to a magnified plaque of Byzantine enamel with the light shining through it. The Byzantine craftsman, or his descendants, at all events, did produce, in addition to the ordinary opaque enamel, a translucent kind, in imitation presumably of precious stones; and it might very well be that it was from thence the glazier first derived the idea of coloured windows. Quite certainly that was nearer to his thoughts than any form of painting, as we understand painting nowadays; and, what is more, had he aimed deliberately at the effect of enamel (as practised in his day), he could not have got much nearer to it. His proceeding was almost identical with that of the enamel worker. In place of vitreous pastes he used glass itself; in place of brass, lead; and, for supplementary detail, in place of engraved lines, lines traced in paint. Side by side with the early European window glazing, and most likely before it, there was practised in the East a form of stained glass window building of which no mention has yet been made. In the East, also, windows were from an early date built up of little pieces of coloured glass; but the Mohammedan law forbidding all attempt at pictorial representation of animate things, there was no temptation to employ painting; the glazier could do all he wanted without it. His plan was to pierce small openings in large slabs of stone, and in the piercings to set numerous little jewels of coloured glass. The Romans, by the way, appear also to have sometimes filled window spaces with slabs of marble framing discs of coloured glass, but these were comparatively wide apart, more like separate window-lets, each glazed with its small sheet of coloured glass. The Oriental windows, on the contrary, were most elaborately designed, the piercings taking the form of intricate patterns, geometric or floral. Sometimes the design would include an inscription ingeniously turned to ornamental use after the manner of the Moorish decorators of the Alhambra (page 15). A further development of the Oriental idea was to imbed the glass in plaster, a process easy enough before the plaster had set hard. This kind of thing is common enough in Cairo to this day, and specimens of it are to be found at the South Kensington Museum.

6. ARAB LATTICE, FLORAL.

M. Vogüé illustrates in his book, *La Syrie Centrale*, an important series of windows in the Mosque of Omar (Temple of Jerusalem), erected in 1528, by Sultan Soliman. The plaster, says M. Vogüé, was strengthened by ribs of iron and rods of cane imbedded in the stouter divisions of the framework, a precaution not necessary in the smaller Cairene lattices (measuring as a rule about four superficial feet), in which the pattern is simply scooped out of the half-dry plaster.

The piercings in these Oriental windows and window lattices are not made at right angles to the slab of stone or plaster, but are cut through at an angle, varying according to the position and height of the window, with a view to as little interference as possible with the coloured light. The glass, however, being fixed nearest the outside of the window, there is always both shadow and reflection from the deep sides of the openings, much to the enhancement of the mellowness and mystery of colour. In the Temple windows referred to, still further subtlety of effect is arrived at by an outer screen or lattice of *faïence*. Thus subdued and tempered, even crude glass may be turned to beautiful account.

Whence the mediaeval Arabs got their glass, and the quality of the material, are matters of conjecture. If we may judge by the not very ancient specimens which reach us in this country, the glass used in Cairene lattices is generally thin and raw; but set, as above described, in jewels as it were, isolated each in its separate shadow cell, the poorest material looks rich. The lattices here illustrated are none of them of very early period; but, where the character of design is so traditional and changes so slowly, the actual date of the work, always difficult to determine, matters little.

7. Arab Glazing in Plaster.

It is more than probable, it is almost certain, that the Venetian glass-workers, who in the tenth century brought their art to France, were familiar with the coloured lattices of the Levant; for, as we know, in the middle-ages Venice was the great trading port of Italy, in constant communication with the East. If that was so, the Italians, always prone to imitate, would be sure to found their practice, as they did in other crafts, more or less upon Persian and Arabian models. At all events, there is every reason to suppose that at first they, practically speaking, only did in lead what the Eastern artificer did in stone or plaster, and that the windows which, according to various trustworthy but vague accounts, adorned the early Christian basilicas as early as the sixth century, bore strong likeness to

Mohammedan glass—Christianised, so to speak. This is not
to unsay what was before said about the affinity of early glass
to enamel. A river has not of necessity one only and unmistakable source; and though we may not be able to trace back
through the distant years the very fountain of this craft, we
may quite certainly affirm that its current was swollen by more
than one side-stream, and that its course was shaped by all
manner of obstinate circumstances and conditions of the time,
before it went to join the broad and brimming stream of early
mediaeval art.

S. ARMS GLAZING IN PLASTER.

One more source, at least, there
was at which the early glazier drew
inspiration—namely, the art of jewel
setting. Coloured glass, as was said
a while ago, was itself probably first
made only in imitation of precious
stones, and, being made in small
pieces, it had to be set somewhat in
the manner of jewellery. In all probability the enameller himself wrought
at first only in imitation of jewellery,
and afterwards in emulation with it.

Just as white glass was called
crystal, and no doubt passed for it,
so coloured glass actually went by
the name of ruby, sapphire, emerald,
and so on. It is recorded even
(falsely, of course) how sapphires
were ground to powder and mixed
with glass to give it its deep blue
colour; indeed, this wilful confusion of terms goes far to explain
the mystery of the monster jewels of which we read in history
or the fable which not so very long ago passed for it. Stories of
diamond thrones and emerald tables seem to lead straight into
fairyland; but the glass-worker explains such fancies, and brings
us back again to reality.

Bearing in mind, then, the preciousness of glass, and the
well-kept secrecy with regard to its composition, it is not
beyond the bounds of supposition that the glazier of the dark
ages not only intended deliberately to imitate jewellery, but
meant that his glass should pass with the ignorant (we forget

how very ignorant the masses were) for veritably precious stones.

Even though we exempt glaziers from all charge of trickery, it was inevitable that they should attempt to rival the work of the jeweller, and to do in large what he had done only in small. That certainly they did, and with such success that, even when it comes to glass of the twelfth, and, indeed, of the thirteenth century, when already pictorial considerations begin to enter the mind of the artist, the resemblance is unmistakable.

6. MOSAIC GLAZING IN PLENITUDE.

Try to describe the effect of an early mosaic window, and you are compelled to liken it to jewellery. Jewelled is the only term which expresses it. And the earlier it is the more jewel-like it is in effect.

So long as the workman looked upon his glass as a species of jewellery, it followed, as a matter of course, from the very estimation in which he held his material, that he did not think of obscuring it by paint—defiling it, as he would have held. It is not so much that he would have been ashamed to depend on the painter to put his colour right, as that the thought of such a thing never entered his mind; he was a glazier. It was the painter first thought of that, and his time had not yet come.

Possibly it may have occurred to the reader, *apropos* of the diagram on page 10, in which it was shown how far the glazier could go towards the production of a map in glass, that that was not far. Certainly he does not go very far towards making a chart of any geographical value, but he does go a long way towards making a window; for the first and foremost qualities in coloured glass are colour and translucency—and for translucent colour the glazier, after the glass-maker, is alone responsible. It is in some respects very much to be deplored that the Gothic craftsman so early took to the use of supplementary painting, which in the end diverted his attention from a possible development of his craft in a direction not only natural to it but big with possibilities never to this day realised.

Of richly jewelled Gothic glass all innocent of paint, no single window remains to us; but there are fairly numerous examples extant of pattern windows glazed in white glass, whether in obedience to the Cistercian rule which forbade colour, or with a view to letting light into the churches—and it is to churches, prevalent as domestic glass may once have been, we must now go for our Gothic windows.

Some of this white pattern work is ascribed to a period almost as early as that of any glass we know; but it is almost impossible to speak positively as to the date of anything so extremely simple in its execution; in which there is no technique of painting to tell tales; and which, when once "storied" windows came into fashion, was probably left to the tender mercies of lesser craftsmen, who may not have disdained to save themselves the trouble of design, and to repeat the old, old patterns.

The earlier glazier, it was said, painted, figuratively speaking, in glass. It is scarcely a figure of speech to say that he drew in leadwork.

This mode of draughtsmanship was employed in all strictly mosaic glass; but it is in the white windows (or the pale green windows, which were the nearest he could get to white, and which it is convenient to call white) that this drawing with the leads is most apparent — in patterns, that is to say, in which the design is formed entirely by the lead-work.

GLAZING IN PLASTER, SOUTH KENSINGTON MUSEUM.

You have only to look at such patterns as Nos. 11 to 17, to see how this was so; they are all designed in outline, and the outline is given in lead. It is perfectly plain there how every separate line the glazier laid down in charcoal upon his bench stood for a strip of lead. And, looking at the glass, we see that it is the lead which makes the pattern. It is no straining of terms to call this designing in the lead.

The ingenuity in designing such patterns as those below and opposite, which is very considerable, consists in so scheming them that every lead line shall fulfil alike a constructive and an artistic function; that is to say, that every line in the design shall be necessary to its artistic effect, that there shall be no lead line which is not an outline, no outline which is not a lead.

It is not always that the glazier was so conscientious as this. M. Viollet le Duc pointed out, in the most helpful article in his famous Dictionary of Architecture, under the head of *Vitrail*, how in the little window from Bonlieu, here illustrated, the mediaeval craftsman resorted to a dodge, more ingenious than ingenuous, by which he managed to economise labour. Each separate lead line there does not enclose a separate piece of glass. The lines are all of lead; but some of them are mere dummies, strips of metal, holding nothing, carried across the face of the glass only, and soldered on to the more businesslike leads at each end.

11. PLAIN GLAZING, BONLIEU.

The extent of *bona fide* glazing is indicated in the right-hand corner of the drawing. I confess I was inclined at first to think that Viollet le Duc might, in ascribing this glass to the twelfth century, very possibly have dated it too far back; for this is the kind of trick one would more naturally expect from the later and more sophisticated workman; but I have since come upon the same device myself, both at Reims and Châlons, in work certainly as old as the thirteenth century. You see, cutting the glass was the difficulty in those days, and sometimes it was shirked.

It should be noted that the subterfuge employed at Bonlieu and in the specimens from Châlons, opposite, was not in order to evade any difficulty in glazing—the designs present none—but

ECONOMY OF CUTTING.

12. CHALONS.

merely to save trouble. There would have been more occasion for evasion in executing the design from Aix-la-Chapelle (14), where the sharp points of the fleur-de-lys give background shapes difficult for the glazier to cut. It will be noticed that to the left of the panel one of the points joins the necking-piece, which holds the fleur-de-lys together. That is a much more practical piece of glazing than the free point, which presents a difficulty in cutting the background, indicative of the late period to which the glass belongs. The earlier mediæval glazier worked with primitive tools, which kept him perforce within the bounds of simplicity and dignified restraint.

In white windows, so called, he did not by any means confine himself wholly to the use of what it is convenient to call "white glass." From a very early date, perhaps from the very first, he would enrich it with some slight amount of colour. Having devised, as it were, a lattice of white lines, as in the left-hand pattern from Salisbury (overleaf), it was a very simple thing to fill here and there a division of his design with a piece of coloured instead of white glass, as in the pattern next to it in order. The third pattern, to the right, shows how he would even introduce a separate jewel of colour, perhaps painted, which had to be connected with the design by leads forming no part of the pattern.

Colour spots are more ingeniously introduced in the example from Brabourne Church, Kent, (said to be Norman) where the darker tints are ingeniously thrown into the background. But here again, although this is perhaps as early a specimen of glazing as we have in this country, the glazier resorts in his central rosettes to the aid of paint.

1. CHALONS.

14. AIX-LA-CHAPELLE.

It will be observed that in the marginal lines which frame this window, and again in the white bands in two out of the three patterns from Salisbury, leads are introduced which have only a constructional use, and rather confuse the design. That they do not absolutely destroy it is due to its marked simplicity, and to the proportion of the narrow bands to the broad spaces. This is yet more clearly marked in the very satisfactory glazing designs from S. Serge at Angers. The fact is, there is a limit to the possibilities of design, such as that from Sens (page 96), in which literally only four leads (viz., those from the points of the central diamond shape) are introduced wholly and solely for strength; and when it comes to windows of any considerable size, such as clerestory windows, to which plain glazing is peculiarly suited, leads which merely strengthen become absolutely

15. SOUTH TRANSEPT, SALISBURY.

16. BRABOURNE CHURCH KENT.

necessary. The art of the designer consists in so scheming them that they shall not seriously interfere with the pattern.

Were the pattern in lines of colour upon white, the crosslines strengthening them would of course be lost in the darker tint; but, as it happens, we do not find in the earliest glazing lines of interlacing colour, though they occur by way of border lines, as at S. Serge (below), where a marginal line of yellow is enclosed between strips of white.

The interlacing character of several of the white glazing patterns illustrated betrays of course Romanesque influence; but there would not have been so many designs consisting of interlacing bands of white upon a white ground, enclosing, at intervals more or less rare, what had best be called jewels of colour, had it not been that the forms of interlacing strap work lend themselves kindly to glazing.

Every time a strap disappears, as it were, behind another, you have just the break in its continuity which the glazier desires, and if only the interlacings are frequent enough (as on page 96) they give him all he wants.

So far the examples illustrated are, for the most part, in outline; that is to say, on a ground of white the pattern appears as a

17. S. SERGE, ANGERS.

network of leads, flowing or geometric as the case may be, emphasised here and there by a touch of dark colour, focussing them as it were. Without such points of colour a design looks sometimes too much like a mere outline, meant to be filled in with colour, and, in short, unfinished; but as yet the darker and lighter tints of white are not used to emphasise the pattern, as they would have done if, for example, the interlacing straps had been glazed in a slightly purer white than the ground. On the contrary, notwithstanding the very great variety in the tints of greenish-white, which resulted from the chemically imperfect manufacture of the glass, they were employed very much at haphazard, and so far from ever defining the design, go to obviate anything harsh or mechanical there may be in it. There is else, of course, a tendency in geometric pattern to look too merely geometric. One wants always to feel it is a window that is there, and not just so many feet of diaper.

Another practical form of design is that in which it is not the network of leads, but the spaces they inclose, which constitutes the pattern; where lines are not so much thought of as masses; where the main consideration is colour, and contour is of quite secondary account. The leads fulfil still their artistic function of marking the division of the colours, as they fulfil the practical one of binding the bits of coloured glass together; the glazier still draws in lead lines; but attention is not called to them especially; indeed, with identically the same lead lines one could produce two or three quite different effects, according as one emphasised by stronger colour one series of shapes or another. In the case of a framework of strictly geometric lines, straight or curved, one gets patterns such as we see in marble inlay. The slab of marble mosaic and the stained glass border opposite are more than alike; the one is simply a carrying further of the other. The glass design might just as well have been executed in marble, or the marble design in glass. In the upper church at Assisi are some borders of geometric inlay, one of which is given on page 96, identical in character with the minute geometric inlay (which, by the way, was also in glass, though opaque), with which the Cosmati illuminated, so to speak, their marble shrines and monuments. This species of pattern work, appropriate as it is to glass mosaic, transparent as well as opaque, does not seem to have been much used in glass, even

18. MARBLE MOSAIC, ROMAN.

in Italy; where it does occur it is in association, as at Assisi and Orvieto, with painted work of the thirteenth or fourteenth century, though from its Byzantine character it might as well be centuries earlier. It appears that this, which was, theoretically, the simplest and most obvious form of leaded pattern work, and might, therefore, well have been the earliest, was never adopted to anything like the extent to which interlacing ornament was carried.

Mediaeval glaziers did not attempt anything like foliated ornament in leaded glass, and for good reason. In such work the difficulty of doing without lines detrimental to the design is greatly increased, whereas abstract forms you can bend to your will, as you can bend your strip of lead. The more natural the forms employed the more nature has to be considered in rendering them, and nature declines to go always in the direction of simple glazing. It might seem easy enough (to those who do not know the difficulty) to glaze together bits of heart-shaped green glass for leaves, and red for petals, with a dot of yellow for the eye of the flower, and to make use of the lead not only for outlines but for the stalks of the leaves and so on, all on a paler ground; but it is not so easy as that. The designer cannot go far without wanting other connecting leads (besides those used for the stalk); and when some leads are meant very emphatically to be seen and some to be ignored, there is no knowing what the actual effect may be; the drawing lines may be quite lost in a network of connecting leads. Again, the mediaeval glazier did not, so far as we have any knowledge, build up in lead glazing a boldly pronounced pattern, light on dark or dark on light.

19. GLASS, GLAZED.

This he might easily have done. On a small scale plain glazing must perforce be modest; but, given a scale large enough, almost any design in silhouette can be expressed in plain glazing. You may want in that case plenty of purely constructional leads, not meant to be seen, or in any case meant to be ignored: but if the contrast between design and background be only strong enough (say colour on white or white on colour), they do not in the least hurt the general effect. On the contrary, they are of the utmost use to the workman who knows his materials, enabling him to get that infinite variety of colour which is the crowning charm of glass.

What the designer of leaded glass had to consider was, in the first place, the difficulty of shaping the pieces. That is now no longer very great, thanks to the diamond, which makes cutting so easy that there is even a danger lest the workman's skill of hand may outrun his judgment, and tempt him to indulge in useless *tours de force*. The absurdity of taking the greatest possible pains to the least possible purpose is obvious. The more important consideration is now, therefore, the substantiality of the window once made. Think of the force of a gale of wind and its pressure upon the window: it is tremendous; and glazing does not long keep a smooth face before it. Except there is a solid iron bar to keep it in place, it soon bulges inwards, and presents a surface as undulous, on a smaller scale, as the pavement of St. Mark's: and, as it begins to yield, snap go the awkwardly shaped pieces of glass which the glazier has been at such pains to cut. The mediaeval artist, therefore, exercised no more than common sense, when he shaped the pieces of glass he employed with a view to security, avoiding sharp turns or elbows in the glass, or very long and narrow strips, or even very acutely pointed wedge-shaped pieces. No doubt the difficulty of cutting helped to keep him in the way he should go; probably, also, he was under no temptation to indulge in pieces of glass so large that, incapable of yielding, they were bound to break under pressure of the wind. That he sometimes used pieces so small as in time to get clogged with dust and dirt, was owing to the natural desire to use up the precious fragments which, under his clumsy system of cutting, must have accumulated in great quantity. Where most he showed his mastery was, in foreseeing where the strain would come, and introducing always a lead joint where the crack might occur, anticipating and warding off the danger to come. He was workman enough frankly to accept the limitations of his trade. Occasionally (as at Bonlieu) he may have shirked work; but he accommodated himself to the nature of his materials. Never pretending to do what he could not, he betrayed neither its weakness nor his own.

Mere *glazing* has here been discussed at a length which perhaps neither existing work of the kind nor the modern practice of the craft (more is the pity) might seem to demand. It is the most modest, the rudest even, of stained glass; but it is the beginning and the foundation of glass window making, and it affects most deeply even the fully developed art of the sixteenth century.

The leading of a window is the framework of its design, the skeleton to be filled out presently and clothed in colour; and, if the anatomy is wrong, nothing will ever make the picture right. The leads are the bones, which it is necessary to study, even though they were intrinsically without interest, for on them depends the form which shall eventually charm us. Beauty is not skin deep: it is the philosophy of the poet which is shallow.

CHAPTER IV.

EARLY MOSAIC WINDOWS.

It has been explained already at how very early a period "stained" glass begins also to be "painted" glass more or less.

But for the fond desire to be something more than an artist—to teach, to preach, to tell a story—the glazier would possibly have been quite content with the mere jewellery of glass, and might have gone on for years, and for generations, using his pot-metal as it left the pot. As it was, working always in the service of the Church, in whose eyes it was of much more importance that a window should be "storied" than that it should be "richly dight," he found it necessary from the first to adopt the use of paint—not, as already explained, for the purpose of giving colour, but of shutting it out, or at most modifying it. His work was still essentially, and in the first place, mosaic. He conceived his window, that is to say, as made up of a multiplicity of little pieces of coloured glass, the outlines supplied, for the most part, by the strong lines of connecting leadwork, and the details traced in lines of opaque pigment. He still designed with the leads, as I have expressed it, and throughout the thirteenth century (though less emphatically than in the twelfth) his design is commonly quite legible at a distance at which the painted detail is altogether lost: but in designing his leads he had always in view, of course, that they were to be helped out by paint.

In the late thirteenth-century or early fourteenth-century figure from Troyes, on page 336, which depends very little indeed upon any painted detail to be deciphered, the lighter figure glazed upon a ground of dark trellis-work is not only readable, but suggestive of considerable feeling; and in the undoubtedly fourteenth-century figure on page 241, where, with the exception of the hands and face, there is absolutely no indication of the paint with which the artist eventually completed his drawing, there is no mistaking the recumbent figure of Jesse, even without any help of colour. But the earlier the glass, the less was there of painting, and the more the burden of design fell upon the glazier. The two figures from Le Mans, here given (generally allowed to belong to about the year 1100) show very plainly both the amount and the character of the painting used, and the extent to which the design depends upon it. There is no mistake about the value of the lead-lines there, or the extreme simplicity of the painted detail.

36. FIGURES FROM ASCENSION, LE MANS.

It will be seen that paint is there used for three purposes: to paint out the ground round about the feet, hands, and faces; to mark the folds of the drapery, and just an indication of shading upon it; and to blacken the hair. It was only in thus rendering the human hair that the earliest craftsman ever used paint as local colour. In that case he had a way of scraping out of it lines of light to indicate detail. If such lines showed too bright, it was easy to tone them down with a film of thinner paint. In these particular figures from Le Mans the artist had not yet arrived at that process; but from the very first it was a quite common custom, instead of painting very small ornamental detail, to obscure the glass with solid pigment, and then scrape out the ornament.

The fact is, that in early windows a much larger proportion of the glass is obscured, and had need to be obscured,

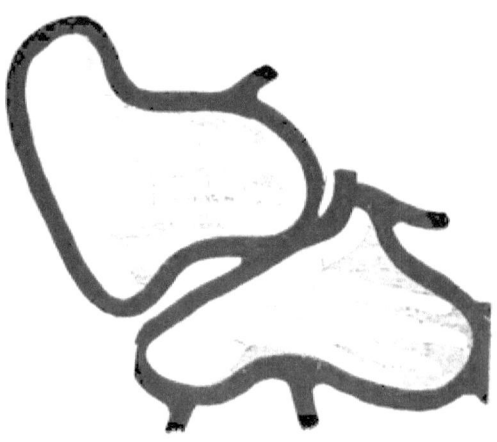

21. Hitchin Church.

than would be supposed. It will be seen what a considerable area of paint surrounds the feet of the two apostles on page 33. This is partly owing to the then difficulty of exactly shaping the pieces of glass employed; but it is largely due to the actual necessity of sufficient area of dark to counteract the tendency of the lighter shades of glass, such as the brownish-pink employed for flesh-tints, to spread their rays and obliterate the drawing. Not only would the extremely attenuated fingers, shown in the scraps from Hitchin Church above look quite well fleshed in the glass, but it was essential that they should be so painted in order to come out satisfactorily—that is, without the aid of shading, to which painters did not yet much resort. On the contrary, they were at first very chary of half-tint—employing it, indeed, for the rounding of flesh and so on, but not to degrade the colour of the glass, small though their palette was.

Something, however, had to be done to prevent especially the whites, yellows, and pale blues, and in some degree all but the dark colours, from taking more than their due part in the general effect. It was not always possible to reduce the area of the glass of an aggressive tint to the dimensions required. To have reduced a line of white, for example, to the narrowness at which it would tell for what was wanted, would have been to

PAINTING OUT AND PICKING OUT.

make it so narrow that the accumulation of dust and dirt between the leads would soon have clogged it and blotted it out altogether. What they did was to paint it heavily with pattern. For example, they would paint out great part of a white line and leave only a row of beads, with so much paint between and around them that certainly not more than one-third of the area of the glass was left clear, and the effect at the right distance (as at Angers, page 116) would be that of a continuous string of pearls. They would in the same way paint a strip of glass solid, and merely pick out a zigzag or some such pattern upon it, with or without a marginal thread of light on each side (Le Mans). Rather than lower the brightness of the glass by a tint of pigment they would coat it with solid brown, and pick out upon it a minute diaper of cross-hatched lines and dots, by that means reducing the volume of transmitted light without much interfering with its purity (S. Remi, Reims, below). Diaper of more interesting kind afforded a ready means of lowering shades of glass which were too light or too bright for the purpose required, and for supplying in effect the deficiencies of the pot-metal palette. Overleaf are some fragments of diaper pattern so picked out, from Canterbury, which would possibly never have been devised if the designer had had to his hand just the shade of blue glass he wanted. Something certainly of the elaboration of pattern which distinguishes the earliest glass comes of the desire to qualify its colour. Viollet le Duc endeavours to explain with scientific precision which are the colours

22. S. REMI, REIMS.

which spread most, and how they spread. His analysis is useful as well as interesting; but absolute definition of the effect of radiation is possible only with regard to a rigidly fixed range of colours to which no colourist would ever confine himself. A man gets by experience to know the value of his colours in their place, and thinks out his scheme accordingly. He puts, as a matter of course, more painting into pale draperies than into dark, and so on; but to a great extent he acts upon that subtle sort of reasoning which we call feeling. Intuition it may be, but it is the intuition of a man who knows.

23. CANTERBURY CATHEDRAL.

The simple method of early execution went hand in hand with equal simplicity of design—the one almost necessitated the other—and the earlier the window the more plainly is its pattern pronounced, light against dark, or, less usually, (as in some most interesting remains of very early glass from Châlons now at the *Musée des Arts Décoratifs* at Paris) in full, strong colour upon white. In twelfth century work especially, figures and ornament alike are always frankly shown *en silhouette*. Witness the design on pages 33 and 115. Similar relief or isolation of the figure against the background is shown in the thirteenth century bishops, occupying two divisions of a rose window at Salisbury, on page 275; and again in the little subject from Lyons, where S. Peter is being led off by the gaoler to prison.

In proportion as the aim of the artist becomes more pictorial he groups his figures more in clumps (you see indications of that at Canterbury), whence comes much of the confusion of effect characteristic of the thirteenth century as it advances, not in this respect in the direction of improvement. In his haste to tell a story he tells it less effectively. Where an early subject is unintelligible (supposing it to be in good preservation)

24. POITIERS CATHEDRAL.
(Compare with 53.)

it is almost invariably owing to the figures not being clearly enough cut out against the background. Isolation of the design seems to be a necessary condition of success in glass of the simple, scarcely painted, kind. In ornament, where the artist had nothing to think of but artistic effect, he invariably and to a much later period defined it unmistakably against contrasting colour. That is illustrated on page 117, part of a thirteenth

25 S. KUNIBERT, COLOGNE.

century window at Salisbury, and in the border below, as well as various others of the period, pages 129, 130, and elsewhere.

It is the almost unanimous verdict of the inexpert that the lead lines very seriously detract from the beauty of early windows. How much more beautiful they would be, it is said, without those ugly black lines! Possibly the expert and the lover of old glass have unconsciously brought themselves not to see what they do not want to see; and the leads may, soberly and judiciously speaking, seriously interfere with the form of the design. But, in the first place, the beauty of early glass is in its colour, not in its form. That is very clearly shown in the illustrations to this chapter and the next; which give, unfortunately, nothing of the beauty and real glory of the glass, but only its design and execution; they appear perhaps in black and white so merely grotesque, that it may be difficult to any one not familiar with the glass itself to understand why so much should be said in its praise. In reality the lack of beauty, especially apparent in the figure drawing of the early glass painters when reduced to monochrome, taken in conjunction with the magnificent effect of many of the earliest windows (which no colourist has ever yet been known to deny) is proof in itself how entirely their art depended upon colour—colour, it should be added, of a quality quite unapproachable by any other medium than that of translucent glass or actual jewellery. No one who appreciates at anything like its full value the magnificence of that colour will think the interference of occasional lead lines a heavy price to pay for it.

For—and this is the second point to be explained in reference to leading—the leads, were they never so objectionable, are actually the price we pay for the glory of early glass. It is by their aid we get those mosaics of pot-metal, the depth and richness of which to this day, with all our science of chemistry, we cannot approach by any process of enamelling. Moreover, though merely constructional leads, taking a direction contrary to the design, may at times disturb the eye, (they scarcely ever disturb the effect) they add to the richness of the glass in a way its unlearned admirers little dream. Not only is the depth and intensity of the colour very greatly enhanced by the deep black setting of lead, a veritable network of shade in which jewels of bright colour are caught, but it is by the use of a multiplicity of small pieces of glass (instead of a single sheet, out of which the drapery of a figure could be cut all in one piece—the ideal of the ignorant!), that the supreme beauty of colour is reached. Examine the bloom of a peach or of a child's complexion, and see how it is made up of specks of blue and grey and purple and yellow amongst the pink and white of which it is supposed to consist. Every artist, of course, knows that a colour is beautiful according to the variety in it; and a "Ruby" background (as it is usually called), which is made up of little bits of glass of various shades of red, not only crimson, scarlet, and orange, but purple and wine-colour of all shades from deepest claret to tawny port, is as far beyond what is possible in a sheet of even red glass as the colour of a lady's hand is beyond the possible competition of pearl powder or a pink kid glove. Not only, therefore, were the small pieces of glass in early windows, and the consequent leads, inevitable, but they are actually at the very root of its beauty; and the artificer of the dark ages was wiser in his generation than the children of this era of enlightenment. He did not butt his head against immovable obstacles, but built upon them as a foundation. Hence his success, and in it a lesson to the glazier for all time—which was taken to heart (as will be shown presently) by craftsmen even of a period too readily supposed to have been given over entirely to painting upon glass.

26. LYONS.

Let there be no misunderstanding about what is claimed for the earliest windows. The method of mosaic, eked out with a minimum of tracing in opaque pigment, does not lend itself very kindly to picture; and it is in ornament that the thirteenth century glazier is pre-eminent. There is even something barbaric about the splendour of his achievement. Might it not be said that in all absolutely ornamental decoration there is something of the barbaric?—which may go to account for the rarity of real ornament, or any true appreciation of it, among modern people.

We might not have to scratch the civilised man very deep to reach the savage in him, but he is, at all events, sophisticated enough to have lost his unaffected delight in strong bright colours and "meaningless" twistings of ornament. Be that as it may, the figure work of the thirteenth century window designer is distinctly less perfect than his scrolls and suchlike, partly, it is true, because of his inadequate figure-drawing, but partly also because his materials were not well adapted to anything remotely like pictorial representation. The figures in his subjects have, as before said, to be cut out against the background in order to be intelligible. Hence a stiff and ultra-formal scheme of design, and also a certain exaggeration of attitude, which in the hands of a *naïve* and sometimes almost childish draughtsman becomes absolutely grotesque. This is most strikingly the case in the larger figures, sometimes considerably over lifesize, standing all in a row in the clerestory lights of some of the great French cathedrals.

The scale of these figures gave opportunity (heads all-of-a-piece show that it did not actually make it a necessity) for glazing the faces in several pieces of glass; and it was quite the usual thing, as at Lyons (opposite) to glaze the flesh in pinkish-brown, the beard in white or grey or yellow or some dark colour—not seldom blue, which had at a distance very much the value of black—and the eyes in white. Sometimes even, as at Reims, the iris of the eye was not represented by a blot of paint but was itself glazed in blue. The effect of this might have been happier if the lines of the painting had been more of the same strength as the leads, and so strong enough to support them. As it is, the great white eyes start out of the picture and spoil it. They have a way of glaring at you fixedly; there is no speculation in their stare; they look more like huge goggles than live eyes. And it is not these only which are grotesque; the smaller figures in subject windows are, for the most part, rude and crude, to a degree which precludes one, or any one but an archæologist *pur sang*, from taking them seriously as figure design. They are often really not so much like human figures as " bogies," ugly enough to frighten a child. What is more to be deplored is that they are so ugly as actually to have frightened away many a would-be artist in glass from the study of them—a study really essential to the proper understanding of his *métier*; for repellant as those bogey figures may be, they show more effectually than later, more attractive, and much more accomplished painting, the direction in which the glass painter should go, and must go, if he wants to make figures tell, say, in the clerestory of a great church.

Apart from the halo of sentiment about the earliest work—and who shall say how much of that sentiment we bring to it ourselves?—apart from the actual picturesqueness—and how much of that is due to age and accident?—there *is* in the earliest glass a feeling for the material and a sense of treatment seldom found in the work of more accomplished glass-painters. If there is not actually more to be learnt from it than from later and more consummate workmanship, there is at least no danger of its teaching a false gospel, as that may do.

From the grossest and most archaic figures, ungainly in form and fantastic in feature, stiff in pose and extravagant in action, out of all proportion to their place in the window, there are at least two invaluable lessons to be learnt—the value of broad patches of unexpected colour, interrupting that monotony of effect to which the best-considered schemes of ornament incline, and the value of simplicity, directness, and downright rigidity of design. Severity of design is essential to largeness of style: it brings the glass into keeping with the grandeur of a noble church, into tune with the solemn chords of the organ. Modern windows may sometimes astound us by their aggressive cleverness, the old soothe and satisfy at the same time that they humble the devout admirer.

The confused effect of Early glass (except when the figures are on a very large scale) is commonly described as "kaleidoscopic." That is not a very clever description, and it is rather a misleading one. For, except in the case of the rose or wheel windows, common in France, Early glass is not designed on the radiating lines which the kaleidoscope inevitably gives. It is enough for the casual observer that the effect is made up of broken bits of bright colour; and if they happen to occupy a circular space the likeness is complete to him. But to know the lines on which an Early Gothic window was built, is to see, through all confusion of effect, the evidence of design, and to resent the implication of thoughtless mechanism implied in the word kaleidoscopic. Nevertheless, little as the mediaeval glaziers meant it—they were lavish of the thought they put into their art—their glass does often delight us, something as the toy amuses children, because the first impression it produces upon us is a sense of colour, in which there is no too definite form to break the charm. There comes a point in our satisfaction in mere beauty (to some it comes sooner than to others—too soon, perhaps) at which we feel the want of a meaning in it—must find one, or our pleasure in it is spoilt; we even go so far as to put a meaning into it if it is not there: but at first it is the mysterious which most attracts the imagination.

And even afterwards, when the mystery is solved, we are not sorry to forget its meaning for a while, to be free to put our own interpretation upon beauty, or to let it sway us without asking why, just as we are moved by music which carries us we know not where, we care not.

CHAPTER V.

PAINTED MOSAIC GLASS.

27. CHARTRES.

THE glass so far vaguely spoken of as "Early" belongs to the period when the glazier designed his leads without thinking too much about painting.

There followed a period when the workman gave about equal thought to the glazing and the painting of his window.

Then came a time when he thought first of painting, and glazing was a secondary consideration with him.

According as we contemplate glass painting from the earlier or the later standpoint, from the point of view of glass or of painting, we are sure to prefer one period to the other, to glory perhaps in the advance of painting, or to regret the lesser part that coloured glass eventually plays in the making of a window. To claim for one or the other manner that it is the true and only way, were to betray the prejudice of the partizan. Each justifies itself by the masterly work done in it, each is admirable in its way. It is not until the painter began, as he eventually did, to take no thought of the glass he was using, and the way it was going to be glazed, that he can be said with certainty to have taken the downward road in craftsmanship. We shall come to that soon enough; meanwhile, throughout the Gothic period at least, he kept true to a craftsmanlike ideal, and never quite forsook the traditions of earlier workmanship; and until well into the fourteenth century he began, we may say, with glazing. In the fourteenth century borders overleaf and in the figure on page 47, no less than in the

28. S. KUNIBERT, COLOGNE.

earlier examples on pages 43 and 46, the glazing lines fulfil a very important part in the design, emphasising the outlines of the forms, if they do not of themselves form an actual pattern. Naturally, once the glazier resorted to the use of paint, he schemed his leads with a view to supplementary painting, and had always a shrewd idea as to the details he meant to add; but it will be clear to any one with the least experience in design that a man might map out the lead work of such borders as those shown below with only the vaguest idea as to how he was going to fill them in with paint, and yet be sure of fitting them with effective foliage. So the architectural canopies on pages 134, 135, 154, were pretty surely first blocked out according to their lead lines; and not till the design was thus mapped out in colour did the designer begin to draw the detail of his pinnacles and crockets. The invariable adherence to a traditional type of design made it the easier for him to keep in mind the detail to come. For he had not so much to imagine as to remember. He was free, however, always to follow any spontaneous impulse of design.

29. S. OUEN, ROUEN.

It was told in Chapter IV. how, in the beginning, pigment was used only to paint out the light, to emphasise drawing, and to give detail—such as the features of the face, the curls of the hair, and so on. That was the ruling idea of procedure. In practice, however, it is not very easy to paint perfectly solid lines on glass. At the end of a stroke always, and whenever the brush is not charged full of colour, the lines insensibly get thin, not perfectly opaque, that is to say; and so, in spite of himself, the painter would continually be obtaining something like translucency—a tint, in fact, and not a solid brown.

Not to have taken advantage of this half tint, would have been to prove himself something less than a good workman, less than a reasonable one; and he did from the first help out his drawing by a smear of paint, more or less in the nature of shading. In flesh painting of the twelfth century (or attributed to that early date) there are indications of such shading, used, however, with great moderation, and only to supplement the strong lines of solid brown in which the face was mainly drawn. The features were first very determinedly drawn in line ("traced" is the technical term), and then, by way of shade, a slight scum of paint was added.

Still, in thirteenth century work, there is frequently no evidence of such shading; the painter has been quite content with the traced line. In the fourteenth century a looser kind of handling is observed. The painter would trace a head in not quite solid lines of brown, and then strengthen them here and there with perfectly opaque colour, producing by that means a much softer quality of line. In any case, the painting until well into the century was at the best rude, and the half tint, such as it was, used, one may say, to be smeared on. Here again practice followed the line of least resistance. It was difficult with the appliances then in use to paint a gradated tint which would give the effect of modelling; and accordingly very little of the kind was attempted. Eventually, however, the painter began to stipple his smear of shadow, at once softening it and letting light into it.

Towards the end of the century this stippling process was carried a step further. It occurred to the workman to coat his glass all over (or all of it except what was meant to remain quite clear) with thin brown, and then, with a big dry brush, dab it until it assumed a granular or stippled surface (darker or lighter, according to the amount of stippling). This was not only more translucent than the smeared colour but more easily graduated, and capable of being so manipulated, and so softened at the edges, as readily to give a very fair amount of modelling. This shading was often supplemented by dark lines or hatchings put in with a brush, as well as by lines scraped out of the tint to lighten it. But in any case there was for a while nothing like heavy shading. Even in work belonging to the fifteenth century, and especially in English glass, as at York, Cirencester, Ross, &c., it is quite a common thing to find

50. SALISBURY.

that the drawing is mainly in line, very delicately done, helped out by the merest hint of shading in tint. This glass is sometimes a little flat in effect, and it is not equal in force to contemporary foreign work; but it is peculiarly refined in execution, and it has qualities of glass-like sparkle and translucency which more than make amends for any lack of solidity in painting. Solidity is just the one thing we can best dispense with in glass.

A comparison of the two borders on pages 38 and 175, both German work, will show how little difference of principle there was between the thirteenth century craftsman and his immediate successor. The difference in style between the two is strikingly marked—the one is quite Romanesque in character, the detail of the other is comparatively naturalistic; but when you come to look at the way they are executed, the way the glazing is mapped out, the way the leads emphasise the outlines, whilst paint is only used to make out details which lead could not give— you will see that the new man has altered his mind more with regard to what he wants to do in glass than as to how he wants to do it. Very much might be said with regard to the two figures on this page and the opposite. The French designer has departed from the archaic composition of the earlier Englishman, and put more life and action into his figure, but there is very little difference in the technique of the two men, less than appears in the illustrations; for, as it happens, one drawing aims at giving the lines of the glass, the other at showing its effect. The fourteenth century figure on page 51 relies more than these last upon painting. The folds of the saint's tunic, for example, are not merely traced in outline, but there is some effect of modelling in them.

It will be instructive also to compare the fourteenth century hop pattern on page 173 with the fourteenth century vine on page 364, and the fifteenth century example on page 345. In the first the method of proceeding is almost as strictly mosaic as though it had been a scroll of the preceding century. Leaves, stalks, and fruits are glazed in light colour upon dark, and bounded by the constructional lines of lead. In the second, though the main forms are still outlined by the leads, much greater use is made of paint: the topmost leaf is in one piece of glass with the stalk of the tree, and all the leaves are relieved by means of shading. In the third the artist has practically drawn his vine scroll, and then thought how best he could glaze it; and the leads come very much as they may.

This last-mentioned proceeding is typical of a period not yet under discussion, but the second illustrates very fairly the supplementary use of paint made in the fourteenth century.

A rather unusual but suggestive form of fourteenth century glazing is shown on page 176. It was the almost invariable practice at this period, as in the preceding centuries, to distinguish the pattern, whether of scroll or border, by relieving it against a background of contrasting colour, usually light against dark; but here the border is varicoloured, without other ground than the opaque pigment used for painting out the forms of the leaves, etc., and filling in between them. The method lends itself only to design in which the forms are so closely packed as to leave not too much ground to be filled in. A fair amount of solid paint about the leaves and stalks does no harm. A good deal was used in Early work, and it results in happier effects than when minute bits of background are laboriously leaded in. The main point is—and it is one the early glaziers very carefully observed—that the glass through which the light is allowed to come should not be made dirty with paint. It was mentioned before (page 35) how, from the first, a background would be painted solid and a diaper picked out of it. Further examples of that are shown overleaf and on pages 88 and 103, though, as will be seen, a considerable portion of the glass is by this means obscured,

ST. S. URBAIN, TROYES.

32. DIAPERS SCRATCHED OUT.

the effect is still brilliant; and in proportion as lighter and brighter tints of glass came into use, it became more and more necessary; in fact, it never died out. The diaper opposite belongs to the fifteenth century, and the minuter of the three diapers above, as well as those on pages 88 and 103, belong to the sixteenth century.

Now that the reader may be presumed to have a perfectly clear idea of the process of the early glazier, and to realise the distinctly mosaic character of old glass, it is time mention should be made of two important intermediate methods of glass staining which presently began to affect the character of stained glass windows.

Allusion has been made (page 2) to the Roman practice of making glass in strata of two colours, which they carved cameo-fashion in imitation of onyx and the like: at least, one *tour de force* of this kind is familiar to every one in the famous Portland vase, in which the outer layer of white glass is in great part ground away, leaving the design in cameo upon dark blue. The mediæval glass-blower seems from the first to have been acquainted with this method of coating a sheet of glass with glass of a different colour. As the Roman coated his dull blue with opaque white glass, so he coated translucent white with rich pot-metal colour. It was not a very difficult operation. He had only to dip his lump of molten white into a pot of coloured glass, and, according to the quantity of coloured material adhering to it, so his bubble of glass (and consequently the sheet into which it was opened out) was spread with a thinner or thicker skin of colour. The Gothic craftsman took advantage of this facility, in so far as he had any occasion for its use. The occasion arose owing to the density of the red glass he employed, which was such that, if he had made it of the thickness of the rest of his glass, it would have been practically opaque. To have made it very much thinner would have been to make it more fragile; and in any case, it was easier to make a good job of the glazing when the glass was all pretty much of a thickness. A layer of red upon white offered a simple and practical way out of the difficulty.

What is called "ruby" glass, therefore, is not red all through, but only throughout one half or a third of its thickness. The colour is only, so to speak, the jam upon the bread; but the red and the white glass are amalgamated at such a temperature as to be all but indivisible, to all intents and purposes as thoroughly one as ordinary pot-metal glass.

For a long while glass painters used this ruby glass and a blue glass made in the same way precisely as though it had been self-coloured. But in shaping a piece of ruby glass, especially with their inadequate appliances, they would be bound sometimes to chip off at the edges little flakes of red, revealing as many little flaws of white. This would be sure to suggest, sooner or later, the deliberate grinding away of the ruby stratum in places where a spot of white was needed smaller than could conveniently be leaded in. As to the precise date at which some ingenious artist may first have used this device, it may be left to archæology to speculate. It must have been a very laborious process; and the early mediæval ideal of design was not one that offered any great temptation to resort to it during the thirteenth or even the fourteenth century. It was not, in fact, until the painting of windows was carried to a point at which there

33. DIAPER SCRATCHED OUT.

was some difficulty in so scheming the lines of the lead that they should not in any way mar its delicacy, that the practice of "flashing" glass, as it is termed, became common. That is why no mention of it has been made till now. It will be seen that it is a perfectly practical and workmanlike process, rendering possible effects not otherwise to be got in glass, but lending itself rather to minuteness of execution and elaboration of detail than to splendour of colour or breadth of effect.

The second intermediate method of staining glass began earlier to affect the design and execution of windows; and the character of fourteenth century glass is distinctly modified by it: and, curiously enough, whilst flashing applied to red and blue glass, this applies to yellow.

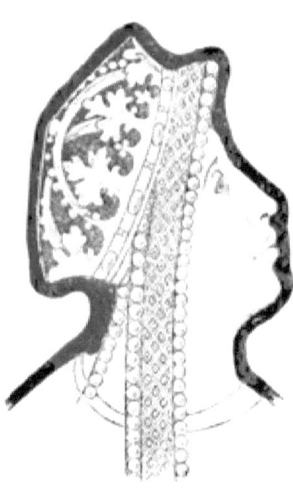

4. QUEEN OF SHEBA, EXETER.

It was discovered about the beginning of the fourteenth century that white glass painted with a solution of silver would take in the kiln a pure transparent stain of yellow, varying, according to its strength and the heat of the furnace, from palest lemon to deepest orange. Observe that this yellow stain is neither an enamel nor a pot-metal colour, but literally a stain, the only stain used upon glass. In pot-metal the stain (if it may be so called) is *in* the glass, this is *upon* it. But it is absolutely indelible: it can only be removed with the surface of the glass itself; time has no more effect upon it than if the glass were coated with yellow pot-metal. This silver stain was not only of a singularly pure and delicate colour, compared to which pot-metal yellows were hot and harsh, but it had all the variety of a wash of water-colour, shading off by imperceptible degrees from dark to light, and that so easily that the difficulty would have been in getting a perfectly flat tint.

Moreover, it could be as readily traced in lines or little touches of colour as it could be floated on in broad surfaces. By its aid it was as easy to render the white pearls on a bishop's golden

35. S. GREGORY. ALL SOULS' COLLEGE, OXFORD.

mitre as to give the golden hair of a white-faced angel, or to relieve a white figure against a yellow ground—and all without the use of intervening lead.

It is not surprising that such a discovery had a very important effect upon the development of the glass painter's practice. By means of it were produced extraordinarily beautiful effects, as of gold and silver, peculiarly characteristic of later Gothic work. The crockets and finials of white canopies would be touched with it as with gold, the hair of angels and the crowns of kings; or the nimbus itself would be stained, the head now being habitually painted on one piece of white glass with the nimbus. The crown and the pearl-edged head-band of the Queen of Sheba, from Fairford, (page 50), are stained upon the white glass out of which the head is cut. In the figure of S. Gregory on page 51 the triple crown is stained yellow, and so is the nimbus of the bull, whose wings also are shaded in stain varying from light to dark.

36. Diaper in White and Stain, All Saints' Church, York.

Of the elaborate diapering of white drapery, with patterns in rich stain, more and more resorted to as the fifteenth century advanced, a specimen is here given, in which the design is figured in white upon a yellow ground, outlined with a delicately traced line of brown. Stain was seldom used on white without such outline.

In the end white and stain predominated. Early glass was likened to jewellery; now the jewels seem to be set in gold and silver. There was a loss in dignity and grandeur, but there was a gain in gaiety and brightness. How far stain encouraged the more abundant use of white glass which prevailed in the fifteenth century it might be rash to say; at any rate, it fitted in to perfection with the tendency of the times, which was ever more and more in the direction of light, until the later Gothic windows became, in many instances, not so much coloured windows as windows of white and stain enclosing panels or pictures in colour. Even in these pictures very often not more than about one-third of the glass was in rich colour. And not only was more white glass used, but the white itself was purer and more silvery, lighter, and at the same time thinner, giving occasion and excuse for that more delicate painting which perhaps was one great reason for the change in its quality. At all events, the more transparent character of the material necessitated more painting than was desirable in the case of the hornier texture of the older make. Hence the prevalence of diaper already referred to.

By the latter half of the fifteenth century painting plays a very important part in stained-glass windows. We have arrived at a period when it is no longer subsidiary to mosaic; still it has not yet begun to take precedence of it. The artist is now a painter, and he relies for much of his effect upon painting; but he is a glazier, too, and careful to make the most of what glass can do. He designs invariably with a view to the glazing of his design, and with full knowledge of what that means. He knows perfectly well what can be done in glass, and what cannot. He has not yet carried painting to the perfection to which it came eventually to be carried, but neither has he begun to rely upon it for what can best be done in mosaic. He can scarcely be said to prefer one medium to another; he uses both to equally workmanlike purpose. He does not, like the early glazier, design in lead any longer, but neither does he leave the consideration of leading till after he has designed his picture, as painters came subsequently to do.

It amounts, it might be thought, to much the same thing whether the artist begins with his lead lines and works up to his painting, as at first he did, or begins with his painting and works up to the leads, as became the practice,—so long as in either case he has always in mind the after-process, and works with a view to it. But the truth seems to be that few men have ever a thing quite so clearly in their minds as when they have it in concrete form before their eyes. The glazier may reckon upon the paint to come, but he does not rely upon it quite so much as the painter who starts with the idea of painting.

The later Gothic artists gradually got into the way of thinking more and more of the painting upon their glass. In the end, they thought of it first, and there resulted from their doing so quite a different kind of design, apart from change due to modifications of architectural style; but so long

37. NATIVITY, GREAT MALVERN.

as the Gothic tradition lasted—and it survived until well into the sixteenth century, in work even which bears the brand of typical Renaissance ornament—so long the glazing of a window was in no degree an after-thought, something not arranged for, which had to be done as best it might. It is apparent always to the eye at all trained in glass design that the composition even of the most pictorial subjects was very much modified, where it was not actually suggested, by considerations of glazing. As more and more white glass came to be used, it was more and more a tax upon the ingenuity of the designer so to compose his figures that his white should be conveniently broken up, and the patches of colour he wanted should be held in place by leads which in no way interfered with his white glass; for it is clear that, in proportion as the white was delicately painted, there would be brutality in crossing it haphazard by strong lines of lead not forming part of the design; and to the last one of the most interesting things in mediæval design is to observe the foresight with which the glass-worker plans his colour for the convenience of glazing.

There is very skilful engineering in the subject from Ross on page 339. It is not by accident that the hands of the hooded figure rest upon the shoulders of S. Edward, or that, together with his gold-brocaded surcoat and its ermine trimming, his hands, and the gilt-edged book he holds in them, they fall into a shape so easy to cut in one piece. Scarcely less artful is the arrangement of the head of the bishop with his crosier and the collar of his robe all in one. The glass painter has only to glance at such subjects as the Nativity from Great Malvern (page 54), or the Day of Creation from the same rich abbey church (page 252), or at the figure of S. Gregory from All Souls', Oxford (page 51), to see how the colour is planned from the beginning, and planned with a view to the disposition of the lead lines. In the Nativity, which is reproduced from a faithful tracing of the glass, and is in the nature of a diagram, the actual map of the glazing is very clear, in spite of its disfigurement by leads which merely represent mending, and form no part of the design. There, too, may clearly be seen how the yellow radiance from the Infant Saviour is on the same piece of whitish glass on which the figure is painted. In the Creation and S. Gregory, which are taken from careful waterdrawings, the effect of the glass is given, and it is perceived how little the leads obtrude themselves upon the observation in the actual windows.*

The Preaching of S. Bernard from S. Mary's, Shrewsbury, opposite, is again disfigured by accidental leads, where the glass

---

* These, together with illustrations 35, 44, 54, 142, 156, 174, 191, 207, 234, are from the admirable collection of studies from old glass very kindly placed at my disposal by Mr. John R. Clayton, himself a master of design in glass.

has been repaired; but it will serve to show how, even when lead lines are as much as possible avoided, they are always allowed for, and even skilfully schemed. Many of the heads, it will be noticed, are painted upon the same pieces of white which does duty also for architectural background; or white draperies are glazed in one piece with the white-and-yellow flooring; yet the lead lines, as originally designed, seem to fall quite naturally into the outlines of the figures.

A very characteristic piece of glazing occurs in the foreground figure, forming a note of strong colour in the centre of the composition. The way the man's face is included in the same piece of glass with the yellow groining of the arch, while his coloured cap connects it with his body, bespeaks a designer most expert in glazing, and intent

38. S. BERNARD PREACHING, S. MARY'S, SHREWSBURY.

upon it always. The danger in connection with a device of this kind, very common in work of about the beginning of the sixteenth century—as, for example, in the very fine Flemish glass at Lichfield—is that, being merely painted upon a white background, and insufficiently supported by leads, the head may seem not to belong to the strongly defined, richly draped figure. It is, of course, very much a question of making the outline strong enough to keep the leads in countenance. The artist of the Shrewsbury glass adopts another expedient at once to support the lead lines, to connect his white and colour, and to get the emphasis of dark touches just where he feels the want of them. He makes occasional use of solid black by way of local colour, as may be seen in the hood of the abbess and the shoes of the men to the right.

In another subject from Shrewsbury (here given), in the bodice of the harpist, and the head gear of the figures on page 104, effective use is made of these points of black. So long as they remain mere points, the end justifies the means, and there is nothing to be said against their introduction;

39. S. Mary's, Shrewsbury.

they are entirely to the good: but such use of solid pigment is valuable mainly in subjects of quite small size, such as these are. It would be obviously objectionable if any considerable area of white glass were thus obscured.

The glass referred to at Shrewsbury, Malvern, and Oxford is of later date than much work in which painting was carried further; but there is here no question of style or period: that is reserved for future consideration (Book II.). The fact it is here desired to emphasise is, that there was a time when glazier and painter took something like equal part in a window, or, to speak more precisely, there were for a while windows in which the two took such equal part that each seemed to rely upon the other; when, if the artist was a painter he was a glazier too. Very likely they were two men. If so, they must have worked together on equal terms, and without rivalry, neither attempting to push his cleverness to the front, each regardful of the other, both working to one end—which was not a mosaic, nor a painting, nor a picture, but a window.

CHAPTER VI.

GLASS PAINTING (MEDIEVAL).

The end of the fifteenth century brings us to the point at which painting and glazing are most evenly matched, and, in so far, to the perfection of stained-and-painted glass, but not yet to the perfection of glass painting. That was reserved for the sixteenth century, when art was under the influence of the Renaissance. Glass painting followed always the current of more modern thought, and drifted picturewards. Even in the fourteenth century it was seen that there was a fashion of naturalism in design, in the fifteenth there was an ever-increasing endeavour to realise natural form, and not natural form alone; for, in order to make the figure stand out in its niche, it became necessary to show the vault in perspective. It was obviously easier to get something like pictorial relief by means of painting than in mosaic, which accordingly fell by degrees into subordination, and the reign of the glass painter began. It must be admitted that at the beginning of the sixteenth century there was still room for improvement in painting, and that to the realisation of the then pictorial ideal stronger painting was actually necessary.

Perhaps the ideal was to blame; but even in Gothic glass, still severely architecturesque in design, more painting became, as before said, necessary, as greater use was made of white, and that painting stronger, in proportion as the material used became thinner and clearer. But though the aim of the glass painter was pictorial, the pictorial ideal was not so easily to be attained in glass; and so, though the painter reigned supreme, his dominion was not absolute. The glazier was in the background, it is true, but he was always there, and his influence is very strongly felt. The pictures of the glass painter are, consequently, still pictures in glass, for the painter was still dependent upon pot-metal for the greater part of his colour; and he knew it, and was wise enough to accept the situation, and, if he did not actually paint his own glass, to design only what could, at all events, be translated into glass. He not only continued to use pot-metal for his colour, but he made every possible use of it to his end, finding in it resources which his predecessors had not developed. His range of colours was extended almost indefinitely, and he used his glass with more discretion. He took every advantage of the accidental variety in the glass itself. No sheet of pot-metal was equal in tint from end to end; it deepened towards the selvedge, and was often much darker at one end than the other. It ranged perhaps from ruby to pale pink, from sea-green to smoky-black.

This gradation of tint wisely used was of great service in giving something like shadow without the aid of paint, and it was used with great effect—in the dragons, for example, which the mediæval artist delighted to depict—as a means of rendering the lighter tones of the creature's belly. Supposing the beast were red, the glass painter would perhaps assist the natural inequality of the glass by abrading the ruby, by which means he could almost model the form in red. If it were a blue dragon he might adopt the same plan; or, if it were green, by staining his blue glass at the same time yellow, he could get every variety of shade from yellow to blue-green.

Every casual variety of colour would be employed to equal purpose. Even the glass-blower's flukes came in most usefully, not merely, as before, to break the colour of a background accidentally, but as local colour. Sheets of glass, for example, which came out, instead of blue or ruby, of some indescribable tint, streaked and flecked with brighter and darker colour, until they were like nothing so much as marble, were introduced with magnificent effect into the pillars of the architecture which now formed so prominent a feature in window design. The beauty and fitness of this marble colour is eventually such as to suggest that the glass-blower must in the end deliberately have fired at this kind of fluke.

Beautiful as were the effects of white and stain produced in the middle of the fourteenth century, it was put now to fuller and more gorgeous use. Draperies were diapered in the most elaborate fashion; a bishop's cope would be as rich as the gold brocade it imitated; patterns were designed in two or even three shades of stain, which, in combination with white and judicious touches of opaque-brown, were really magnificent. Occasionally, as at Montmorency—but this is rarer—the painter did not merely introduce his varied stain in two or three separate shades, nor yet float it on so as to get accidental variety, but he actually painted in it, modelling his armour in it, until it had very much the effect of embossed gold.

In some ornamental arabesque, which does duty for canopy work at Conches, in Normandy, this painting in stain is carried still further, the high lights being scraped out so as to give glittering points of white among the yellow. The result of this is not always very successful; but where it is skilfully and delicately done nothing could be more brilliantly golden in effect. It is curious that this silver came to be used in glass just as goldleaf was used in other decorative painting; in fact, its appearance is more accurately described as golden than as yellow, just as the white glass of the sixteenth century has a quality which inevitably suggests silver.

It was stated just now that blue glass could be stained green. It is not every kind of glass which takes kindly to the yellow stain. A glass with much soda in its composition, for example, seems to resist the action of the silver; but such resistance is entirely a question of its chemical ingredients, and has only to do with its colour in so far as that may depend upon them.

Apart from glass of such antipathetic constitution, it is quite as easy to stain upon coloured glass as upon white; and, if the coloured glass be not too dark in colour to be affected by it, precisely the same effect is produced as by a glaze or wash of yellow in oil or water-colour.

Thus we get blue draperies diapered with green, blue-green diapered with yellow-green, and purple with olive, in addition to quite a new development of landscape treatment. A subject was no longer represented on a background of ruby or dense blue, but against a pale grey-blue glass, which stood for sky, and upon it was often a delicately painted landscape, the trees and distant hills stained to green. Stain was no less useful in the foreground. By the use of blue glass stained, instead of pot-metal green, it was easy to sprinkle the green grass with blue flowers, all without lead.

It was by the combination of stain with abrasion that the most elaborately varied effects were produced. The painter could now not only stain his blue glass green (and just so much of it as he wanted green), but he could abrade the blue, so as to get both yellow, where the glass was stained, and white where it was not. Thus on the same piece of glass he could depict among the grass white daisies and yellow buttercups and bluebells blue as nature, he could give even the yellow eye of the daisy and its green calyx ; and, by judicious modification of his stain, he could make the leaves of the flowers a different shade of green from the grass about them. The drawing of the flowers and leaves and blades of grass, it need hardly be said, he would get in the usual way, tracing the outline with brown, slightly shading with half tint, and painting out only just enough of the ground to give value to his detail.

In spite of the tediousness of the process, abrasion was now largely used—not only for the purpose of getting here and there a spot of white, as in the eyes of some fiery devil in the representation of the Last Judgment, but extensively in the form of diaper work, oftenest in the forms of dots and spots (the spotted petticoat of the woman taken in adultery in one of the windows at Arezzo seems happily chosen to show that she is a woman of the people), but also very frequently in the form of scroll or arabesque, stained to look like a gold tissue, or even to represent a garment stiff with embroidery and pearls. Often the pattern is in gold-and-white upon ruby or deep goldenbrown, or in white-and-gold and green upon blue, and so on. In heraldry it is no uncommon thing to see the ground abraded and the charge left in ruby upon white. Sometimes a small head would be painted upon ruby glass, all of the colour being abraded except just one jewel in a man's cap.

Stain and abrasion, by means of which either of the three primaries can be got upon white, afford, it will be seen, a workmanlike way of avoiding leadwork. But there are other ways. There is a window at Montmorency in which the stigmata in the hands and foot of S. Francis are represented by spots of ruby glass inlaid or let into the white flesh, with only a ring of lead to hold them in place. It would never have occurred to a fourteenth century glazier to do that. He would have felt bound to connect that ring of lead with the nearest glazing lines, at whatever risk of marring his flesh painting ; but then, his painting would not have been so delicate, and would not in any case have suffered so much.

Indeed, the more delicate painting implies a certain avoidance of lead lines crossing it, and hence some very difficult feats of glazing. This kind of inlaying was never very largely used, but on occasion not only a spot but even a ring of glass round it would be let in in this way. There is a window at Bourges in which the glories of the saints are inlaid with jewels of red, blue, green, and violet, which have more the effect of jewellery than if they had been glazed in the usual way. Whether it was worth the pains is another question.

A more usual, and less excusable, way of getting jewels of colour upon white glass was actually to anneal them to it. By abrading the ground it was possible to represent rubies or sapphires, surrounded by pearls, in a setting of gold, but not both rubies and sapphires. In order to get this combination they would cut out little jewels of red and blue, fix them temporarily in their place, and fire the glass until these smaller (and thinner) pieces melted on to and almost into it; the fusion, however, was seldom complete. At this date some of the jewels—as, for example, at S. Michael's, Spurrier Gate, York—are usually missing—but for which accident one would have been puzzled to know for certain how this effect was produced. The insecurity of this process of annealing is inevitable. Glass is in a perpetual state of contraction and expansion, according to the variation of our changeable climate. The white glass and the coloured cannot be relied upon to contract and expand in equal degree; they are seldom, in fact, truly married. The wedding ring of lead was safer. Sooner or later incompatibility of temper asserts itself, and in the course of time they fidget themselves asunder.

All these contrivances to get rid of leads are evidence that the painter is coming more and more to the front in glass, and that the glazier is retiring more and more into the background. The avoidance of glazing follows, as was said, upon ultra-delicacy of painting, and dependence upon paint follows from the doing away with leads. We have thus not two new systems of work, but two manifestations of one idea—pictorial glass. The pictorial ideal inspired some of the finest glass painting—the windows of William of Marseilles, at Arezzo, to mention only one instance among many. With the early Renaissance glass we arrive at masterly drawing, perfection of painting, and pictorial design, which is yet not incompatible with glass. One may prefer to it, personally, a more downright kind of work; but to deny such work its place, and a very high place, in art is to write oneself down a bigot at the least, if not an ass.

It is not until the painter took to depending upon paint for strength as well as delicacy of effect, trusting to it for the relief of his design, that it is quite safe to say he was on the wrong tack.

Towards the sixteenth century much more pronounced effects of modelling are aimed at, and reached, by the painter. Even in distinctly Gothic work the flesh is strongly painted, but not heavily. In flesh painting, at all events, the necessity of keeping the tone of the glass comparatively light was a safeguard, as yet, against overpainting.

The actual method of workmanship became less and less like ordinary oil or water-colour painting. It developed into a process of rubbing out rather than of laying on pigment. It was told how the glass painter in place of smear shadow began to use a stippled tint. The later glass painters made most characteristic use of "matt," as it was called. Having traced the outlines of a face, and fixed it in the fire, they would cover the glass with a uniform matt tint; and, when it was dry, with a stiff hoghair brush scrub out the lights. The high lights they would entirely wipe out, the half tints they would brush partly away, and so get their modelling, always by a process of eliminating shadow. The conscientious painter who meant to make sure his delicate tints would stand would submit this to a rather fierce fire, out of which would come, perhaps, only the ghost of the face. This he would strengthen by another matt brushed out in the same way as before, and fire it again. Possibly it would require a third painting and a third fire; that would depend upon the combined strength and delicacy at which he was aiming, and upon the method of the man. For, though one may indicate the technique in vogue at a given time, no one will suppose that painters at any time worked all in the same way. Some men no doubt could get more out of a single painting than others out of two; some were daring in their method, some timid; some made more use than others of the stick for scraping out lines of light; some depended more upon crisp touches with the sable "tracer," necessary, in any case, for the more delicate pencilling of the features; some would venture upon the ticklish operation of passing a thin wash of colour over matt or stippling before it was fired, at the risk of undoing all they had done—and so on, each man according to his skill and according to his temperament. But with whatever aid of scratching out lights, or touching in darks, or floating on tints, the practice in the sixteenth century was mainly, by a process of scrubbing lights out of matted or washed tints of brown, to get very considerable modelling, especially in flesh painting and in white draperies.

It is impossible in illustrations of the size here given to exemplify in any adequate manner the technique of the Early Renaissance glass-painters, but it is clear that the man who painted the small subject from the life of S. Bonnet, in the church dedicated to that saint at Bourges, (page 210) was a painter of marked power. A still finer example of painting is to be found in the head of William de Montmorency (opposite) from the church of S. Martin at Montmorency near Paris, really a masterpiece of portraiture, full of character, and strikingly distinguished in treatment. There is at the Louvre a painting of the same head which might well be the original of the glass. If the glass painter painted the picture he was worthy to rank with the best painters of his day. If the glass painter only copied it, he was not far short of that, for his skill is quite remarkable; and the simple means by which he has rendered such details as the chain armour and the collar, and the Order of S. Michael, supplementing the most delicate painting with touches of opaque colour, which in less skilful hands would have been brutal, show the master artist in glass painting.

Here, towards the end of the first quarter of the sixteenth century, we have glass painting carried about as far as it can go, and yet not straying beyond the limits of what can best be done in glass. The apologists for the Renaissance would attribute all such work as this to the new revival. That would be as far wide of the mark as to claim for it that it was Gothic. The truth is, there is no marked dividing line between Gothic and Renaissance. It is only by the character of some perhaps quite slight monumental or architectural detail that we can safely classify a window of the early sixteenth century as belonging to one or the other style. It belongs, in fact, to neither. It is work of the transition period between the two. Gothic traditions lingered in the glass painter's shop almost as long as good work continued to be done there; so much so, that we may almost say that with those Gothic traditions died the art itself. For all that, it is not to be disputed that the most brilliant achievements in glass painting were certainly in the new style and inspired by the new enthusiasm for art.

40 GUILLAUME DE MONTMORENCY, MONTMORENCY

CHAPTER VII.

GLASS PAINTING (RENAISSANCE).

THE quality *par excellence* of Renaissance glass was its painting; its dependence upon paint was its defect. Until about the middle of the sixteenth century the painter goes on perfecting himself in his special direction, neglecting, to some extent, considerations of construction on the one hand, and of colour upon the other, which cannot with impunity be ignored in glass, but achieving pictorially such conspicuous success that there may be question, among all but ardent admirers of glass that is essentially glass-like, as to whether the loss, alike in depth and in translucency of colour, as well as of constructional fitness, may not be fully compensated for by the gain in fulness of pictorial expression. According as we value most the qualities of glass in glass, or the qualities of a picture in no matter what material, will our verdict be. But there comes a point when the painter so far oversteps the limit of consistency, so clearly attempts to do in glass what cannot be done in it, so plainly sacrifices to qualities which he cannot get the qualities which stained glass offers him, that he ceases to be any longer working in glass, and is only attempting upon glass what had very much better have been done in some other and more congenial medium.

The event goes to prove the seductiveness of the pictorial idea, and illustrates once more the danger of calling to your assistance a rival craft, which, by-and-by, may oust you from your own workshop. The consideration of the possibilities in the way of pictorial glass is reserved for a chapter by itself. It concerns us for the moment only in so far as the pictorial intention affected, as it very seriously did, the technique of glass painting.

In pursuit of the pictorial the painter strayed from his allegiance to glass. He learnt to depend upon his manipulation instead of upon his material; and that facility of his in painting led him astray. He not only began to use paint where before he would, as a matter of course, have glazed-in coloured glass, but to lay it on so heavily as seriously to detract from that translucency which is the glory of glass.

It is rash to say, at a glance, whether glass has been too heavily painted or not. I once made a careful note, in writing, that certain windows in the church of S. Alpin, at Châlons, were over-painted. After a lapse of two or three years I made another equally careful note to the effect that they were thin, and wanted stronger painting. It was not until, determined to solve the mystery of these contradictory memoranda, I went a third time to Châlons, that I discovered, that with the light shining full upon them the windows were thin, that by a dull light they were heavy, and that by a certain just sufficiently subdued light they were all that could be desired. There is indiscretion, at least, in painting in such a key that only one particular light does justice to your work; but the artist in glass is always very much at the mercy of chance in this respect. He cannot choose the light in which his work shall be seen, and the painter of Châlons may have been more unfortunate than in any way to blame. There comes, however, a degree of heaviness in painted glass about which there can be no discussion. When the paint is laid on so thick that under ordinary conditions of light the glass is obscure, or when it is so heavy that the light necessary to illuminate it is more than is good for the rest of the window, the bounds of moderation have surely been passed. And in the latter half of the sixteenth century it was less and less the custom to take heed of considerations other than pictorial; so that by degrees the translucency of glass was sacrificed habitually to strength of effect depending not so much upon colour, which is the strength of glass, as upon the relief obtained by shadow—just the one quality not to be obtained in glass painting. For the quality of shadow depends upon its transparency; and shadow painted upon glass, through which the light is to come, must needs be obscure, must lack, in proportion as it is dark, the mysterious quality of light in darkness, which is the charm of shadow. The misuse of shading which eventually prevailed may best be explained by reference to its beginnings, already in the first half of the century, when most consummate work was yet being done. For example, in the masterpieces of Bernard van Orley, at S. Gudule, Brussels—one of which is illustrated overleaf; it is a mere diagram, giving no idea of the splendour of the glass, but it is enough to serve our purpose.

The execution of the window is, in its kind, equal to the breadth and dignity of the design. The painter has done, if not quite all that he proposed to do, all that was possible in paint upon glass. Any fault to find in him, then, must be with what he meant to do, not what he did. To speak justly, there is no fault to find with any one, but only with the condition of things. We have here, associated with the glass painter, a more famous artist, the greatest of his time in Flanders, pupil of Michael Angelo, court painter, and otherwise distinguished. It was not to be expected that he should be learned in all the wisdom of the glass painter, nor yet, human nature being what it is, that he should submit himself, lowly and reverently, to the man better acquainted with the capacities of glass. All that the glass painter could do was to translate the design of the master into glass as best he might, not perhaps as best he could have done had there been no great master to consult in the matter.

This was not the first time, by any means, that the designer and painter of a window were two men. There is no saying how soon that much sub-division of labour entered the glass worker's shop; but so long as they were both practical men, versed each in his art, and, to some extent, each in the technique of the other, it did not so much matter. When the painter from outside was called in to design, it mattered everything. What could he be expected to care for technique other than his own? What did he know about it? He was only an amateur so far as glass was concerned; and his influence made against workmanlikeness. He may have done marvels; he did marvels; but his very mastery made things worse. He bore himself so superbly that it was not seen what dangerous ground he trod on. Lesser men must needs all stumble along in his footsteps, until they fell; and in their fall they dragged their art with them.

The fault inherent in such work as the Brussels windows is neither Van Orley's nor the glass painter's; it is in the mistaken aim of the designer striving less for colour in his windows than for relief. He succeeds in getting quite extraordinary relief, but at the expense of colour, which in glass is the most important

41. Mosaic Glass, Arezzo.

thing. The figures in the window illustrated are so strongly painted that even the white portions of their drapery stand out in dark relief against the pale-grey sky. That is not done, you may be sure, without considerable sacrifice of the light-giving quality of the glass. It is at a similar cost that the white-and-gold architecture stands out in almost the solidity of actual stone against the plain white diamond panes above, giving very much the false impression that it is placed in the window, and that you see through its arches and behind it into space. Another very striking thing in the composition is the telling mass of shadow on the soffit of the central arch. It produces its effect, and a very strong one. The festoons of yellow arabesque hanging in front of it tell out against it like beaten gold, and the rather poorish grey-blue background to the figures beneath it has by comparison an almost atmospheric quality. It is all very skilfully planned as light and dark; but there is absolutely no reason why that shadow should have been produced by heavy paint. Under certain conditions of light there are, it is true, gleams of light amidst this shadow. You can make out that the roof is coffered, and can perceive just a glow of warm colour; but most days and most of the day it is dead, dull, lifeless, colourless. The points to note are: (1) that this painted shadow must of necessity be dull; and (2) that on work of this scale at all events (the figures here are very much over lifesize), this abandonment of the mosaic method was not in the slightest degree called for. On the contrary, the simpler, easier, and more workmanlike thing to do would have been to glaze-in the shadow with deep rich pot-metal glass. That was done in earlier glass, and in glass of about the same period as this.

41. RENAISSANCE WINDOW, S. GUDULE, BRUSSELS.

For example, at Liège, where there are beautiful windows of about the same period, very similar in design, the glass is altogether lighter and more brilliant, partly owing to the use of paint with a much lighter hand, but yet more to greater reliance upon pot-metal. In the Church of S. Jacques, as at S. Gudule, there are arched canopies with festoons in bright relief against a background of shadowed soffit; but there the shadow is obtained by glazing-in pot-metal, which has all the necessary depth, and is yet luminous and full of colour.

So also the deeply shadowed architectural background to the representation of the Daughter of Herodias dancing before Herod, in the Church of S. Vincent, at Rouen (overleaf), is leaded up in deep purple glass, through which you get peeps of distant atmospheric blue beyond. And this was quite a common practice among French glass painters of the early half of the sixteenth century—as at Auch, at Ecouen, at Beauvais, at Conches, where the architecture in shadow is leaded in shades of purple or purplish glass, which leave little for the painter to do upon the pot-metal. At Freiburg, in Germany, there is a window designed on lines very similar indeed to Van Orley's work, in which the shadowed parts are glazed in shades of deep blue and purple. In Italy it was the custom, already in the fifteenth century, to lead-in deep shadows in pot-metal; and they did not readily depart from it. Surely that is the way to get strong effects, and not by paint. You may take it as a test of workmanlike treatment, that the darks have been glazed-in, where it was possible, and not merely painted upon the glass.

There is some misconception about what is called Renaissance glass. Glass painting was not native to Italy, and was never thoroughly acclimatised there, any more than Gothic architecture, to which it was—the handmaid I was going to say, but better say the standard-bearer. Much glass was accordingly executed in Italy in defiance, not only of all tradition, but of all consistency and self-restraint. But even in Italy you will find sixteenth century glass as workmanlike as can be. The details from Arezzo and Bologna, above, overleaf, and on page 266, are pronouncedly Renaissance in type, but the method employed by the glass painter is as thoroughly mosaic as though he had worked in the thirteenth century. Not less glazier-like in treatment are the French Renaissance details from Rouen, on pages 75 and 347, from which it may be seen that a workmanlike treatment of glass was not confined to Gothic glaziers. It was less a question of style, in the historic sense, than of the men's acquaintance with the traditions of good work, and their readiness to accept the situation.

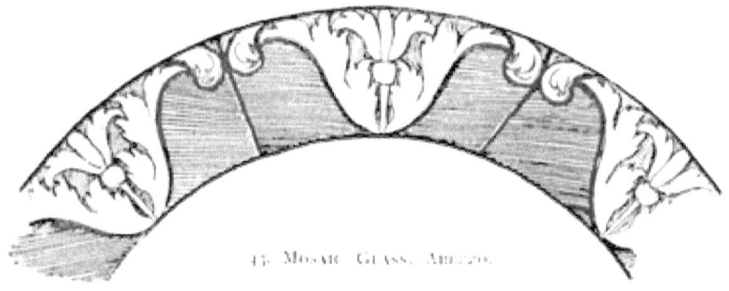

43. MOSAIC GLASS, AREZZO.

Possibly the Netherlandish love of light and shade—and especially of shade—may account for the character of the Brussels glass. Against that it should be said that, elsewhere in Flanders, splendid glass was being done about the same time, less open to the charge of being too heavily painted—at Liège, for example. But everywhere, and perhaps more than anywhere in the Netherlands, which became presently a great centre of glass painting, the tendency, towards the latter part of the century, was in the direction of undue reliance upon paint; of which came inevitably one of two things—either the shaded parts were heavy, dirty, and opaque, or they were weak and washy in effect. If, by means of painting, an artist can get (as he can) something worth getting not otherwise to be got, though we may differ as to the relative value of what he gains and what he sacrifices, it would be hard to deny him his preference, and his right to follow it; but if by painting on glass he attempts to get what could better be expressed by working in it, then clearly he has strayed (as Van Orley did) from the straight path, as glass workers read the map.

It is rather a curious thing that the avoidance of leading, the dependence upon glazing and paint, should manifest itself especially in windows designed on such a scale that it would have been quite easy to get all that was got in paint, and more, by the introduction of coloured glass; in windows, for example, on the scale of those at King's College, Cambridge, with figures much over lifesize, where the artist, you can see, has been afraid of leading, and has shirked it. Evidently he did not realise

44. SALOME, S. VINCENT, ROUEN

for how little the leads would count in the glass. He does not in that case fall into the error of painting with too heavy a hand, but he trusts too much to paint—a trust so little founded that the paint has oftentimes perished, much to the disfigurement of his picture.

The French glass painters of about the same period, though working upon a smaller scale, did not depart in the same way from the use of glazing; and where they did resort to painting, it was often with a view to a refinement of detail not otherwise to be obtained, as in the case of the delicate landscape backgrounds painted upon pale blue, which have a beauty all their own.

There is here

45. RENAISSANCE MOSAIC GLASS.

no intention whatever of disparaging such work as that at S. Gudule. Any one capable of appreciating what is strongest and most delicate in glass must have had such keen delight in them that there is something almost like ingratitude in saying anything of them but what is in their praise. But the truth remains. Here is a branching off from old use; here the painter begins to wander from the path, and to lead after him generations of glass painters to come. It takes, perhaps, genius to lead men hopelessly astray!

CHAPTER VIII.

ENAMEL PAINTING.

THE excessive use of opaque paint was not so much a new departure as the exaggeration of a tendency which had grown with the growth of glass painting itself. The really new thing in glass painting about this time was the introduction of enamel.

When glass painters were resorting, not only to opaque painting, but to abrasion, annealing, or whatever would relieve them from the difficulty of getting in mosaic glass the pictorial effect which was more and more their ruling thought, when glazing had become to them a difficulty (to the early glass workers it was a resource), it was inevitable that they should think about painting on glass in colour. Accordingly towards the middle of the sixteenth century they began to use enamel. This was the decisive turning-point of the art.

In theory the process of painting in enamel is simple enough. You have only to grind coloured glass to impalpable dust, mix it with "fat oil," or gum-and-water, and paint with it upon white or tinted glass: in the furnace the medium will be fired away, and the particles of coloured glass will melt and adhere, more or less firmly, to the heated sheet of glass to which they have been applied. This theory glass painters began to put into practice. In the beginning they used enamel only tentatively, first of all in the flesh tints. It had been the custom since the fourteenth century to paint flesh always upon white or whitish glass in the ordinary brown pigment; and something of the simple dignity and monumental character of old glass is due, no doubt, to that and similar removedness from nature. Gradually the fashion was introduced of painting the flesh in red instead of brown. In one sense this was no such very new thing to do. The ordinary brown pigment spoken of all along is itself enamel, although it has been thought better not to speak of it by that name for fear of confusion. Inasmuch, however, as this was the use of a pigment to get not merely flesh painting but flesh tint—that is to say, colour—it was a step in quite a new direction. Pictorially it offered considerable advantages to the painter. He could not only get, without lead, contrast of colour between a head and the white ground upon which it was painted, or the white drapery about it, but he could very readily give the effect of white hair or beard in contrast to ruddy flesh, and so on. There is a fragment at the Musée des Arts Décoratifs at Paris, attributed to Jean Cousin, 1531, in which a turbaned head appears to have been cut out of a piece of purplish-blue glass, the flesh abraded, and then painted in red, the lips still redder, whilst the beard is painted on the blue, which shades off into the cheeks in the most realistic manner. Very clever things were done in this way, always in the realistic direction; but down to the middle of the century, and even later, there were always some painters who remained faithful to the traditional cool brown colour. A rather happy mean between warm and cold flesh is found at Auch (1513), where warmish enamel upon grey-blue or greenish glass gives modelling and variety of colour in the flesh, which is yet never hot. Well-chosen pieces of glass are made use of, in which the darker half comes in happily for the bearded part of a man's face. So, also, the head of the Virgin at the foot of the cross is painted upon grey, which tells as such in her coif, shaded with a cooler brown, but only deepens and saddens her face, and intensifies the contrast with the Magdalen. Occasionally one of these heads comes out too blue, but at the worst it is better than the hot, foxy flesh painting which became the rule.

Painting in colour upon glass could naturally not stop at flesh red. It was used for pale blue skies, at first only to get a more delicate gradation from pale pot-metal colour to white, but eventually for the sky throughout the picture. In connection with yellow stain it gave a green for distant landscape.

Enamel was used in ornament to give the colour of fruits and flowers in garlands and the like, and generally for elaboration of detail, which, if not trivial, was of small account in serious decoration. For a while there were glass painters who remained proof against its seduction. It was not till the latter half of the sixteenth century that glass painters generally began seriously to substitute enamel for pot-metal, and to rely upon paint, translucent as well as opaque. Even then they could not do without pot-metal, avoid it as they might. The really strong men, such as the Crabeth Brothers, at Gouda, by no means abandoned the old method, but they relied so much upon paint as to greatly obscure the glory of their glass. The Gouda windows, which bring us to the seventeenth century, contain among them the most daring things in glass extant. They prove that a subject can be rendered more pictorially than one would have conceived to be possible in glass, but they

36. THE BAPTISM, GOUDA.

show also what cannot be done in it; in fact, they may be said to indicate, as nearly as can be, the limits of the practicable. What artists of this calibre could not do we may safely pronounce to be beyond the scope of glass painting, even with the aid of enamel.

No skill of painting could make otherwise than dull the masses of heavily painted white glass employed to represent the deep shade of the receding architecture in the upper part of the window on page 242; so, the mass of masonry which serves in the lower half of the window on this page as a background to the Donor and his patron saint and some shields of arms, represented as it is by a thick scum of brown paint, could not but lack lustre. Think of the extent of all that uninteresting paint; what a sacrifice it means of colour and translucency!

Enamel painting did not lead to much. The colours obtained by that means had neither the purity nor the richness and volume of pot-metal. They had to be strengthened with brown, which still further dulled them; and, the taste for light and shade predominating as it did in the seventeenth century, the glass painter was eventually lured to the destruction of all glass-like quality in his glass.

There are some windows in the cathedral at Brussels, in the

chapel opposite that of the Holy Sacrament, where are Van Orley's windows, which bear witness to the terrible decline that had taken place during something like a century—not that they are badly executed in their way. The texture of silk, for example, is given by the glass painter perfectly : but, in the struggle for picturesque effects of light and shade, all consistency of treatment is abandoned. The painter is here let loose ; and he can no more withstand the attractions of paint than a boy can resist the temptation of fresh fallen snow. The one must throw snowballs at somebody, the other must lay about him with pigment. Here he lays about him with it recklessly. He is reckless, that is, of the obscurity of the glass he covers with it. At moments, when the sun shines fiercely upon it, you dimly see what he was aiming at ; nine-tenths of the time all is blackness. Slabs of white glass are coated literally by the yard with dense brown pigment through which the light rarely shines.

It had become the practice now to glaze a window mainly in rectangular panes of considerable size. Where pot-metal colour was used at all, it had of necessity to be surrounded with a leaden line : but within the area of the coloured mass the leading was usually in these upright and horizontal lines, and not at all according to the folds of the drapery or what not. If the glazier went out of his way to take a lead line round a face, instead of across it, that was as much as he would do : if it was merely the face of a cherub, however delicately painted, he would, perhaps, as at S. Jacques, Antwerp, cut brutally across it ; and even where structural lead lines compelled him to use separate pieces of material, he by no means always took advantage of the opportunity of getting colour in his glass, but, as at Antwerp, contentedly accepted his rectangular panes of white, as something to paint on—to the exclusion of no matter how much light. It simplified matters, no doubt, for the painter thus to throw away opportunities, and just depend upon his brush ; but it resulted at the best only in an imitation of oil painting, lacking the qualities of oil paint.

The French glass painters were less reckless. At Troyes, indeed, there is plenty of seventeenth century glass in which a workman can still find considerable interest. That of Linard Gontier, in particular, has deservedly a great reputation. He was a painter who could get with a wash of colour, and seemingly with ease, effects which most glass painters could

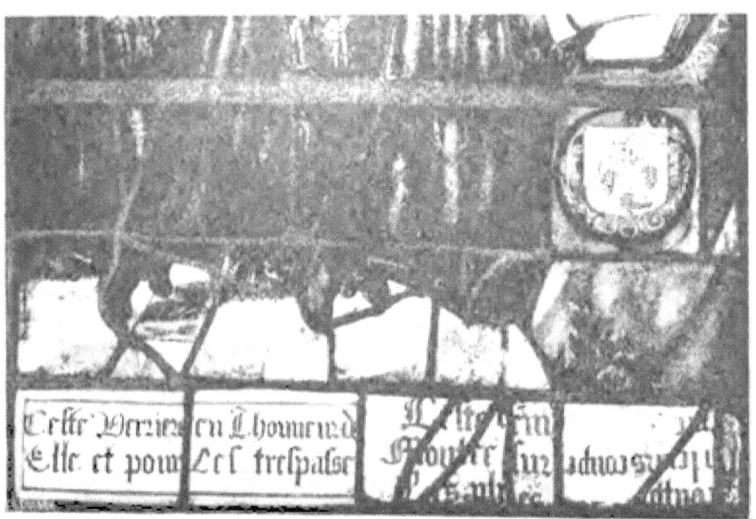

17. S. MARTIN ES VIGNES, TROYES.

only get at by stippling, hatching, and picking out; and he managed his enamel very cleverly, floating it on with great dexterity. But it is rarely that he gets what artists would call colour out of it. Even in the hands of a man of his prodigious skill the method proclaims its inherent weakness. The work is thinner, duller, altogether poorer, than the earlier glass of much less consummate workmen, who worked upon sounder and severer principles. The strength and the weakness of the painter are exemplified in the group of Donors above.

The painting is admirable, not only in the heads, but in the texture of the men's cloaks; those cloaks, however, are painted in black paint. When the light is quite favourable they look like velvet: they never look like glass.

There is here the excuse, for what it may be worth, of texture and perhaps other pictorial qualities. Even that is often wanting in seventeenth century work, as when, at S. Jacques, Antwerp, the background to a design in white and stain is glazed in panes of white glass solidly coated with brown paint. This is obscuration out of pure wilfulness.

It was not only when the artist sought to get strong effects in enamel painting that the method fell short of success. The delicacy that might be got by means of it was neutralised by the necessity of some sort of glazing, and matters were not mended by glazing the windows in panes. It is impossible to take much satisfaction in the most delicately painted glass picture when it is so scored over with coarse black lines of lead or iron that it is as if you were looking at it through a grill. That is very much the effect seen in Sir Joshua Reynolds' famous window in the ante-chapel at New College, Oxford (two lights of which are shown opposite), where the Virtues are seen imprisoned, you may say, within iron bars. They look very much better there than in the glass, which, for all the graceful draughtsmanship of the artist and the delicate workmanship of the painter, is ineffective to the last degree. It has no more brilliancy or sparkle than a huge engraving seen against the light; square feet of white glass are muddied over with paint.

It was not Sir Joshua's fault, of course, that the traditions of the glazier's craft were in his day well-nigh extinct; but Sir Horace Walpole was quite right when he described these vaunted Virtues as "washy." To say that they are infinitely more pleasing in the artist's designs is the strongest condemnation of the glass.

There was one use made of enamel which promised to be of real help to the glazier— that of painting the necessary shadows on pot metal in shades of the same colour as the glass. Since enamel of some kind had to be used, why not employ a colour more akin to the glass itself than mere brown? It would seem as if by so doing one might get depth of colour with less danger of heaviness than by the use of brown; but the glass painted in

48. VIRTUES, BY SIR J. REYNOLDS, NEW COLL., OXFORD.

that way (by the Van Lingen, for example, a family of Flemings established in England, whose work may be seen at Wadham and Balliol Colleges, Oxford) was by no means free from heaviness. Enamel then, it will be seen, was never really of any great use in glass painting, and it led to the degradation of the art to something very much like the painting of transparencies, as they are called, on linen blinds.

Let us note categorically the objections to it. A glazier objects to it, that it is an evasion of the difficulty of working in glass, and not a frank solution of it. That may be sentimental more or less. A colourist objects to it, because it is impossible to get in it the depth and richness of strong pot-metal, or the brilliancy of the more delicate shades of self-coloured material. That, it may be urged, remains to be proved, but the enamel painter practically undertook to prove the contrary, and failed. Admirers of consistency object to it, that it succeeds so ill in reconciling the delicacy of painting aimed at with the brutality of the glazing employed. That, again, is a question of artistic appreciation, not so easily proved to those who do not feel the discord. Lovers of good work, of work that will stand, object to it that it is not lasting. This is a point that can be easily proved.

The process of enamel painting has been explained above (page 77). The one thing necessary to the safe performance of the operation is that the various glass pigments shall be of such consistency as to melt at a lower temperature than the glass on which they are painted. That, of course, must keep its shape in the kiln, or all would be spoilt. The melting of the pigment is, as a matter of fact, made easier by the admixture of some substance less unyielding than glass itself—such as borax—to make it flow. This "flux," as it is called, makes the glass with which it is mixed appreciably softer than the glass to which it is apparently quite safely fixed by the fire. It is thus more susceptible to the action of the atmosphere: it does not contract and expand equally with that; and in the course of time, perhaps no very long time, it scales off. Excepting in Swiss work (to which reference is made in Chapter IX.) this is so commonly so, that you may usually detect the use of enamel by the specks of white among the colour, where the pigment has worked itself free, altogether to the destruction of pictorial illusion. And it is not only with transparent enamel that this happens, but also with the brown used by the later painters for shading.

The brown tracing and painting colour was originally a hard metallic colour which required intense heat to make it flow. The glass had to be made almost red-hot, at which great heat there was always a possibility that the pigment might be fired away altogether, and the painter's labour lost. In the case of the thirteenth century painter's work the danger was not very serious. Thanks to the downright and sometimes even brutal way in which he was accustomed to lay on the paint, solidly and without subtlety of shade, his work was pretty well able to take care of itself in the kiln. It was the more delicate painting avoid all possibility of any such catastrophe. The easiest way which was most in danger of being burnt away; and in proportion as men learnt to carry their painting further, and to get delicate modelling, they became increasingly anxious to of doing this was (as in the case of transparent enamel) to soften this colour with flux. That enabled them to fire their glass at a much lower heat, at which there was no risk of losing the painting, and they were able so to make sure of getting the soft gradations of shade they wanted; and the more the painter strove to get pictorial effects the more he was tempted to soften his pigment; but, according as the flux made the colour easier to manage in the fire, it made it less to be depended upon afterwards; and the later the work, and the more pictorial its character, the more surely the painting proves at this date to have lost its hold upon the glass. In many a seventeenth century window the Donors were depicted in their Sunday suits of black velvet and fur, the texture quite wonderfully given; now their garments are very much the worse for wear, more than threadbare. The black or brown is rich no longer, it is pitted with specks of raw white light; sometimes the colour has peeled off *en masse*. Time has dealt comparatively kindly with the gentlemen on page 81, but in the glass there is an air of decay about their sable cloaks which takes considerably away from their dignity. It is one characteristic of enamelled windows that they do not mellow with age, like mosaic glass, but only get shabby.

Any one altogether unacquainted with the characteristics of style is apt to be very much at fault as to the date of a window. The later windows are in so much more dilapidated a condition than the earlier that they are quite commonly mistaken for the older.

It has to be borne in mind that most of the devices adopted by the glass painters—the use, namely, of large sheets of fragile glass, and the avoidance of strengthening leads, no less than the resort to soft enamel, whether for colour or for shading—all go to make it more perishable.

It may be said that the decay of the later painting is due not so much to the use of enamel as to the employment of soft flux. That is true. But when it comes to the painting of texture and the like, the temptation to use soft colour has generally proved to be irresistible. One is forced to the conclusion that the aim of the later glass painter was entirely wrong; that for the sake of pictorial advantages—which went for very little in a scheme of effective church decoration, even if they did not always detract from the breadth of the work—he gave up the qualities which go at once to make glass glorious, and to give it permanence. Whatever the merits of seventeenth century glass painting they are not the merits of glass; there is little about it that counts for glass, little that is suggestive of glass—except the breakages it has suffered.

What is said of seventeenth century glass applies also to that of the eighteenth century, only with more force. Sir Joshua and Benjamin West were quite helpless to raise the art out of the slough into which it had fallen, for they were themselves ignorant of its technique, and did not know what could be done in glass. It was not until the Gothic revival in our own century, and a return to mosaic principles, that stained glass awoke to new life.

CHAPTER IX.

THE NEEDLE POINT IN GLASS PAINTING.

ALLUSION has been made to the glass painter's use of the point for scraping out lights, and especially diapers upon glass coated with pigment. These are often quite lace-like in their delicacy. That would be a poor compliment if it meant that the glass painter had had no more wit than to imitate the effects produced in a material absolutely unlike glass. But it is not merely for want of a better word that the term lace-like is used. It is strictly appropriate, and for a very good reason. It was explained how from the first the glass painter would use the stick end of his brush to scrape out sharp lights in his painting, or even diaper patterns out of a tint. The latest glass painters made more and more use of the point, and of a finer point than the brush end, until, in Swiss work, they adopted the pen and the needle itself. It is not surprising, then, that point-work should resemble point-work, though the one be in thread and the other on glass. The strange thing would have been if it were not so. Thus it comes about that much of the Swiss diaper work is most aptly described as lace-like in effect.

The field of a small shield is frequently diapered with a pattern so fine that it could only have been produced with a fine point. Some of the diapers opposite may be identified as portions of heraldic shields. On a shield it may be taken to represent the engraving of the metal surface of the thing itself; and, indeed, here again is a significant resemblance between two technical processes.

To scratch with a needle or with a graver is much the same thing; and thus many a Swiss diaper suggests damascening, and might just as well have been executed in bright lines of gold or silver filigree, beaten into lines graven in steel or iron, as scraped out of a tint on glass.

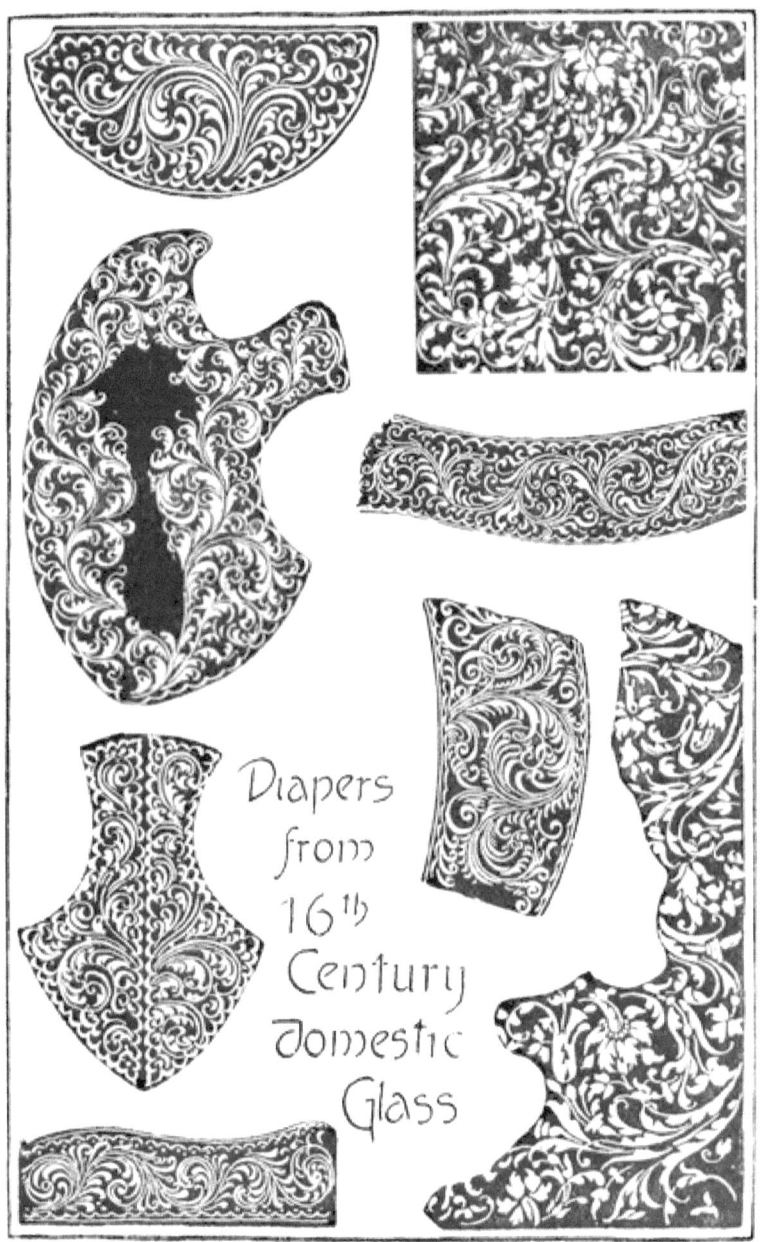

49. EXAMPLES OF SCRATCHING OUT.

But the use of the point was by no means reserved for ornamental detail. It became the main resource of the painter, and so much so, that this technique, or this development of technique, is the most striking characteristic of Swiss glass painting—if that should be called painting which has really more affinity with etching.

For the laying on of the paint in the form of solid colour, or of matted tint, or of skilfully floated wash, is only the groundwork of the Swiss glass painter's method. It scarcely needs to be explained how admirably the point adapted itself to the representation of hair, fur, feathers, and the like. The familiar bears, for example, the device of the city of Berne, which occur very frequently in Swiss heraldic work, are rendered at Lucerne in the most marvellously skilful manner. First a juicy wash of colour is floated all over the body of the beast, more or less translucent, but judiciously varied so as to give *à peu près* the modelling of the creature. Then with a fine point the lines of the fur are scraped out, always with an eye to the further development of the modelling. Finally, the sharp lights are softened, where necessary, with delicate tint, and a few fine hair-lines are put in with a brush in dark brown.

By no conceivable method of execution could certain textures be better rendered than this. A similar process is adopted in rendering the damascened surface of slightly rounded shields; but in that case the modelling of the ground is first obtained by means of matt, not wash.

Black as a local colour, whether by way of heraldic tincture or to represent velvet in costume, was very generally used; but in such small quantities always as entirely to justify its use. The practice, that is to say, referred to on page 57, with reference to the German work at Shrewsbury, was carried further. This was quite a different thing from what occurs, for example, in a late window at Montmorency, where four brown Benedictine monks are frocked in muddy paint: that is a fault of judgment no skill in execution could make good. In the case of black used by way of local colour the drawing lines were of course scraped out in clear glass, and toned, if need were, with tint. The hair, cap, and feathers of the figure opposite illustrate the processes of execution above described; the chain armour about the man's neck is also very deftly suggested.

The use of the point went further than rendering the texture

50. NEEDLE-POINT WORK, SWISS

of hair, and so on. It was used for the rendering of all texture and the completion of modelling everywhere. The Swiss glass painter did very much what is done in large when one draws on brown or grey paper in white and black; only instead of black chalk he used brown paint, and instead of putting on white chalk he scraped away a half tint with which he had begun by coating the glass; and of course he worked in small.

One knows by experience how much more telling the white crayon is than the black, how much more modelling you seem to get with very little drawing; and so it is in glass; and so it was that the glass painter depended so much more upon taking out lights than upon putting in darks. The difference between the Swiss manner and the process already described in reference to Renaissance church glass was mainly that, working upon so much smaller a scale, the artist depended so much more upon the point. His work is, in fact, a kind of etching. It is the exact reverse of drawing in pen and ink, where the draughtsman works line by line up to his darkest shadow. Here he works line by line to clearest light, precisely as the etcher draws his negative upon copper, only on glass it is the positive picture which is produced. So far as manipulation is concerned the two processes are identical. It is indeed quite within the bounds of possibility that the method of the glass painter (and not that of the damascener, as generally supposed) may first have put the etcher upon the track of his technique.

The method of workmanship employed by the painter is shown pretty clearly on page 90. In spite of a certain granular surface given by the stone employed by the lithographer in reproducing the design, it is quite clearly seen how the man's armour and the texture of the silk in his sleeves is all obtained by the point. The trace of the needle is not clearly shown in the flesh, except in the hand upon his hip; but on page 93 it is everywhere apparent—in the shading of the architecture, at the top of the page, in the damascening of the tops of shields below, in the drawing of the pastoral staff, in the modelling of the mitre and the representation of the jewels upon it, no less than in the rendering of the texture of the silk.

This ultra-delicacy of workmanship was naturally carried to its furthest extent upon white glass or upon white and stain, but the same method was employed with pot-metal colour; and, during the early part of the sixteenth century at least, pot-metal colour was used when it conveniently could be, and the leading was sometimes cleverly schemed, though the glass employed was often crude in colour. Eventually, in Switzerland as everywhere, enamel colour succeeded pot-metal, by which, of course, it would have been impossible correctly to render the tinctures of elaborately quartered shields on the minute scale to which they were customarily drawn. At Lucerne, for example, there are some small circular medallions with coats of arms not much bigger than occur on the back of an old-fashioned watchcase. Needless to say that there the drawing is done entirely with a point. This kind of thing is, of course, glass painting in miniature; it is not meant to say that it is effective; but it is none the less marvellously done. It was at its best, roughly speaking, from 1530 to a little later than 1600. Some of the very best that was ever done, now at the Rath-haus at Lucerne, bears date from 1606—1609; there is some also at the Hof-kirche there; but that is out of the reach of ordinary sight, and this is placed where it can conveniently be studied. The point work, it should be understood, is still always scraped out of brown, or it may be black. The enamel that may be used with it is floated on independently of this; and as time went on enamel was of course very largely used, especially in the seventeenth century. To the credit of the Swiss it should be said that, alone among later glass painters, they were at once conscientious and expert in the chemistry of their art, and used enamel which has been proof against time. They knew their trade, and practised it devotedly. Possibly it was the small scale upon which they worked which enabled them to fuse the enamel thoroughly with the glass. It is due to them also to say that, though their style may have been finikin, there was nothing feeble about their workmanship; that was masterly. And they remain the masters of delicate manipulation and finish in glass painting.

Although the needle point was used to most effective purpose in Swiss glass it did not of course entirely supersede other methods. At the Germanic Museum at Nuremberg (where there is a fair amount of good work, 1502—1672) there is some matted tint which is shaded and then lined in brown, much after the manner of one of Dürer's woodcuts. It has very much the appearance of a pen drawing shaded, as many of the old masters' drawings were, in brown wash.

51. NEEDLE-POINT WORK, SWISS.

A fair amount of simple figure work in white and stain continued to be done, in which outline went for a good deal, and matted shadow was only here and there helped out with the point. In landscape backgrounds shade tint was sometimes broadly and directly floated on. But as often as not shading was executed to a great extent with the needle, whilst local colour was painted with enamel. Even in association with admirable heraldry and figure work, one finds distant figure groups and landscapes painted in this way. They look more like coloured magic-lantern slides than painted window glass.

Sometimes subtlety of workmanship was carried rather beyond the bounds of discretion, as when at Nuremberg (1530) faces were painted in tint against clear glass, without outline, the mere shading, delicate as it is, being depended upon to relieve them from the ground. It must be confessed that, near to the eye, it does that; but the practice does not recommend itself.

It is remarkable how very faint a matt of colour on the surface of transparent glass gives a sort of opacity to it which distinguishes it from the clear ground. Sometimes white enamel is used, sometimes perhaps a mere coat of flux: it is difficult to say what it is, but there is often on the lightest portions of the painted glass no more than the veriest film, to show that it has been painted.

It is obvious that glass of the most delicate character described must be the work of the designer; and it seems clear, from numerous drawings extant, which are evidently the cartoons for Swiss window panes, that the draughtsman contemplated carrying out his design himself. At all events, he frequently left so much out of these drawings, that, if he trusted to the painting of another, no little of the credit of the draughtsmanship was due to that other, and he was at least part designer of the window. In glass where painting is carried to a high state of perfection it goes without saying that the painter must be an artist second only to the designer. Invention and technical power do not always go together. But if the designer can paint his own glass, and will, so much the better. It is more than probable that the best glass is the autograph work of the designer.

CHAPTER X.

THE RESOURCES OF THE GLASS PAINTER—A RECAPITULATION.

Having followed the course of technique thus far, it may be as well to survey the situation and see where we now stand. Suppose an artist altogether without experience in glass had occasion to design a window. The first thing he would want to know would be the means at his command at this present moment, and what dependence he could place upon them. That is what it is intended briefly to set forth in this chapter, quite without reference to date or style or anything but the capacities of the material. The question is, what can be done with it? Not until a man knows that is he in a position to make up his mind as to what he will do.

If he ask, as artists will, why cannot he do just what he likes, and as he likes, the answer is: because glass was not made for him, and will only do what he wants on condition of his demands upon it being reasonable. He might find it pleasanter if the world revolved round him; but it does not. If he would make a window he must go the way of glass: and the way of glass is this:—

In the first place, it is mosaic. It may be a mosaic of white glass or of the pearly tints which go to make what is termed grisaille, in which case the leads which bind the glass together form the pattern, or, at all events, a feature in it. Or it may be of coloured glass, or of white and colour, in which case the glass forms the pattern, and the lead joints are more or less lost in the outline of the design.

If the pattern is in white upon a deep coloured ground the lead joints crossing the pattern and not forming part of it are, as it were, eaten up by the spreading rays of white light, and, supposing them to be judiciously contrived, do not count for much. On the other hand, the lead joints crossing the coloured ground are lost in its depth. Advantage is taken of this to break up the ground more than would be necessary for convenience of glazing, or of strength when glazed, and so to get

52. PLAIN GLAZING, EARLY FRENCH.

that variety of pot-metal upon which so much of the beauty of glass colour depends.

To give satisfactory colour the best of pot-metal glass is essential. Structural conditions which a man is bound to take into account in his design are—that the shapes he draws must be such as can readily be cut by the glazier; that his lead joints must be so schemed as, where not lost in the glass, to form part of the design, strengthening, for example, the outlines; that his plan must at intervals include provision for substantial iron bars which shall not interfere with the drawing.

He must understand that each separate colour in his composition is represented by a separate piece of glass, cut out of a sheet of the required colour. There may, and should, however, be variety in it. A sheet of glass varies in depth of tone according to its thickness, which in the best glass is never even; moreover, it may be streaked or otherwise accidentally varied; and so considerable play of tint may be got in a well-selected piece of pot-metal. Should a tint be required which the palette of the glazier does not supply it may sometimes be obtained by leading up two thicknesses of glass together. This expedient is called "plating."

There are two very workmanlike ways in which white and colour may be obtained in one piece of glass. If the glass is not coloured throughout its thickness, but only a part of the way through, the coloured part may be eaten away in places by acid (it used formerly to be

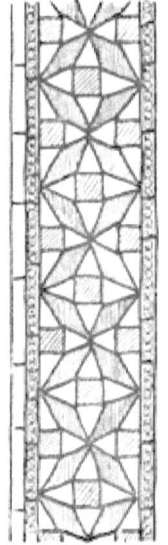

53. MOSAIC GLASS, ASSISI.

tediously abraded): and so a pattern of white may be traced upon a ground of blue, for example, or, as is more common, ruby.

A piece of white or pale coloured glass may further be *stained*, but only, so far, of one colour, yellow. The window opposite is all in white and golden-yellow. This result is produced by the action of silver upon it, which, at a sufficient temperature, develops a tint varying from lemon to orange of beautiful quality, and as imperishable as the glass; but one cannot be quite certain always as to the precise shade it will take in the fire. On blue it gives green, and so on.

By the combination of these two processes three tints may be obtained, or even four upon the same piece of glass—say white, green, and yellow all upon a blue ground.

There is a third method of avoiding lead glazing. If little jewels of coloured glass be cut out of various sheets and placed upon white glass they become fused at a sufficient heat in the kiln, and adhere more or less firmly to the glass on which they are laid; but this process of "annealing" is not very safe. Still less to be depended upon is the fourth process of "enamelling." In that case the coloured glass is applied in the form of a paint upon a sheet of white. Fusing at a comparatively low temperature, it rarely gets quite firmly fixed. Nor has it the depth of pot-metal colour. The three processes of staining, annealing, and enamelling, entail, it will be seen, the burning of the glass. Literally this is the limit of what can be done in stained glass.

The term stained glass, however, is generally used to include painting, which from the first has been associated with it. This painting (not to be confounded with the above-mentioned enamelling) is a second process, which the glass undergoes after it is cut and before it is fired. It is not in the least what a painter understands by painting. It is, in the first place, a means of giving in solid brown pigment, which effectually stops out the light, detail smaller than mere glazing would permit, such as the features of a face or the veining of a leaf: it gives the foils of the foliage, and marks the individual berries in the border overleaf. In the next it is used partially to obscure the glass, so as to give shading. The pigment is not used as colour, but for drawing and shading only. Local colour is represented by the pieces of pot-metal glass employed; the painting fulfils precisely the part of the engraving in a print coloured by hand. The various methods of painting are

54. WINDOW IN WHITE AND STAIN, WARWICK CASTLE.

55. AUXERRE.

explained on pages 45, 64, 89. In some respects they have more affinity with line drawing, mezzotint, and etching than with oil or water-colour painting.

It is extremely difficult to get delicacy of modelling or high finish at one painting—to all but a consummate glass-painter impossible. Many a time the work has to be painted several times over, each painting being separately burnt in, always at some risk. Painting that is not sufficiently fired peels off in time. If it is fired too much it may be burnt quite away.

The effect of paint in the form of shading is naturally to obscure the glass. Up to a certain point there is not much harm in that; it counts for nothing as compared with the facilities of expression it affords. But that point is soon reached. Then it becomes a question of the relative value of, on the one hand, purity and translucency of glass colour, and, on the other, of pictorial qualities. The problem is to get the utmost of modelling or expression with the minimum of obscuration. Much depends upon the method of painting adopted. So long as the light is allowed to get through it, one may indulge in a fair amount of shading, but a deep even tint, leaving none of the glass clear, is inevitably heavy. The more one can represent shadows by deeper tinted glass the more brilliant the result will be.

This painting, although, strictly speaking, in brown enamel, is not, as was said, what is usually meant by enamel painting: that is described on page 77. A window may be painted altogether in enamel; and, when the mosaic method went out, designs were painted in enamel upon panes of plain white glass; but, for the most part, since the pieces had to be connected by lead, it was found convenient to use pot-metal for some of the stronger colours. In recent times, however, owing to the introduction of large sheets of thicker glass, to improved glass kilns, and also to more accurate knowledge of the chemistry of enamel colours, it is possible to paint a picture window on one sheet of glass. That has been done with extraordinary skill at Sèvres. You may see really marvellous results in this kind in the Chapel of the Bourbons at Dreux. If you want neither more nor less than a picture upon glass, and are content with a picture in which the shadows are opaque and the lights transparent, that is the way to get it. You will not get the qualities of glass. Within the last two or three years there seems to have been very considerable improvement in the purity, translucency, and depth of enamel colours. How far they are lasting remains to be proved. Anyway, brilliant as they are, they have not by any means the intensity of pot-metal glass, and it does not seem, humanly speaking, possible that a film of coloured glass upon a sheet of white can ever compete in strength and volume with colour in the body of the glass itself.

If, therefore, we want the qualities of deep, rich, luminous and translucent colour, which glass better than any other medium can give, we must resort to the use of pot-metal—that is to say, to glazing—assisted more or less by brown paint, used, not to get colour, but to stop it out, or to tone it down.

According to the more or less of your dependence upon paint your method may be described as mosaic or pictorial.

Starting upon the mosaic system, you rough out your design in coloured glass (or what stands for it upon paper), and then consider how, by use of paint, as above mentioned, you may get further detail, shading, harmony of tone.

Starting upon the pictorial system you sketch in your design, shade it, and colour it, and then bethink you how you can get the glass to take those lines.

In either case you have, of course, from the first, a very distinct idea as to the assistance you will get from the supplementary process; but it makes all the difference whether you think first of the glass or of the painting. Upon that will depend the character of your window. If you want all that glass can give in the way of colour, begin with the mosaic. If you want pictorial effect, think first of your painting. If you want to get both, balance the two considerations equally in your mind from the first. Only, to do that, you must be a master of your trade.

A first consideration in the design of a window are the bars which are to support it. The skilled designer begins by setting these out upon his paper, nearer or closer together, according to the width of the opening, from nine to eighteen inches asunder. In a wide window it may be as well to make every second or third bar extra strong. Upright stanchions may also be introduced. Exigencies of design may make it necessary to alter the arrangement of bars with which you set out. You may have occasionally to bend one of them to escape a face, or other important feature; but, if you begin with them, this will not often be necessary. Bars may be shaped to follow the lines of the design. There is nothing against that, except that it is rather costly to do; and, on the whole, it is hardly worth doing. In big windows, such as those at King's College, Cambridge, raised some feet above the level of the eye, stout bars have, in effect, only about the value of strong lead lines, whilst lead lines disappear.

The points to be observed with regard to glazing are these: Since leads must form lines, it is as well to throw them as much as possible into outlines. In a cleverly glazed window the design will tell even when the paint has perished. To glaze a picture in squares, regardless of the drawing, is mere brutality. Because by aid of the diamond glass may actually be cut to almost any shape, it is not advisable, therefore, to design shapes awkward to cut, but rather to design the lead lines of a window with a view to simplicity of cutting and strength of glazing. Pieces of glass difficult to cut are the first to break. It is the business of the designer to anticipate breakage by introducing a lead just where it would occur. *Tours de force* in glazing are not worth doing. It is a mistake to be afraid of leads. Skilfully introduced, they help the effect; and, except in work which comes very near the eye, they are lost in the glass.

The quality of pot-metal glass is all important. It should never be mechanically flat and even. The mechanically imperfect material made in the Middle Ages is so infinitely superior to the perfect manufacture of our day, that we have had deliberately to aim at the accidents of colour and surface which followed naturally from the ruder appliances and less accurate science of those days. There are legends about lost secrets of glass making, to which much modern produce gives an appearance of truth. But, as a matter of fact, though old glass undoubtedly owes something of its charm to weathering, better and more beautiful glass was never made than is now produced; but it is not of the cheapest, and it wants choosing.

The choice of glass is a very serious matter. What are called "spoilt" sheets are invaluable. It takes an artist to pick the pieces. But without experience in glass the judgment even of a colourist will often be at fault. Some colours spread unduly, so that the effect of the juxtaposition of any two is not by any means the same as it would be in painting. It is only by practical experiment that a man learns, for example, how much red will, in conjunction with blue, run into purple, and which shade of either colour best holds its own. Effects of this kind have been more or less scientifically explained—by M. Viollet le Duc for one—but, in order to profit by any such explanation, a man must have experience also.

Referring to "flashed" glass, all kinds of double-glass are now made: red and blue = purple, yellow and blue = green, and so on; but there is not, except, perhaps, in work on quite a small scale, much to be gained by this. In fact, it is not well in work on a fairly large scale to depend too much upon etching pattern out of coated glass. In a window breadth of effect is of more account than minuteness of detail. Damask or other patterns in draperies might, more often than they are, be leaded up in pot-metal. It would compel simplicity on the part of the designer, and the effect of the glass would be richer.

With the increasing variety of coloured glass now made, plating becomes less necessary than once it was. The drawback to the practice is that dust and dirt may insinuate themselves between the two pieces of glass, and deaden the colour. The safe plan is to fuse the two pieces of glass together.

Good glass is more than half the battle. Raw glass may be toned down by paint, but poor glass cannot be made rich by it. The Italian glass painters often used crude greens and purples, and softened them with brown. They might do that with comparative safety under an Italian sky; but the deeper tones produced that way have not the purity and lusciousness of juicy pot-metal, and the paint is liable to peel off and betray the poverty of the cheap material. It is the fundamental mistake of the painter, because by means of paint he can do so much, to depend upon it for more than it can do. The toning of local colour with brown paint is only a makeshift for more thoroughly mosaic work; but it is an ever-present temptation to the painter, and one against which he should be on his guard.

The actual technique of glass painting, it has been explained already, is quite different from painting as the painter understands it; often it is not so much painting as scraping out paint. The artist may, nay must, choose his own technique. He will get his effect in the way most sympathetic to him. What he has to remember is, that, except where he wants actually to stop out light, he must get light into his shadows—whether by stippling the wet colour, or by scrubbing it when dry with a hog tool, or by scraping with a point, is his affair. For example, if he wants to lower the tint of a piece of glass, the worst thing he could do would be to coat it with an even film of paint. It would be better to stipple it so that in parts more light came through. But the best way of preserving the brilliancy of the glass would be either to paint the glass with cross hatched lines, or to scrape bright lines out of a coat of paint.

In draperies, backgrounds, and so on, this is most effectively done in the form of a diaper, often as minute as damascening, which scarcely counts much as pattern. Bold or delicate, a diaper is quite the most effective means of lowering colour; even hard lines seldom appear hard in glass, owing to the spreading of the light as it comes through; but the inevitable hardness of lines scraped out may be mitigated by dabbing the wet paint so as to make it uneven, or by rubbing off part of the paint after the lines have been scraped out. Another and yet another delicate film of paint may be passed over the painted diaper by a skilful hand, but out of each film lights should be scraped if the full value of the glass is to be preserved.

Solid pigment as local colour is a thing to indulge in only with extreme moderation. The strong black lead lines often want lines or touches of black strong enough to keep them in countenance (that is not sufficiently remem-

56. SCRATCHED DIAPER.

bered, and it is when it is forgotten that the leads assert their harshness in white glass), and here and there, in work on a small scale, a point of black (a velvet cap, a bag, a shoe, as shown overleaf,) is very valuable as local colour; but, when the scale allows, it is better always to get this mass in dark-toned glass, which gives the necessary depth of colour most easily, most safely, and with most luminous effect.

The thing not to do, is to paint the robes of black-draped

figures in black, a common practice in the seventeenth century. On the other hand, a robe of black richly embroidered with gold and pearls may quite well be rendered, as it was in late Gothic work, by solid paint, because the pearls being only delicately painted, and the gold being in great part perfectly clear yellow stain, plenty of light shines through.

As to the means of getting delicate painting in glass, the utmost delicacy can be got, but it costs patient labour, and there is risk of its going for nothing.

The only quite safe way of getting very delicate effects of painting is to paint much stronger than it is meant to appear. A very fierce fire will then reduce that to a mere ghost of what it was; possibly it will burn it away altogether. Upon this ghost of your first painting you may paint once again, strengthening it (and indeed exaggerating it) in all but quite the most delicate parts. A strong fire will, as before, reduce this without affecting the first painting. Possibly a third or even a fourth painting may be necessary to an effect of high finish. When you have it, it is as lasting as the glass itself.

37. S. MARY'S, SHREWSBURY.

This painstaking process, however, is found to be tedious. A much easier plan is to add to the pigment a quantity of borax, or other substance which will make it flow easily in the kiln. That necessitates only a gentle fire, in which there is no risk of burning away the work done, and enables you to do in one or two operations what would have taken three or four. But the gentle fire required to fix soft flux only fixes it gently. Securely to fix the pigment, the glass should have been raised to almost red heat, to the point, in fact, at which it just begins to melt, and the colour actually sinks into it, and becomes one with it. A heat anything like that would have wiped out soft colour altogether. Moreover, the borax flux itself is very readily decomposed by the moisture of a climate like ours. Accordingly the more easily executed work cannot possibly be fast. It fades, they say. That is not the case. It simply crumbles off, sooner or later; but eventually the atmosphere has its way with it. That is how we see in modern windows faces in which the features grow dim and disappear.

We have got to reckon with this certainty, that if we want our painting to last we must fire it very severely. What will not stand a fierce oven will not stand the weather.

In view of the labour and risk involved in very delicate painting it becomes a question how far it is worth while. That will depend upon the artist's purpose. But the moral seems to be that, for purposes of decoration generally, it would be better not to aim at too great delicacy of effect, which is after all not the quality most valuable, any more than it is most readily attainable, in glass.

Only those who have had actual experience in glass appreciate the value of silver stain. It gives the purest and most beautiful quality of yellow, from lemon to orange, brilliant as gold. There is some risk with it. One kind of glass will take it kindly, another will reject it; you have to choose your glass with reference to it. The fire may bring it to a deeper colour than is wanted. It may even come out so heavy and obscure that it has to be removed with acid, and renewed. Some all but inevitable uncertainty as to its tint, renders this peculiar yellow more suitable for use where absolute certainty of tint is not essential. Nevertheless, the skilled glass painter makes no difficulty of doubling the process, and staining a dark yellow upon a lighter, with very beautiful results. Occasionally a master of his craft has gone so far as literally to paint in stain, scraping out his high lights in white, and giving, for example, the very picture of embossed goldsmith's work.

In the diapering of draperies and the like stain is of great service, and again in landscape upon blue. But it has not been used for all it is worth as a means of qualifying colour which is not precisely right, apart altogether from pattern. Many a time where a scum of paint has been employed to reduce a tint, a judicious blur of stain, not appreciable as such, would have done it more satisfactorily, without in the least obscuring the glass.

Nowhere is silver stain more invaluable than in windows of white glass or *grisaille*, the quality of which is not sufficiently appreciated. The mother-of-pearl-like tints of what is called white glass lend themselves, in experienced hands, to effects of opalescent colour as beautiful in their way as the deeper pot-metal tones.

There is no great difficulty in combining *grisaille* and colour, provided the white be not too thin nor the colour too deep; but the happiest combinations are where one or the other is distinctly predominant. With very deep rich glass, such as that used in the thirteenth century, it is most difficult to use white in anything like a patch (for the flesh, for example, in figure work). Unless very heavily painted it asserts itself too much, and heavy paint destroys its quality. Practically the only thing to do is to use glass of really rather strong tint, which in its place has very much the value of white. The "whites" in Early windows are a long way from purity. They are greenish, bone colour, horny; but they have much more the effect of white than has, for example, pure white glass reduced by paint to a granular tint of umber.

Flesh tints present a difficulty always, unless you are content to accept a quite conventional rendering of it. In connection with strong colour you may use flesh-tinted glass; but that is just the one tint which it is most difficult to get in glass. It is usually too pink. Painting on white glass in brown produces the most invariably happy results, and in windows into which white largely enters that is quite the best expedient to adopt. In practice it proves ordinarily a mistake to adopt a warmer brown for flesh tint, or to paint it in brown and red, as was done in the sixteenth century and after that. It looks always unpleasantly hot. When flesh wants relieving against white it is better to use a colder white glass for the background. The only condition under which warm-tinted flesh is quite acceptable is when it is in the midst of strong red and yellow. The use of red enamel for flesh seems to be a weak, unnecessary, and unavailing concession to the pictorial. It does not give the effect of actual flesh, and it does not help the effect of the window. Since you cannot get actual flesh tones it is as well to accept the convention of white flesh, which gives breadth and dignity to the glass. There is a sort of frivolity about enamelled flesh-pink. It is, in a way, pretty, but out of key with the monumental character of a window. Glass lends itself best to strong, large work. The quality of pot-metal gives the colour chord. The leads give the key to the scale of design—the pitch, as it were, of the artist's voice. That these are strong (it is seldom worth while resorting to extra thin leads) does not argue that design must be coarse. You have to balance them with strong work, with patches, perhaps, as well as strong lines, of dark paint, to carry off any appearance of brutality in them. This done, much delicate detail may be introduced. A strong design need not shout any more than a speaker need, who knows how to manage his voice. That is the condition: you must know your instrument, and have it under control.

Experience seems to show that a certain formality of design befits stained glass. Formality of colour arrangement soon becomes tedious; but it is seldom, if ever, that the design of glass strikes one as unduly formal.

Mosaic glass is designed, it was said above, with a view to glazing. The skilled artist designs, so to speak, in leads; but they are not the design; in fact, they count only as contours, and, except in mere glazing, they should not be expected to give lines. It is a common fault to make leads take a part in the design which they will not play in the glass.

In drawing, strong, firm, even angular lines are valuable, if not imperative. The radiating light softens them. Drawing which is already suave is likely to be too soft in the glass, to want accent. Only experience will tell you how much you must attenuate fingers and the like in your drawing in order that the light shall fill them out, and give them just their normal plumpness. The beginner never allows enough for the spreading of light.

Glass painters who know what they are about use plenty of solid painting-out; but it takes experience to do it cunningly. An artist whose *métier* is really glass is not careful of the appearance of his drawings. Cartoons are nothing but plans of glass, not intrinsically of any account. Really good glass is better than the drawings for it—necessary as good sketches may be to please the ignorant patron.

New departures in technique will suggest themselves to every inventive mind. They may even be forced upon a man—as, by his own confession, they were forced upon Mr. Lafarge—by the inadequacy of the materials within his reach, or the incompetence of the workmen on whom he has to depend. Mr. Lafarge's glass is sometimes very beautiful in colour, and is strikingly unlike modern European manufacture: but it is not so absolutely original in method as Americans appear to think. He seems to have discovered for himself some practices which he might have learnt from old or even modern work, and to have carried others a step further than was done before. The basis of his first idea, he explains, was in a large way to recall the inlay of precious stones that are set in jade by Eastern artists. That was practically the notion of the earliest Byzantine workers in glass. His use of other materials than glass in windows he might have learnt from China, Java, or Japan, where they use oyster, tortoise, and crocodile shell; or from ancient Rome, where mica, shells, and alabaster were employed. There is nothing very new in blended, streaked, or even wrinkled glass, except that moderns do by deliberate intention what the mediaeval glass maker could not help but do, and carry it farther than they. In chipping flakes or chunks out of a solid lump of glass, Mr. Lafarge certainly struck out an idea which had probably occurred to no one since, in prehistoric ages, man shaped his arrow heads and so on out of flint. He has produced very beautiful and jewel-like effects by means of this chipping, though the material lends itself best to a more barbaric style of design than the artist has usually been content to adopt. He has appreciated, no one better, the quality of glass, but not the fact that so characteristic a material as he adopts must rule the design. The attempt to get pictorial, atmospheric, or other naturalistic effects by means of it, soon brings you to its limitations. At the rendering of flesh it comes to a full stop.

The experiment has been tried by Mr. Lafarge of a minute mosaic of little pieces of glass between two sheets of white, all fused into one; but it appears to be too costly, if not too uncertain an expedient, to be really practical as a means of rendering the human face, more especially if you want to get expression, which is there of more importance than natural colour. Another new departure, the device of blowing glass into shapes, so as to get modelling in them, results so far in rather dumb and indeterminate form.

It is quite possible to melt together a mosaic of glass without the use of lead. That practice may yet come into use in window panes, but they will be as costly as they are fragile. In larger work there is no real artistic reason why lead or its equivalent should be avoided. How much old glass would have remained to us if it had been executed in huge sheets? Here and there perhaps a broken scrap in a museum.

It is not meant to suggest that we should do in the nineteenth century only what was done in times gone by. Our means are ampler now, our wants are more. We can follow tradition only so far as it suits our wants: and, in carrying it further, we are sure to arrive at something so different that it may be called a new thing. If old methods do not meet new conditions we must invent others. The problem of our day is how to reconcile manufacture with anything like art: or failing that, whether there is a livelihood for the independent artist-craftsman?

Whoever it may be that is to make our stained glass windows in the future, he will have to make them fit the times. He may discover new materials. Meanwhile it is of no use quarrelling with those he has. He must know them and humour them. Bars have to be accepted as needful supports, leads to be acknowledged as convenient joints; glass must be allowed its translucency, and painting kept to what it can best do. A window should own itself a window.

And what is the aim and use of a stained glass window? To "exclude the light," said the poet, sarcastically. Yes, to subdue its garishness, soften its glare, tinge it with colour, animate it with form perhaps.

The man who means to do good work in windows will devote as serious study to old glass as a painter to the old masters. He will not rest satisfied without knowing what has been done, how it was done, and why it was done so; but he will not blind himself to new possibilities because they have never yet been tried. The pity is that often the antiquary is so bigoted, the glass painter so mechanical, the artist so ignorant of glass. The three men want fusing into one. The ideal craftsman is a man familiar with good work, old and new, a master of his trade, and an artist all the while: a man too appreciative of the best to be easily satisfied with his own work, too confident in himself to accept what has been done as final; a man experimenting always, but basing his experiments upon experience, and proving his reverence for the great men who light the way for him by daring, as a man has always dared, to be himself.

BOOK II.

CHAPTER XI.

THE DESIGN OF EARLY GLASS.

DESIGN in glass developed itself on lines almost parallel to the progress of technique. Each, of course, affected the other—how and why it is now proposed to show.

It is not intended at present to say more than is absolutely necessary about "Style," in the historic sense—that is reserved for a chapter by itself—but, as it is convenient to refer to a period of design by its name, it will be as well at this stage briefly to enumerate the historic "Periods."

Glass follows, inevitably, the style of architecture of the period. Accordingly it is divided broadly into Gothic and Renaissance. Gothic, in its turn, is divided by Rickman (who first attempted to discriminate between the styles of architecture in England) into three periods. Winston, who did for English glass what Rickman did for English architecture, adopts his classification as follows:—Early Gothic—to about 1280. Decorated Gothic—to about 1380. Perpendicular Gothic—to about 1530.

Renaissance art has been classified in Italy according to the century, and in France has been named after the reigning sovereign—François Premier, Henri Deux, and so on. In England also we make use of the terms Tudor, Elizabethan, Jacobean, and the like. No one, however, has attempted to draw subtle distinctions between the periods of Renaissance glass, for the obvious reason that the best of it was done within a comparatively short period, and the rest is not of much account. It is enough, therefore, to mark off two divisions of Renaissance glass. The first (which overlaps the latest Gothic) may be called Sixteenth Century, or by the Italian name Cinque Cento, or simply Renaissance; whilst the second, which includes seventeenth century and later work, is sufficiently described as Late glass.

The development of style in other countries was not quite parallel with its march on this side of the water. The French were always in advance of us, whether in Gothic or Renaissance; the Germans lagged behind, at all events in Gothic; but the pace is equal enough for us to group windows generally into three Gothic and two Renaissance periods—Early, Middle, and Late Gothic; Early and Late Renaissance. If we do that it will concern us less, that Early German work is more Romanesque than Gothic, that Late French work is not Perpendicular but Flamboyant, and so on.

The accepted classification is determined mainly by the character of the architectural or ornamental detail of the design. Such architectural or other detail—that of costume, for example—is of the very greatest use as a clue to the date of glass. That is a question of archæology; but it is not so much the dates that artists or workmen have to do with as with the course of craftsmanship, the development of art. It is convenient for us to mark here and there a point where art or workmanship has clearly reached a new stage; it gives us breathing time, a starting-point on some fresh voyage of discovery; but such points need be few. The less we bother ourselves by arbitrary subdivisions of style the better; and Winston himself allows that his divisions are arbitrary.

The student need not very seriously concern himself about dates or names. People are much too anxious to get a term for everything, and when they can use the term glibly they fancy they know all about the thing. It is no doubt easier to commit to memory a few names and a few dates than to know anything about a craft; but the one accomplishment will not do in place of the other. A very little real knowledge of art or practical workmanship will lead you to suspect, what is the truth, that there is a good deal of fee-fi-fo-fum about the jargon of styles. It is handy to talk of old work as belonging to this or that broadly marked historic period; and it is well worth the while of any one interested in the course of art to master the characteristics of style. The student should master them as a matter of course; but he must not take the consideration of period for more than it is worth. Really we give far too much

WINDOW SHAPE AND GLASS DESIGN.

attention to these fashions of bygone days—fashions, it must be allowed, on a more or less colossal scale, compared to ours, but still only fashions.

It is proposed then to allude here only so far to the styles as may be necessary to explain the progress of design, and especially the design of stained glass windows.

In dividing Gothic into Early, Middle, and Late Gothic, corresponding roughly with the thirteenth, fourteenth, and fifteenth centuries, it is not forgotten that there is an earlier Gothic of the twelfth and perhaps eleventh centuries, more or less reminiscent of the Romanesque period preceding it; but English glass begins, to all intents and purposes, with the thirteenth century, and even in France there is not a very great quantity of characteristically earlier glass. What there is differs from thirteenth century work mainly in the Romanesque character of the figure drawing and ornamental detail, in its deliberately simple composition, and in the spontaneity of its design. The glazier was still feeling his way. Any composition to be found in a Byzantine ivory-carving, enamel, illuminated manuscript, or what not, might just as well occur in glass. The more familiar types of early Gothic window-design had not yet settled down into orthodoxy.

38. POITIERS.

The lines on which the oldest windows extant were set out are in the main those of the thirteenth century also. They were more or less suggested by the shape of the window opening, which, it will be seen, had always had a good deal to say as to the direction glass design should take.

The window openings in Romanesque or Norman-French churches were single lights, round or pointed arched, rather broad in proportion to their width. Stained glass, it has been explained, has to be held in its place by copper wires, soldered to the lead work, and attached to iron bars let into the masonry for that purpose. In the case of a very narrow lancet, such bars would naturally be placed at convenient intervals across the opening. But for the most part windows were the reverse of narrow, and the horizontal bars had to be supplemented by vertical stanchions, so that the window space was divided into rectangular divisions. As a matter of construction the glass was

59. POITIERS, EAST WINDOW.
(Compare with 243.)

made in panels, corresponding to these, and attached to them. It is not surprising, therefore, that these divisions should often have been accepted as part of the design, or that the design of the glass should to some extent have followed them. On page 113 is the skeleton of the upper part of a twelfth century window. The strong black lines in the diagram show the bars, the finer ones indicate the main divisions of the design of the glass. It will be seen that the four strips into which the upright bars divide the window are not equal, but that the outer divisions are narrower than the inner, so as to accommodate themselves to the width of the border. Naturally that was determined always by the proportion of the window; such borders measured often one-sixth part, or more, of the entire width. The way in which the central circular shape in the glass breaks across in front of the border is an instance of the spontaneity and unexpectedness of design characteristic of the earliest existing work; later one series of forms would repeat themselves without interruption throughout the length of the window. When, as above, the centre of a window is occupied by a great crucifix, or, as below, other such irregularity occurs, it is safe to conclude that the glass, if not prior to the thirteenth century, belongs to its first years. It is characteristic of the very early date of the glass that the bars in the diagrams given do not go out of their way to follow the outline of the circles, vesicas, quatrefoils, and other shapes, but on occasion cut relentlessly across them.

The filling out of such a skeleton as those given would in many respects be much the same in the eleventh, twelfth, or thirteenth

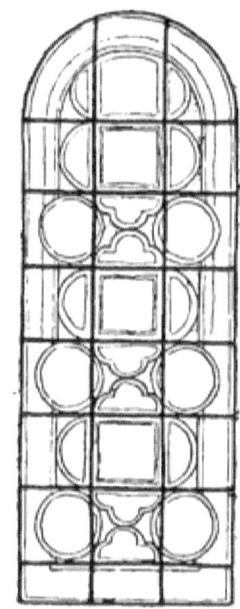

60. POITIERS, NORTH TRANSEPT.

century; and in each case it would be in direct pursuance of the traditions of Early Christian design. You may see in Byzantine ivories and enamels precisely the kind of thing that was done in glass; and in the Romanesque Michaelis Kirche at Hildesheim, is a painted roof, the design of which might have been carried out, just as it is, in a giant window.

The main divisions of the centre part of such a window would

61. BORDER, ANGERS.

62. BORDER, ANGERS.

each contain its little "subject" or glass picture; the border and the interstices between the pictures would be occupied with foliated ornament: only, the earlier the work, the more pronounced would be the Romanesque character, alike of the ornament and the figure work. The broad borders from Angers, above, and the narrower one from Le Mans (page 327) differ materially from the accepted thirteenth century type (page 117). Witness how in the Angers glass the stalks of the foliage frame little panels in the border, and how in the Le Mans work the stalks take the form of straps, patterned with painted ornament. This elaboration of the stalks with painted zig-zag, pearlwork, and so on, is precisely the kind of thing one sees in Byzantine carving and inlay. The very early spandril from Angers, below, if not markedly Romanesque in character is yet not of the distinctively Early Gothic type.

65. ANGERS.

The shape of each medallion would be emphasised by a series of coloured lines or fillets framing it. In quite early work the broader of these would be broken up into blocks of alternating colour; they would be patterned probably (which in the thirteenth century they would probably not be), and altogether the effect of the ornament would be more jewelled. One of these broken and patterned margins is shown in the vesica-shaped framing to the figure on page 37 —belonging, by the way, to the window given in skeleton on page 114.

The difference between twelfth and thirteenth century pictures is in the lingering of Byzantine traditions of design in the earlier work, and in the strictly simple disposition of the figures *en silhouette* against the background, as well as in the way the drapery is wrapped closely round them, so that the figure always explains itself. There is an expression and a "go" about some of the earliest figures for which we look in vain later in the thirteenth century. The figures of the Apostles from the Ascension at Le Mans on page 33 are altogether more alive than the thirteenth century bishops, for example, on page 276, who seem by comparison tame and altogether respectable. A certain exaggeration there is, no doubt, about the action of these earliest figures, a certain brutality of rendering, as there is also a certain barbaric quality in the ornament, and, indeed, in the whole effect; but of its superlative richness there is no manner of doubt. One is even led to speculate, when one compares it with later work, whether a certain barbaric character of design does not go to that unrivalled brilliancy. In the absolute glory of rich colour the very earliest glass has never been equalled. The advance of glass painting was at the cost of this, perhaps barbaric, quality.

In the earliest windows the subjects were not invariably enclosed in medallions; sometimes the square lines of the

117

64. EARLY ORNAMENT, SALISBURY.

bars would be accepted as division enough; these would be framed with lines of colour, and the design of the portion of the window within the border would consist (as occasionally at Chartres) of a series of square subjects, each with its marginal lines, ranged one above the other. For the most part, however, the design of the earliest richly coloured windows extant took the shape of little pictures in panels or medallions. Another favourite scheme was to delineate the Tree of Jesse. The upper portion of such a window is given on page 117; but further consideration of Jesse windows is reserved for a separate chapter.

From the earliest period, no doubt, clerestory or other lights were often occupied each with a separate figure standing upright; but such of these as may remain in their places are not readily distinguishable from thirteenth century work; and the undoubtedly earlier figures—such, for example, as those in S. Remi at Reims—have been re-set in framework more or less old, but so as not to tell us anything very authentic about the setting out of the original windows. Again at Augsburg, where the figures in the clerestory are said to be the oldest in Germany (to belong, in fact, to about the year 1000), the windows are bordered with modern glazing in white. At Reims we have very rudely drawn figures in rich colour against a deep background, standing with splayed feet upon little rounds or half rings of colour, re-

65. S. REMI, REIMS.

presenting the earth, their names inscribed in bold lettering, which forms a band of yellow behind their heads. At Augsburg the figures, equally rude in drawing, equally splay-footed, are in white and colour upon a white ground. They stand upon little hemispheres of Byzantine ornament, and their names are writ large in black letters upon the white glass around their heads. Presumably they were framed in a border of pattern-work similar to that surrounding the medallion windows. The ornamental work in the windows at S. Remi may not always have formed part of the same window with the figure work—it does not go very happily with it now—but it is probably of about the same date; and it illustrates, together with some similar work at S. Denis, near Paris (so " thoroughly restored " as to have lost its historic value), a kind of pattern-work peculiar to the earliest glass.

As a rule, early glass divides itself naturally into two classes: work in rich colour, which is what we have hitherto been discussing, and work in " grisaille," as it is called ; that is to say, in which the glass is chiefly white, or whitish, relieved only here and there by a line or a jewel of colour.

Occasionally, as at Auxerre, Reims, and Poitiers, rich figure work is found set in grisaille or framed by it; and in some fragments from Châlons, now at the *Musée des Arts Décoratifs* at Paris, coloured figures are found on a white ground.

You find also in France rich colour-work surrounded by white glass—the work of a period when the powers that were became possessed of the idea that they must lighten the interior of their churches, and accordingly removed so much of the coloured glass as seemed good to their ignorance, and replaced it with plain glazing. But, as a rule, and apart from the tinkering of the latter-day ecclesiastic, rich colour and grisaille were kept apart in early mediaeval churches; that is to say, a coloured window has not enough white in it perceptibly to affect the depth and richness of its colour, nor a grisaille window enough colour to disturb the general impression of white light. At Reims and S. Denis, however, you find ornament in which white and colour are so evenly balanced that they belong to neither category. The amount of colour introduced into grisaille was never at any time a fixed quantity; one has to allow something for the predilection of the artist; but here the amount of colour makes itself so distinctly felt that the term grisaille no longer serves to express it.

The design of these patterns was of a rather mechanical type (pages 35, 118, 120) and not in any case very interesting; but it would have been difficult under any circumstances to produce a very satisfactory effect by so equally balancing white and colour. The designer falls between two stools. The well-known gryphon medallions at S. Denis seem at first to promise something rather amusing in design, but there is no variety in them: —and no wonder! the greater number of them prove to be new, and they have all been rearranged by Viollet le Duc. That is as much as to say, some of the gryphons are of Abbot Suger's time, but the design of the window is Viollet le Duc's. White and colour are again too evenly mixed in the heavy-looking English glass at Lincoln shown on page 121, but that is of the thirteenth century.

66. S. REMI, REIMS.

It need hardly be said that the earlier the work, the simpler was the character of the painting, the more deliberately was pigment reserved for painting out the light, the more strictly was the shading in lines. But the painted detail was often small; glass was used in small pieces; subjects themselves were ordinarily small in scale. The largeness of effect was due first to the actual simplicity of the main lines of the design, and then to breadth of colour, a breadth of colour all the more remarkable seeing the small pieces of glass of which the broad surfaces were of necessity made up.

Of course, too, the earlier the work the more the design was influenced by the technique of glazing, the more clearly it can be seen how the glazier designed (as was explained on page 44) in lead-lines, and only made use of paint to fill them out.

In twelfth century glass the white was greenish and rather horny in texture; ruby was sometimes streaky, and often tawny or inclined to orange; blue varied from deep indigo to pale grey, occasionally it was of the colour of turquoise; yellow, dark or pale, was usually brassy; green ranged from bluish to pale apple, and from dull to emerald. These colours, with a rich brownish-purple, the lighter shades of which served always as flesh tint, made up the glazier's palette. Happily there was considerable inequality of colour in the material. It deepened, for example, towards the selvage of the sheet where it was thickest; it had streaks and bubbles in it; no two batches ever came out of the pot quite alike; and altogether the rudely made pot-metal was chemically most imperfect and artistically all that glass should be.

67. LINCOLN.

It would be rash in the extreme to formulate any theory as to early schemes of colour; probably the glazier's main thought was to get somehow a deep, rich, solemn effect of colour. He secured this very often by not confusing his tints, and by allowing a single colour so to predominate that the window impressed you at once as bluish or greenish or reddish in tone. He was on the whole happiest when he kept his colour cool; but he produced also red windows which are never to be forgotten.

In the cathedral at Poitiers, where many of the beautiful medallion windows belong to the very early part of the thirteenth century, the scheme is usually to adopt a blue background, alike for the medallions and for the spaces between, relying upon a broad band of ruby, edged with white pearling, to mark the medallion shapes, which it effectively does; but these are not the most beautiful windows in the church. One recognises their date rather by the individuality and spontaneity of the design than by any distinctly Romanesque character in the detail. It should be mentioned, also, that at Poitiers, even in windows which seem not so emphatically to belong to the very beginning of the century, the early practice of using only straight upright and cross bars is adhered to. There may be something of local conservatism in that.

68. BARS IN EARLY MEDALLION WINDOWS.

CHAPTER XII.

MEDALLION WINDOWS.

IN the thirteenth century the practice of the earlier glaziers stiffened into something like a tradition, and design took almost inevitably the form of (1) the Medallion window, (2) the Single Figure window, (3) Ornamental Grisaille.

The full-blown thirteenth century Medallion window differed from what had gone before in that it was more orthodox. The designer begins as before by marking off a broad border to his glass, defined on the inner side by an iron bar, and proceeds to fill the space within the border with medallion shapes. But he now adapts the medallions more regularly to the spaces between the bars. At most two alternating shapes occur throughout the length of the light, without break or interruption, such as occurs in earlier work, and as a rule they keep strictly within the lines of the border. In all the nine examples here given, taken at random from Chartres, Bourges, Canterbury, and elsewhere, only in one case does a medallion cut boldly across the border in the head of the light. The slight overlapping of the quatrefoils in one case is not really an overlapping of the border but only of the marginal lines to it, not shown in the diagram above, but clearly enough explained on page 132, which shows the completion of a corner of the window, less its side border. In the window with large circular medallions divided into four, there is no upright bar to define the border, faintly indicated by a dotted line.

It will be seen from these diagrams, which illustrate at once the main divisions of the glass and the position of the iron-work, what a change came over the construction of windows in the thirteenth century. The window is no longer ruled off by upright and horizontal bars into panels into which the design is fitted; it is the bars which are made to follow the main lines

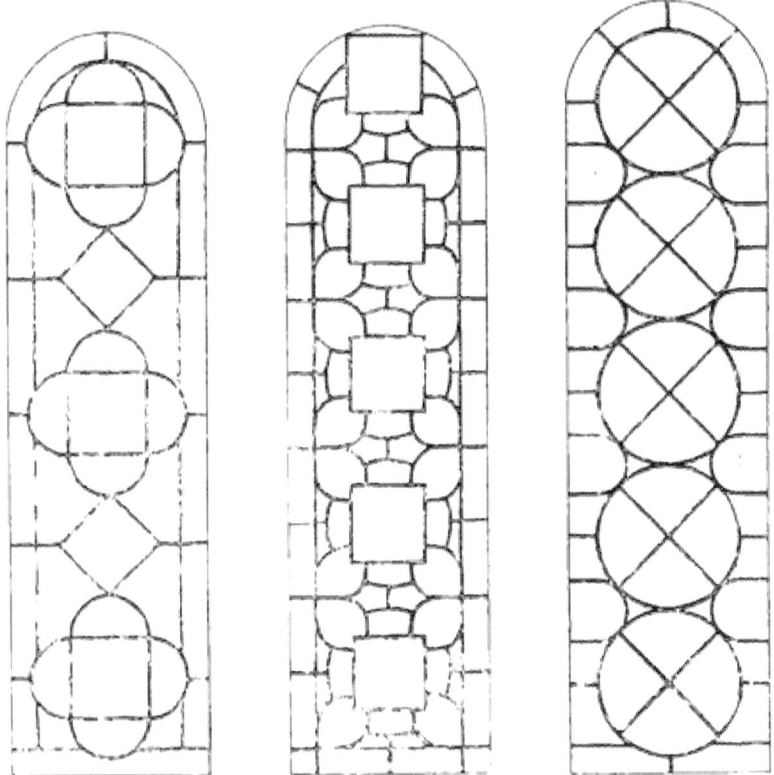

69. BARS IN EARLY MEDALLION WINDOWS.

of the design, and to emphasise the forms of the medallions. The rare exceptions to this rule (as at Bourges, overleaf) may generally be taken to betray either the beginning or the end of the period; but at Poitiers they seem to have passed through the early period without ever arriving at shaped bars. The early glazier, it was said, first blocked out his design according to his leading; here he begins with the bars. The iron frame-work forms, itself, in many of these windows, a quite satisfactory

S.G.

pattern, and one which proudly asserts itself in the finished
window. The designs of the period are not of course all equally
ingenious. Sometimes, in order to strengthen a circle or quatrefoil of great size, the glazier, instead of breaking up the shape
ornamentally as was the rule, merely supports it by cross bars;
not only that, but he accepts the awkward shapes given by them
as separate picture spaces. Of this comes one of two evils: either
he frames his little pictures with sufficient borders-lines to keep

70. SPANDRILS OF MEDALLION WINDOW, BOURGES.

them distinct, and so draws attention to the shapes, an attention
they do not deserve; or he has to accept the bars, with perhaps
a fillet of colour, as sufficient frame, which they are not, and
his pictures run together, to the bewilderment of whoever would
decipher them.

It is matter for regret that the French did not accept the
full shape of even the largest medallion, and fill it with
one bold subject: over and over again one feels that the
subjects in medallion windows are not only too small to be
readable, but so small that the figures are out of scale with
the ornamental detail. The scale of the church has, of
course, to be taken into account; but the French churches
are big enough to warrant figures thrice the size of those
which ordinarily occur in medallions. In our narrower
"Early English" lancet windows the medallions naturally
came small.

To divide a window into eccentric divisions (halves or
quarters of circles, quatrefoils, and the like) and then to take

these awkward shapes as separate picture frames, is an archaic method of design much in need of excuse. The more reasonable thing to do would have been to make use of such incomplete forms only in some secondary position, and as framework for ornament, or at least quite subsidiary figures.

Apart from shapes which are really only segments of medallions, the only awkward medallion shapes occurring in Early glass are those which are broader than they are high, such as occur, for example, at Soissons. These have always the uncomfortable appearance of having been crushed.

How the iron skeleton of a medallion window is filled out with leaded glass; how the border and the medallion shapes are strengthened by bands of colour; how the medallions themselves are occupied with little figure subjects, and how the interspaces are filled in with ornament, is indicated opposite and on pages 132, 325.

By way of variation upon the monotony of design, the designer will sometimes reverse the order of things. At Bourges, for example, you will find the centre of a light devoted to insignificant and uninteresting ornament, whilst the figure subjects are edged out into half quatrefoils at the sides of the window; and, again, at Chartres and Le Mans you may occasionally see the pictures similarly ousted from their natural position by rather mechanical ornament. One can sympathise with an artist's impatience with the too, too regular distribution of the stereotyped medallion window. There is undoubtedly a monotony about it which the designer is tempted to get rid of at any price; but consistency is a heavy price to pay for the slight relief afforded by the treatment just described.

This striving after strangeness results not only in very ugly picture shapes—no one would deliberately design such a shape as that which frames the picture of the Dream of Charlemagne (overleaf)—but it produces a very uncomfortable impression of perversity. It is quite conceivable that ornament may be better worth looking at than some pictures; but a picture refuses to occupy the subordinate position; it will not do as a frame to ornament. There is no occasion to illustrate very fully the design of Early figure medallions; they are often of very great interest, historical, legendary and human, but there is little variation in the system of design. The picture is of the

I 2

simplest, perhaps the baldest, kind. The figures, as before stated, are clearly defined against a strong background, usually blue or ruby; a strip or two of coloured glass represents the earth upon which they stand; a turret or a gable tells you that the scene is in a city; a foliated sprig or two indicate that it is out of doors, a forest, perhaps; a waving band of grey ornament upon the blue tells you that the blue background stands for sky, for this is a cloud upon it.

71. THE DREAM OF CHARLEMAGNE, CHARTRES.

The extremely ornamental form which conventional trees may assume is shown in Mr. T. M. Rooke's sketch from a medallion at Bourges, opposite. In the medallions from Chartres (page 325) are instances of simpler and less interesting tree forms, and in the upper part of the larger of the two, a bank of conventional cloudwork. Explanatory inscriptions are sometimes introduced into the background, as in the dream of Charlemagne (above), or in the margin of the medallions, as in the Canterbury window on page 132, fulfilling in either case an ornamental as well as an elucidatory function.

In the Canterbury glass it will be seen the figures are more crowded than in the French work illustrated. This is not a peculiarity of English glass, but a mark of period; as a rule the clump or compact group of personages proclaims a later date than figures isolated against the background. There is no surer sign of very early work than the obvious display of the figures against the background, light against dark or dark against light. Another indication of the date of the Canterbury figures is that their draperies do not cling quite so closely about them as in figures (page 33) in which the Byzantine tradition is more plainly to be traced.

There is no mistaking a medallion window, the type is fixed: within a border of foliated ornament a series of circles, quatrefoils, or other medallion shapes, for the most part occupied by figure subjects on a rather minute scale, and between these ornament again.

The border might be wider or narrower, according to the proportion of the window, though a wide border was rather characteristic of quite early glass. A twelfth century border (Angers) will sometimes measure more than a quarter of the entire width of the window. The borders from Canterbury, Beverley, Auxerre, and Chartres (overleaf) are of the thirteenth. A border of sufficient dimensions will sometimes include medallion shapes as on pages 115, 325, and even occasionally little subject medallions at intervals, or it may be half-circles, each containing a little figure; but such interruption of the running border is rare. In so far as it counts against monotony it is to the good.

In narrower windows, such as more frequently occur in this

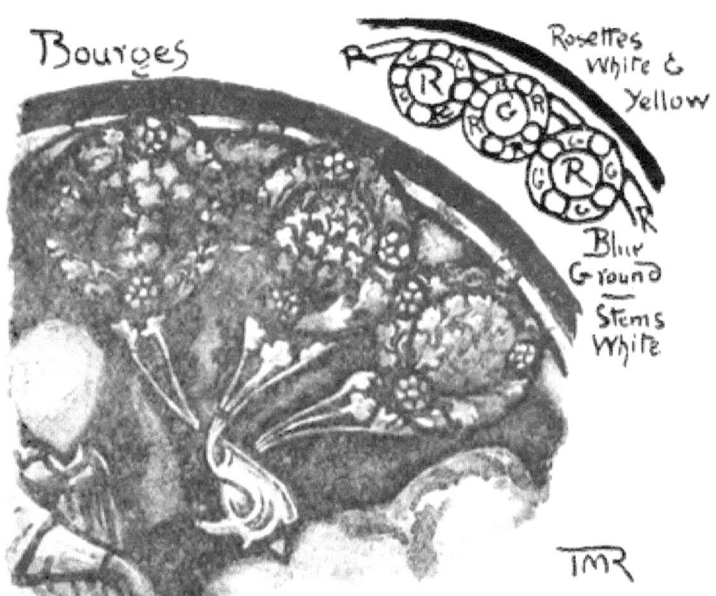

72. DETAIL FROM AN EARLY MEDALLION.

73. CANTERBURY.

country, where, as the Gothic style of architecture supplanted the Norman, lancet lights took a characteristically tall and slender shape, the border was reduced to less imposing proportions, as for example at Beverley;—there was no room for a wide frame to the medallions, nor any fear, it may be added, that these should be so large as to require breaking up into segments, as in much French glass, or at Canterbury: there the window openings, as was to be expected of a French architect, are more characteristically Norman than English in proportion. In a very narrow light in the one-time cathedral at Carcassonne the medallions break in front of a not very wide border; but then this, though a medallion window, belongs probably by date to the Second Gothic period.

Medallions themselves may be simple or fantastic in shape. They may be devoted each to a single picture, or subdivided into a series of four or five; they may be closely packed, and supported by segments of other medallions, also devoted to figure work, or they may be separated by considerable intervals of ornament. The character of that ornament takes two distinct forms.

In the examples given (pages 132, 325) it takes the form of foliated scrollwork, very much of a piece with the ornament in the borders, except that there is more scope for its growth. In actual detail it varies, according to its date and whereabouts, from something very much like Romanesque strapwork to the more or less trefoiled foliage typical of Early Gothic ornament, whether French or English. Further examples of the last are shown in the borders from Auxerre and Chartres (page 328). The one from Chartres illustrates the transition from the Romanesque; it is intermediate between the two. The borders from S. Kunibert's, Cologne, are quite Romanesque in character, though they

74. BEVERLEY MINSTER.

THIRTEENTH CENTURY ORNAMENT.

75. AUXERRE.   76. CHARTRES.

are of the thirteenth century; but then it has to be remembered that the Romanesque style of architecture was flourishing on the Rhine long after the Gothic style had developed itself in France and England. Many of the details from Canterbury—which, by-the-bye, are almost identical with contemporary French ornament—show a lingering influence of the pre-Gothic period, but the scroll occupying the spandril on page 132 is pronouncedly of Early Gothic type. Of much the same character is the detail from Salisbury on page 117, which forms no part of a medallion window, but more likely of a tree of Jesse.

It was in this ornamental kind of design that the thirteenth century glaziers were most conspicuously successful. One no longer feels here, as one does with regard to their figure work, that they mean much better than their powers enable them to do. And it is with scrollery of this kind, either growing free or springing from the margin of the medallion, that the Early English designers occupied the intervals between the medallions in their windows. In France it became the commoner practice to substitute for it a diaper of geometric pattern. Other expedients were occasionally adopted. There is a window at S. Denis in which there is foliated scrollwork on a background of geometric diaper, although this last is so much "restored" that, for all one can tell, Viollet le Duc may be entirely responsible for it.

At Soissons is a window in which the interspaces between the medallions are filled with deep blue, broken only here and there by a spot of ruby; at Poitiers also the ornament in spandrils is often just a quatrefoil or so, barely foliated, if at all: at Bourges there is an instance of spandrils (page 125) occupied by

77. S. KUNIBERT, COLOGNE.

78. FRENCH MOSAIC DIAPERS.

bare curling stalks and rosette-like flowers; at Poitiers the bands which frame the medallions have a way of interlacing, not in the simple fashion shown in the example from Canterbury below, but so as to form a kind of pattern in the spandrils in front of the geometric filling; and there are other variations on the accustomed medallion tunes; but as a rule the ornament consists either of the usual Early Gothic foliation, closely akin to that in the borders, such as is shown on pages 129, 130, 328, 330, or of geometric pattern, such as is here given. The rarity of the mosaic diaper in this country may be gathered from the fact that in the whole series of Early medallion windows at Canterbury it is found only once, its frequency in France from the fact that in the choir alone of Bourges Cathedral it occurs in no

79. CANTERBURY.

less than twenty-two instances; again at Chartres, out of twenty-seven great windows, not more than four have scrollwork; at Poitiers, on the other hand, there is little geometric diaper, but the ornament is of the simplest, and barely foliated. This device of geometric diaper-filling was possibly inspired by the idea of utilising the small chips of precious glass, which, with the then method of working, must have accumulated in great

80. FRENCH MOSAIC DIAPERS.

81. DETAIL OF MEDALLION WINDOW, CANTERBURY.

quantity. In any case, it must have been encouraged by that consideration, if not actually suggested by it. Apart from economy, which is a condition of craftsmanlike work, there does seem a sort of artistic logic in the use of merely geometric design for quite subordinate filling, to act as a foil to figure work; but there was no occasion to put the mosaic of fragments quite so regularly, not to say mechanically, together, as was the custom to do.

82. FRENCH MOSAIC DIAPER.

That is shown in a rather unusual instance in a window of the Lower Church at Assisi; there occurs there a diaper of circles with blue interstices, where the circles, though all alike painted with a star pattern, vary in colour in a seemingly accidental way, and are red, yellow, green, brown, just as it took the fancy of the glazier.

It follows inevitably from the small scale on which these patterns are set out, and from the radiation of the coloured light, that unless very great discretion is exercised the rays get mixed, with a result which is often the reverse of pleasing. And the worst of it was that the French glaziers particularly affectioned a combination of red and blue most difficult to manage. A very favourite pattern consisted of cross bands of ruby (as above), enclosing squares or diamonds of blue, with dots of white at the intersection of the ruby bands, which persists always in running to purple.

Instances of this unpleasant cast of colour are of continual occurrence, but they are never otherwise than crude and plummy in effect. The rather unusual combination of red and green mosaic diaper occurs, however, pretty frequently at Carcassonne. The diapers illustrated indicate the variety of geometric pattern to be found at Bourges, Chartres, Le Mans, and Notre Dame at Paris, and elsewhere. In proportion as there is in them a preponderance of blue and ruby the effect is that of an aggressive purple. The safest plan seems to be in associating with the blue plenty of green, or with the ruby plenty of yellow glass; or a similar result may be obtained by the choice of a deep neutral blue and of an orange shade of red, taking care always that the two contrasting colours shall not be of anything like equal strength.

At the best these diapers compare very unfavourably with

scrollwork. They are, in the nature of things, more monotonous and less interesting than a growth of foliage; they are apt also to run to gaudy colour, which by its mass overpowers the pictures set in it. Compare, in any French church, the windows in which there is geometric mosaic and those in which there is scrollwork; and, though they may be all of the same period, and presumably the work of the same men, you will almost certainly have to marvel how artists who at one moment hold you spellbound by the magic of their colour can in the next disturb your eyesight with a glare of purple produced by the parody of a Scotch plaid. Many of these diapers are very minute in scale; the smaller the scale on which they are designed the greater the certainty of the colours running together.

S. S. PETER DELIVERED FROM PRISON, LYONS.

It is to the very small scale of the figures, also, that the confusion of effect in medallion subjects, in spite of their comparatively flat treatment, is to be attributed. At Bourges, at Canterbury, everywhere, the medallion subjects are on far too minute a scale to be made out by mortals of ordinary patience, or, to speak accurately, impatience. Often, even in windows which come close enough to the eye for study, it is only the more conventionally familiar pictures which explain themselves readily; and those you recognise almost by anticipation. You have no difficulty in deciphering the Nativity, the Crucifixion, the Ascension, and so on, because you expect to find them. A certain muddle of effect must be accepted as characteristic of medallion windows.

It is not to be wondered at, that, considering the difficulty of making out the ordinary medallion subjects in the lower windows, where they are usually found, some other scheme of composition should have been adopted for clerestory windows where those would have been more than ever unintelligible. Accordingly, in that position, the single figure treatment was adopted, and carried further than in the preceding century. The figure was now, not for the first time, but more invariably, enclosed in something like an architectural niche—a practice borrowed from the sculptor, who habitually protected the carved figures enriching the portals of great churches by a projecting canopy, giving them at the same time a pedestal or base of some kind to stand upon.

In glass there was clearly no occasion for such architectural shelter or support; but the pretended niche and base offered a means of occupying the whole length of the space within the border, which, without some additional ornament, would often have been too long in proportion to the figure, the mere band of inscription under its feet not being enough to fill out the length. These very rudimentary canopies, specimens of which are given here, are usually very insignificant. It takes sometimes an expert to realise that the broken colour about the head of the saint (page 46) stands for architecture. The forms, when you come to look at them closely, may be ugly as well as childish, but they go for so little that it seems hardly worth while to take exception to them. It is only as indication of a practice (later to be carried to absurd excess) of making shift with sham architecture for the ornamental setting necessary to bring the figure into relation and into proportion with the window it is to occupy, that the device of thus enshrining a figure as yet deserves attention. As the beginning of canopy work in glass it marks a very eventful departure in design. All that need here be said about the Early Gothic canopy is that it would have been easy to have devised decorative forms at once more frankly ornamental, more interesting in themselves, and more beautiful, not to say less suggestive of a child's building with a box of bricks.

84. LYONS.

Sometimes, as at Chartres and elsewhere, the base of the canopy would itself take the form of a little subordinate niche enclosing a figure in small of the Donor, or perhaps only of his shield of arms. Sometimes it would take the form of a panel of inscription, boldly leaded in yellow letters upon blue or ruby.

An alternative idea was to represent the Saints, or other holy personages, sitting. The figure on page 135 belongs actually to the beginning of the fourteenth century; but, except for a slightly more naturalistic character in the drawing of the drapery, it might almost have belonged to the same period as the standing figure on page 46. In longer lights two saints are often figured, sitting one above the other. This may be seen in the clerestory at Canterbury; but the effect is usually less satisfactory than that of the single figure on a larger scale. The standing position is also much better suited to the foreshortened view which one necessarily gets of clerestory windows. A curious variation upon the ordinary theme occurs in four of the huge lancets in the south transept at Chartres, where the Major Prophets are represented each bearing on his shoulders an Evangelist. The same idea recurs at Notre Dame, Paris, under the south rose. That is all very well in idea—iconographically it is only right that the Old Testament should uphold the New—but reduced to picture it is absurd, especially as the Evangelists are drawn to a smaller scale than the Prophets, and irresistibly suggest boys having a ride upon their fathers' shoulders. Dignity of effect there can be none. Not now for the first time, seemingly, is art sacrificed to what we call the literary idea.

It shakes one's faith somewhat in the sincerity of the early mediæval artist to find that in the serried ranks of Kings, Prophets, Bishops, and other holy men, keeping guard over the church in the clerestory lights, one figure often does duty for a variety of personages, the colour only, and perhaps the face, being changed. At Reims there are as many as six in a row, all precisely of the same pattern, though the fraud may not be detected until one examines them from the triforium gallery. At Lyons, again, it looks as if the same thing occurred; but one cannot get near enough to them to be quite certain. None the less they are fine in colour. Thirteenth century glass was capable of great things in the way of colour; and the rows of Kings and Prophets looking down upon you from the clerestory of a great church like Bourges, archaic though the drawing be, are truly solemn and imposing.

CHAPTER XIII.

EARLY GRISAILLE.

WITH grisaille glass begins a new chapter in the history of glass painting, and a most important one—not only because of the beautiful work which was done from the first in white, but also because coloured glass grew, so to speak, always towards the light.

85. S. SERGE, ANGERS.

The first coloured windows were intense in colour, rich, and even heavy. The note they struck was deep, solemn, suited to the church and to the times. Neither priest nor parishioner was afraid to sacrifice a certain amount of light. It was the business of a window to shut in those that worshipped from the outer world, and wrap them in mysterious and beautiful gloom. With other days, however, came other ideals. As time went on, and men emerged from the dark ages, the problem of the glazier was how more and more to lighten his glass; until at last white glass predominated, and the question was how to introduce colour into it. Meanwhile the thirteenth century glaziers resorted, where they wanted light, to the use of windows in grisaille, in absolute contrast to the rich picture glass in the same church.

86. S. SERGE, ANGERS.

The model for grisaille design was readily found in the earlier pattern work in plain glazing.

This last never quite went out of use. But already in the thirteenth century, and probably in the twelfth, it began to be supplemented, for the most part, by painting. The exceptionally graceful work at S. Serge, Angers, for example, on this page and the last, is probably not very much later than the year 1200. You can see at a glance how this is only a carrying further of the unpainted work in the same church (page 27) attributed to the thirteenth century. There may be found indeed amidst the plain glazing scraps of painted work; but they never happen to fit, and have pretty certainly found their way into the window in course of repairs. The unpainted window seems to be of greener and more silvery glass than the painted, to which perhaps the cross-hatching gives a rather horny look.

87. S. JEAN-AUX-BOIS.

The one way of painting grisaille in the thirteenth century was to trace the design (which of course followed the traditional lines) boldly upon the white glass, and then to cross-hatch the ground, more or less delicately according to the scale of the work and its distance from the eye, as here shown. By this means the pattern was made to stand out clear and light against the background, which had now the value of a

88. S. Jean-aux-Bois.

tint, only a much more brilliant one than could have been got by a film or wash of colour. Very occasionally a feature, such as the group of four crowns which form the centre of the circle, above, might be emphasised by filling in the ground about them in solid pigment; but that was never done to any large extent. The rule was always to cross-hatch the ground.

With the introduction of colour into grisaille comes always the question as to how much or how little of it there shall be. There is a good deal of Early French work, which, on the face of it, was designed first as a sort of strapwork of interlacing bands in plain glazing, and then further enriched with painted

89. Soissons.

work, not growing from it, except by way of exception. This is seen in the example here given. The painter indulged in slight modifications of detail as he went on. He had a model which he copied more or less throughout the window; but he allowed himself the liberty of playing variations, and he even departed from it at times. By this means he

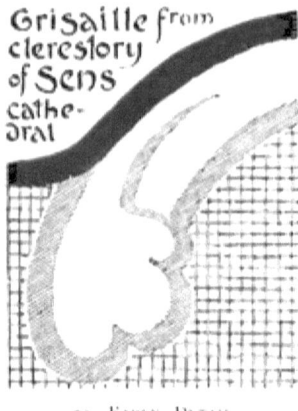

90. EARLY DETAIL.

adapted himself to the glass, which did not always take just the same lines, and at the same time he amused himself, and us, more than if he had multiplied one pattern with monotonous precision. His painting was strong enough to keep the leads in countenance; that is to say, his main outlines would be as thick (see opposite) as lead lines.

Patterns such as those on pages 138, 139, and below, from Soissons, Reims, S. Jean-aux-Bois, would make good glazed windows apart from the painting on them. Indeed, the painting is there comparatively insignificant in design. In the Soissons work, in particular, it consists of little more than cross-hatching upon the background, to throw up the interlacing of the glazed bands; for, with the exception of just a touch of colour in the one opposite, these designs are executed entirely in white glass.

91. SOISSONS.

The geometric glazing shapes so completely convey the design, that the painted detail might almost be an afterthought.

In much of the earliest grisaille there is absolutely no colour but the greenish hue belonging to what we are agreed to call white glass, and the effect of it is invariably so satisfactory as to show that colour is by no means indispensable. And, at all events in France, the colour was at first very

92. REIMS.

WHITE BANDS AND COLOURED JEWELS.

sparingly used, except in those twelfth century patterns (pages 35, 118, 120) which cannot fairly be called grisaille. In the window on page 137 the colour is, practically speaking, enclosed in small spaces ingeniously contrived

95. LINCOLN.

94. WATER PERRY, OXON. S.G.

between the interlacing bands of white; in that on page 138 it is introduced in half rings, which form part of the marginal line, and in spots or jewels; but in either case there is little of it, and it is most judiciously introduced. The interlacing of bands of plain white upon a ground of cross-hatching, itself enriched with scrollwork clear upon it, is characteristically French. Similar bands of white occur, though not interlacing, in the comparatively clumsy panel from Lincoln (above), but the more usual English way was to make the bands of white broader, and to paint a pattern upon them, as in the lancet from Water Perry, Oxfordshire (opposite), or in the much more satisfactory light from Lincoln (overleaf), leaving only a margin of clear glass next the cross-hatched background. A similar kind of thing occurs in the church

EARLY GRISAILLE.

95. LINCOLN.

of S. Pierre at Chartres (below). A yet more usual plan with us was to make the strapwork in colour, as at Salisbury. In the patterns on this page the straps do not interlace. In that on page 143 they not only interlace one with the other, but the painted ornament, which now takes the form of more elaborate scrollwork than heretofore, is intertwined with them. This is an extremely good example of Early English grisaille. Altogether Salisbury Cathedral is rich in white glass windows of this period (pages 143, 148, 329, 332).

The grisaille in the clerestory at Bourges is similar to the Salisbury work, but it is not possible to get near enough to it to make careful comparison. The scrollwork on page 143 may be profitably compared with the very unusual white window at S. Jean-aux-Bois (overleaf). There the design consists altogether of scrolls in white upon a cross-hatched ground. It is as if the designer had set out to glaze up a pattern in white upon a white ground, cross-hatched. But it is obvious that, as there is

96. S. PIERRE, CHARTRES.

97. GRISAILLE, SALISBURY CATHEDRAL.

no change of colour, it was no longer necessary always to cut the ornament out of a separate piece of glass from the ground. We find consequently that, wherever it is convenient, a painted line is used to save leading. That, it has been already explained (page 24), was a practice from the first; and it was resorted to more and more. It came in very conveniently in the French windows, in which the design consisted largely of white strapwork. It was adopted in the example from Châlons here given, though it does not appear in the sketch, any more than it does in the glass until you examine it very carefully. However, in the sketches from the great clerestory window from Reims Cathedral (overleaf), and in the smaller one from

98. CHÂLONS.

S. Jean-aux-Bois (facing it), the economy of glazing is easy to perceive; whilst in that from Coutances (page 147) the glazier is already so sparing of his leads that they no longer always follow or define the main lines of the pattern.

In a remarkable window in the choir of Chartres Cathedral (page 150) the design includes interlacing bands both of white and colour, the coloured ones flanked with strips of white; but the white bands are not glazed separately. They are throughout included in the same piece of glass as the crosshatching, which defines them. This ingenious and very graceful pattern window is still of the thirteenth century, though clearly of much later date than, for example, the windows of S. Jean-aux-Bois, which might indeed almost belong to the twelfth.

In several of the Salisbury windows (pages 148, 386) thin straps of colour are bounded on the outer side by broader bands of white painted with pattern. And here it should be noticed the bands no longer interlace at all; on the contrary, the ornamental forms are superposed one upon the other. This is very markedly the case on page 148. In the centre of the light is a series of circular discs, and at the sides of these a row of

99. CLERESTORY, REIMS.

zigzags, which, as it were, disappear behind them, whilst at the edges of the window, again, is an array of segments of smaller circles losing themselves behind these. In such cases, it will be seen, the broad white bands fulfil the very useful purpose of keeping the coloured lines apart, and separating one series of shapes from the other. In this window, as in the narrow light on page 386, where the vesica shape is occupied once more with flowing scrollwork, and as in all but one of the windows on that page, the background of cross-hatching is for the first time omitted, and the pencilled pattern is by so much the less effective. As a rule, patterns traced in mere outline like this belong to a later date; but these windows are certainly of the thirteenth century. It is seldom safe to say that this or that practice belonged exclusively to any one period. The white glass on page 335, almost entirely without paint, might have been executed in the twelfth century, but its border indicates more likely the latter part of the thirteenth.

105. S. JEAN-AUX-BOIS.

Quite the simplest form of glazing was to lead the glass together in squares or diamonds. These "quarries," as they are called (from the French *carré*) are associated sometimes with rosettes and bands of other pattern-work, as at Lincoln (pages 284, 287); but more ordinarily the ornamental part of the window is made up entirely of them. "Quarry" is a term to be remembered. It plays in the next century an important part in the design of windows.

The best-known grisaille windows in England are the famous group of long lancets, ending the north transept of York Minster, which are known by the name of the Five Sisters. You remember the legend about them. The "inimitable Boz" relates it at length in "Nicholas Nickleby"; but it is nonsense, all the same. The story tells how in the reign of Henry the Fourth five maiden ladies worked the designs in embroidery, and sent them abroad to be carried out in glass. But, as it happens, they belong to the latter part of the thirteenth century; they are unmistakably English work; and, what is more, no woman, maiden, wife, or widow, ever had, or could have had, a hand in their design. Their authorship is written on the face of them. Every line in their composition shows them to be the work of a strong man, and a practical glazier, who worked according to the traditions that had come down to him. A designer recognises in it a man who knew his trade, and knew it thoroughly. The notion that any glazier ever worked from an embroidered design is too absurd. As well might the needlewoman go to the glazier to design her stitchery. But such is the popular ignorance of workmanship, and of its intimate connection with design, that no doubt the vergers will go on repeating their apocryphal tale as long as vergers continue to fill the office of personal conductors.

COUTANCES.

The Five Sisters are rather looser and freer in design than the Salisbury glass, and have broad borders of white. In detail they are certainly not superior to that, nor in general design, so far as one can make it out at all; but, from their very size and position, they produce a much more imposing effect. Whoever is not impressed by the Five Sisters is not likely ever to be moved by grisaille. They form one huge fivefold screen of silvery glass. The patterns are only with great difficulty to be deciphered. It is with these as with many others of the most fascinating windows in grisaille: the glass is corroded on the surface, black with the dirt and lichen of ages, cracked and crossed with leads introduced by the repairing glazier, until the design is about as intelligible as would be a conglomeration of huge spiders' webs. But, for all that, nay, partly because of it, it is a thing of absolute

102. GRISAILLE, SALISBURY CATHEDRAL.

103. CHARTRES CATHEDRAL.

beauty, as beautiful as a spider's web, beaded with dewdrops, glistening in the sun on a frosty winter's morning. It is a dream of silvery light: who cares for details of design? But it is all this, because it was designed, because it was planned by a glazier for glazing, and has all that gives glass its charm.

Stained glass, like the men who design it, has always the defects of its qualities. It is the first business of those who work in it to see that it has at least the qualities of its defects.

CHAPTER XIV.

WINDOWS OF MANY LIGHTS.

THE merry life of the medallion window was a short one. It reigned during the Early Gothic period supreme; but after the end of the thirteenth century it soon went quite out of fashion, and with it the practice of shaping the bars to suit the pattern of the window—a practice, it will have been noticed, not followed in grisaille windows, though it might very well have been.

With the change which came over the spirit of later thirteenth century architecture some new departure in the design of glass became inevitable. The windows spoken of till now were all single lights, broader or narrower, as the case might be, but each so far off from the other that it had to be complete in itself, and might just as well be designed with no more than general reference to its neighbours. But in time it began to be felt in France that the broad Norman window was too broad, and so they divided it into two by a central shaft, or mullion as it is called, of stone. In England equally it began to be felt that the long narrow lancet lights were too much in the nature of isolated piercings in the bare wall, and so the builder brought them closer and closer together, until they also were divided by narrow mullions.

In this way, and in answer especially to the growing demand for more light in churches, and consequently for more windows, it became the custom to group them. Eventually the window group resolved itself into a single window of several, sometimes of many, lights, divided only by narrow stone mullions. Or, to account for it in another way, windows of considerable size coming into vogue, it became necessary, for constructional no less than for artistic reasons, to subdivide them by mullions into two or more lights. The arched window-head was broken up into smaller fancifully shaped "tracery" lights, as they are called; and so we arrive at the typical "Decorated" Gothic window.

The height of these windows being naturally in proportion to their width, the separate lights into which they were divided were apt to be exceedingly long. To have treated them after the Early medallion manner, each with its broad border, would have been to draw attention to this, and even to exaggerate their length. The problem now to be solved in glass was, how best to counteract the effect of insecurity likely to result from the thinness of the upright lines of the stone and the narrowness of the openings between them. It is not meant to say that the medallion window expired without a spasm. For a while Decorated windows were treated very much after the fashion of the earlier medallion windows. The medallions were necessarily smaller, and usually long in proportion to their width, although they extended now to the edge of the stonework, the narrowish border to the lights passing, as it were, behind them. This is very amply illustrated in the windows in the choir clerestory at Tours. Occasionally there is no border but a line of white and colour, and the whole interval between the elongated hexagonal or octagonal panels is given up to mosaic diaper.

104. DECORATED MEDALLION WINDOW, GERMAN.

The medallions naturally range themselves in horizontal order throughout the three or four lights of the window, giving just the indication of a horizontal line across them. By way of exception, the subject of the Last Supper extends through all three lights of the East window, the tablecloth forming a conspicuous band of light across it. This glass at Tours is deep and rich throughout, as intense sometimes as in earlier work, though warmer in colour, owing to the greater amount of yellow glass employed. That was not to last long.

It lingered longest in Germany. There is a curious two-light window in Cologne Cathedral, with queer rectangular medallions, of considerable interest, which is probably not very early in date. A not very common type of Decorated medallion window is illustrated above. The cutting across the border by medallion or other subjects, is a common thing in fourteenth century glass (below and opposite), just because such encroachment is obviously a most useful device in dealing with narrow spaces. It occurs in some medallion windows (also of the fourteenth century) at the church of Santa Croce, at Florence.

But this was not enough. The Germans went a step further, and carried the medallions boldly across two lights, treating them as a single medallion window with a stone mullion instead of an iron bar up the centre. There is an instance of this at S. Sebald's Church, Nuremberg, and another, more curious than beautiful to see, at Strassburg. They went further still, and carried the medallions across a three-light window. There is one such at Augsburg, where the medallions almost fill the window, extending to the extreme edge of the outer lights. Indeed, a broad outer border of angels surrounding the great circles is cut short by the side walls. This is at least a means of getting rid of the littleness resulting sometimes from the small medallion treatment, and it is in fact most effective. The broad, sweeping, circular lines also have the appearance of holding the lights together and strengthening them.

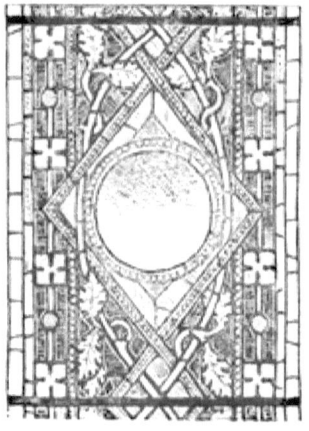

105. FREIBURG.

This was a thing most needful to be done in Decorated glass. It was needed sometimes already in Early work. At Clermont-Ferrand the narrow lancets at the end of the South transept are filled, except for a thin white beaded border, with diaper work in rich colour, interrupted at intervals by big rosettes of white, which form two bands of light across the series, and make them seem one group.

The deliberate use of horizontal lines (or features giving such lines) in glass, was clearly the most effective way of counteracting the too upright tendency of the masonry, or rather of preventing it from appearing unduly drawn out; and it became the custom. Even in a comparatively small Decorated window, for example, the figures would usually form a band across it, distinguished from the ornamental shrinework

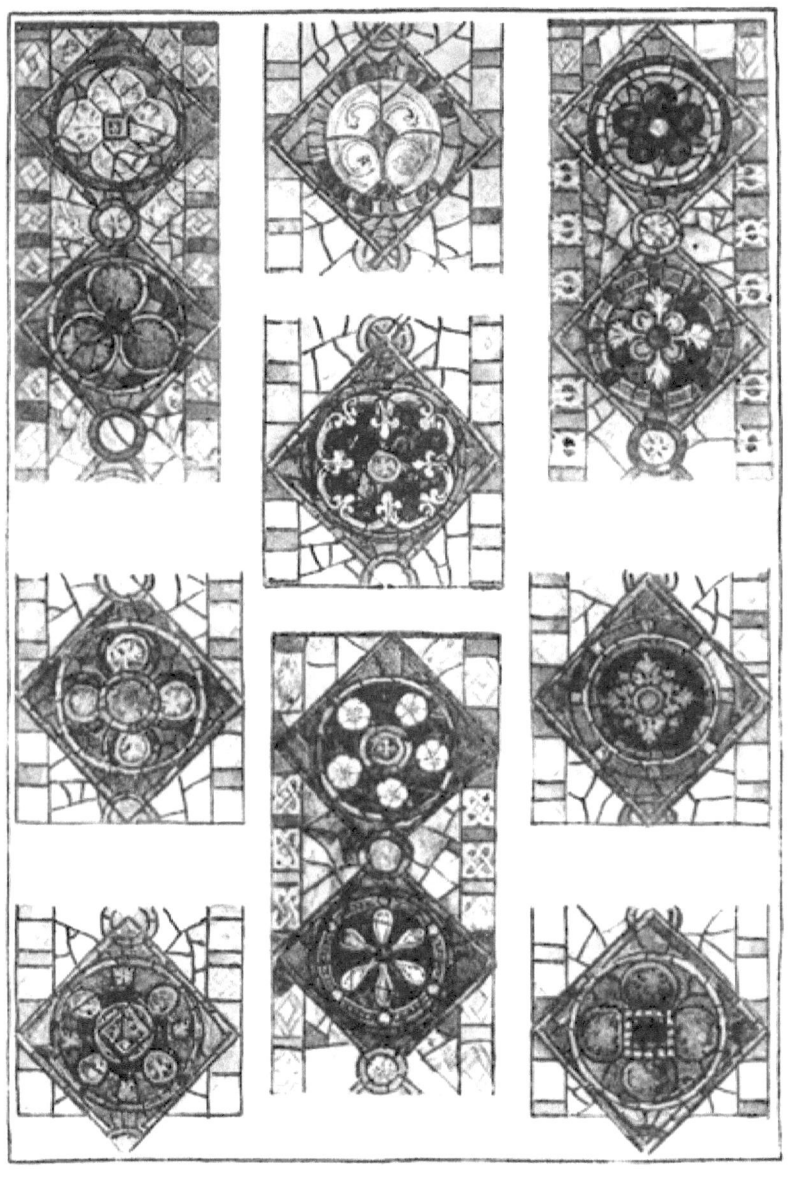

106. DETAILS OF DEC. GERMAN GLASS.

DECORATED CANOPIES.

107. TYPICAL DECORATED CANOPY.

above and below it by a marked difference in colour. In a taller window there would be two, or possibly three, such bands of figures, in marked contrast to their framing. In Germany very often one big frame would cross the window, or the figure subjects would be separated—as at Strassburg, for example—by bands of arcading, out of which peeped little saints each with a descriptive label in his hand.

A typical English canopy of the period is given on this page. It was commonly enclosed, as here shown, within a border, wide enough to be some sort of acknowledgment of the subdivision of the window, but not wide enough to prevent the colour of the canopy from forming a distinct band across the window. The predominance of a powerful, rather brassy, yellow in the canopy work, and a contrast in colour between its background and that of the figures, carried the eye without fail across the window. A notable exception to the usual brassiness of the Decorated canopy occurs at Toulouse, where a number of high-pitched gables of the ordinary design, stronger in colour than usual, have crockets and finials of a fresh bright green.

The Decorated canopy, with its high-pitched gable and tall

108. S. URBAIN, TROYES.

flying buttresses, its hard lines, and its brassy colour was a characteristic, but never a very beautiful feature in design; and it grew to quite absurd proportions. It was in Germany that it was carried to greatest excess, extending to a height three or four times that of the figure and more; but with us also it was commonly tall enough altogether to dwarf the poor little figure it pretended to protect.

Even when it was not preposterously tall, its detail was usually out of all proportion to the figure. Your fourteenth century draughtsman would have no hesitation in making the finial of his canopy bigger than the head (nimbus and all) of the saint under it. Clumsiness of this kind is so much the rule, and disproportion is so characteristic of the middle of the fourteenth century, that, but for some distinctly good ornamental glass of the period, one might dismiss it as merely transitional, and not worthy of a chapter to itself in the history of glass design.

Our distinctions of style, as was said, are at the best arbitrary. We may devise a classification which shall serve to distinguish one marked type from another, but it is quite impossible to draw any hard-and-fast line between the later examples of one kind and the earlier of another one. We may choose to divide Gothic art into three classes, as we may

109. NEW COLLEGE, OXFORD.

subdivide the spectrum into so
many positive colours, but the
indeterminate shades by which
they gradate each into the other
defy classification or description.

Certainly the best figure work
of the middle period is that
which might quite fairly be
claimed as belonging, on the
one hand, to the end of the
Early, or on the other to the
beginning of the Late, Gothic
period. In the figures from
Troyes, for example (page 47
and opposite), the Early tradition lingers; in those from New
College (also opposite) the characteristics of Late work begin
to appear. In the figure of the
headsman on this page there is
certainly no sense of proportion.
In all the wealth of Decorated
figure-and-canopy-work at York
Minster there is nothing to rank

116. EXECUTIONER OF S. JOHN
BAPTIST, 14TH CENTURY.

for a moment with the best Early or Perpendicular glass. Nor
in France, though there is Decorated work in most of the
great churches, is there anything conspicuously fine. Even at
S. Ouen, at Rouen, there is nothing particularly worthy of note.
It is true that the period of the English occupation and the
troubles which followed it was not the time when we should
expect the arts to flourish there.

A most characteristic thing in glass of this intermediate
period was the way in which colour and grisaille were
associated. It has been already told how, before then, white
and colour had been used together in the same light—at
Auxerre, for example, where, within a broad border of colour,
you find an inner frame of grisaille, enclosing a central figure
panel of colour. Quite at the beginning of the fourteenth century,
if not already at the end of the thirteenth, you find, as at
S. Radegonde, Poitiers, upon a ground of grisaille, coloured
medallion subjects, or more happily still, little figures, as it were,

inlaid, breaking the white surface very pleasantly with patches of unevenly but judiciously dispersed colour—the whole enclosed in a coloured border. But in the fourteenth century the more even combination of white and colour was quite a common thing. Naturally it was introduced in the form of the horizontal bands already mentioned. And indeed it is in windows into which grisaille enters that this band-wise distribution of design is most apparent, and most typical. The designer very commonly conceived his window as in grisaille, crossed by a band or bands of colour, binding the lights together.

111. DECORATED BORDERS.

That may be seen in the chapter-house at York, where you have several series of little subjects, more or less in the shape of medallions, forming so many belts of colour across the five-light grisaille windows, which belts the eye insensibly follows right round the building.

That is the theory of design. Its practical construction may be better described otherwise. The iron horizontal bars, to the use of which the glaziers had by this time come back, divide the lights each into a series of panels, which panels are filled at York alternately with coloured subjects and ornamental grisaille. Elsewhere perhaps two panels are filled with colour

112. GRISAILLE AND FIGURE

to one of grisaille, or three to one, or *vice versâ*. In any case these alternate panels of white and colour, occurring always on the same level throughout the lights composing the window (and often through all the windows along the aisle of a church), range themselves in pronounced horizontal strips or bands.

This acceptance of the bars as a starting-point in design, and this deliberate counterchange of light and dark, may appear to indicate a very rough-and-ready scheme of design. But any brutality there might be in it is done away with by the introduction of a sufficient amount of white into the coloured bands and of a certain modicum of colour in the bands of white. And that was habitually the plan adopted. Into the subjects it was easy to introduce just as much white as seemed necessary. A little white might be there already in the flesh, which was no longer always represented in flesh-coloured glass but more and more commonly in white. The usual border at the sides of the grisaille — now reduced to quite modest proportions—perhaps a simple leaf border, as on pages 44, 158, perhaps a still simpler "block" border, as above, served to frame the white, at the same time that it was an acknowledgment once more of the fact that each light forms a separate division of the window. In most cases the introduction of a little colour into the grisaille panel, very often in the form of a rosette, went further to prevent any possible appearance of disconnection between the figures and their ornamental setting. As a matter of fact, so little obvious is the plan of such windows in the actual glass that it often takes one some time to perceive it.

113. EVREUX.

In the nave at York Minster the grisaille is crossed by two bands of coloured figure work. Elsewhere it is crossed by one; but where the figures have canopies, as they often have, that makes again a horizontal subdivision in the coloured portion of the glass. Sometimes the topmost pinnacles of the coloured canopies will extend into the grisaille above, breaking the harshness of the dividing line; but it is seldom that it appears harsh in the glass. The fact seems to be that the upward tendency of the long lights is so marked, and the mullions make such a break in any cross line, that there is no fear of horizontal forms pronouncing themselves too strongly; the difficulty is rather to make them marked enough. Architects came eventually to feel the want of some more sternly horizontal feature than the glazier could contrive, when they introduced the stone transom, which was a feature of the later Gothic period.

When it was a question of glazing a broad single-light of earlier construction, the fourteenth century artist designed his glass accordingly. Not that he then adopted the thirteenth century manner—it never entered his mind to work in any other style than that which was current in his day: the affectation of bygone styles is a comparatively modern heresy—but he adapted his design equally to help, if not to correct, the shape of the window opening. Accustomed as he was to narrower lights, the broad window of an earlier age appeared to him unduly broad, and his first thought was to make it look narrower. This he did by dividing it into vertical (instead of horizontal) strips of white and colour. That is shown in the window from Troyes (page 159), in which the centre strip of the window, occupied by figures and canopies in colour, is flanked by broad strips of grisaille, and that again by a coloured border. There, as usual, you find some white in the figure work and some colour in the grisaille, always the surest way of making the window look one.

The judicious treatment of a belated lancet window like this goes to show that it was of set purpose that the tall lights of a Decorated window were bound together by ties of coloured glass. So long as windows were built in many lights, that plan of holding them together was never abandoned. There is a very notable instance of this at Berne, where the four long lights of a Late Gothic window are crossed by lines of canopy work, taking not horizontal but arched lines (a device common enough in German glass), effectually counteracting the lean and lanky look of the window. Still markedly horizontal lines of subdivision in glass design are more characteristic of the second Gothic period than of any other.

CHAPTER XV.

MIDDLE GOTHIC GLASS.

Towards the fourteenth century, it seems, a wave of realism swept over Gothic art. So much is this so that a relatively speaking naturalistic form of ornamental detail is the most marked feature of the Decorated period, giving it its name, and, indeed, its claim to be a style.

No great stress has been laid in the foregoing chapters upon this new departure in naturalism, because it did not so very vitally affect design. When it is said that glass followed always the fashion of architecture, that is as much as to say that, as the sculptors took to natural instead of conventional foliage, so did the glass painters; and there is not much more to tell. To trace the development of naturalistic design would lead us far astray. Enough to say that, by the naturalistic turn of its ornamental foliage you may recognise the period called "Decorated." How far that naturalism of Decorated detail may be to the good is a

114. NORBURY, DERBYSHIRE.

question there is no need here to dispute. It was a new departure. The new work lacked something of the simple dignity and self-restraint which marked the earlier, and it had not yet the style and character which came in the next century of more consistently workmanlike treatment. In so far it was a kind of prelude to Perpendicular work. This is not to deny that excellent work was done in the Decorated period, especially perhaps in glass, where naturalism, at its crudest, is less offensive than in wood or stone. But there is no getting over the fact that the period was intermediate; and Decorated glass is in a state of transition (1) between the archaism of the early and

115. S. PIERRE, CHARTRES.

the accomplishment of the later Gothic; (2) between the conventional ornament which merely suggests nature and natural foliage conventionally treated; (3) between strong rich colour and delicate silvery glass. The transition of style is nowhere more plainly to be traced than in the grisaille of the period. At first the character of fourteenth century grisaille did not greatly differ from earlier work, except in the form of the painted detail. That from S. Urbain, Troyes, on page 333, is a typical instance of Early French Transition foliage, in which the scroll is only less strong and vigorous than before. Precisely the same kind of detail is shown again in the lower of the two instances, likewise from Troyes, opposite; but already natural leaves begin to mingle with it; whilst in the illustration above it, though the mosaic border is characteristically early, the foliage in grisaille is deliberately naturalistic. The grisaille at Troyes, by the way, often reminds one of that at York Minster. It is mainly by the naturalistic character of the ivy scroll, or perhaps it would be nearer the mark to say of the leaves upon it, that the design from Norbury, Derbyshire (page 162), betrays its later date, by that and the absence of cross-hatching on the

116. DEC. GRISAILLE, S. URBAIN, TROYES.

TRANSITION.

117. CHARTRES.

background. The glazing of the window is still thoroughly mosaic.

There is a different indication of transition in the little panel from S. Pierre at Chartres, almost entirely in white glass, on page 163. The foliated ornament is here still early in character; but, it will be seen, there is no longer any pretence of leading up the bands of clear glass in separate strips. They are only bounded on one side by a lead line. That is so again in the three designs from Chartres Cathedral above, where, further,

118. EVREUX.   119. ROUEN CATHEDRAL.

L 2

the background is clear of paint; and in those from Evreux, on pages 165, 284. There the background is cross-hatched; but in one case the foliage is naturalistic.

The coloured strapwork in the grisaille from the Lady Chapel of Rouen Cathedral on page 165 is frankly mosaic; but the foliated ends of the straps, gathered together into a central quatrefoil in a quite unusual fashion, indicates the new spirit. The white glass is there painted with trailing foliage in outline upon a clear ground, not shown in the sketch, which is merely a diagram of the glazing. The grisaille from Stanton S. John, Oxford, here given, still hesitates rather between two opinions. The foliage is naturalistic, but the background is cross-hatched; the broad diagonal bands, patterned with paint, are glazed in colour; the rings of white are not separately leaded.

138. STANTON S. JOHN, OXFORD.

That sort of thing has occurred, as already pointed out, before; but it was not till the fourteenth century, or thereabouts, that the strapwork of white lines, forming so characteristic a feature in Decorated grisaille, are systematically indicated by painted outlines and not glazed in if it could be helped.

You have only to examine the crossing of the white lines in any of these last-mentioned patterns to see that, now that they are not separately glazed, they do not really interlace as before. It is out of the question that they should.

It is easy enough to glaze up bands so that they shall interlace; but, when some of the drawing lines are lead and some paint, it occurs continually that you want a leaded line to pass

121. Châlons.

behind a line of clear glass —which, of course, is a physical impossibility. It follows that the pretended interlacing comes to grief. The pattern is confused (it is worse when there is no hatched background) by the occurrence of leads, stronger than the painted lines, which, so far from playing any part in the design, occur just at the points where they most interfere with it.

That this did not deter them, that they made a shift with interlacing which does not truly interlace, marks a falling off in what may be called the conscientiousness of the Gothic designers. French and English Decorated grisaille, effective as it often is in the window, is distinctly less satisfactory in design than the common run of earlier work. Its charm is never in its detail.

The patterns may be ingenious and not without grace, but they are never altogether admirable, any more than are the figures.

What you most enjoy in it is the distribution of white and colour; and you enjoy it most when you do not too curiously examine into the detail of the design, when you are satisfied to enjoy the colour, and do not look for form, which after all is of less account in glass.

122. Châlons.

So far as effect only is concerned, quarry work, the mere glazing in squares, answers in many places (such, for example, as the clerestories of narrow churches, where you could not possibly enjoy any detail of design that might be there) all the purpose of grisaille; and it was commonly resorted to. But the painting upon such quarries counts for very little; it is far too small and fine in detail to have any effect further than to tone the glass a little, which would have been unnecessary if the glass employed had been less clear. In fact, delicate paint on distant clerestory glass is much ado about very little; and one cannot help thinking that plain glazing would there have answered all the purpose of the most delicately painted pattern work. The fourteenth century glaziers seldom complicated their quarry work by the introduction of bands or straps of colour between the quarries, or by the introduction of colour other than such as might occur in rosettes or shields and so on, planted upon them, rather than worked into the design. Occasionally, however, as at Châlons-sur-Marne, you come upon an ornamental window (page 167) in which quarries are separated by bands of clear white, a certain amount of colour being introduced in the form of yellow quarries substituted at regular intervals for the white. On the same page is another coloured diaper window designed on quarry lines, also at Châlons. In that quarries of white and yellow are separated by a trellis of blue. Something of the sort is to be seen also at S. Radegonde, Poitiers.

REGENSBURG.

MUNICH MUSEUM.

In these cases the painting, as will be seen, is strong enough to hold its own at a considerable distance from the eye, but the effect is not very happy. When, by the way, it was said that delicate painting on distant quarries was lost, it was not meant to imply that strong painting on quarries would be a happy solution of the difficulty. As a matter of experience, it is seldom satisfactory. On the other hand, the common expedient of leading up the coloured backgrounds to figure work in small squares of ruby, green, and so on, was generally the means of securing good broken colour.

It can hardly be said that geometric pattern windows in strong colour are ever very successful. The Germans, who, it should be remembered, call their second Gothic period the "Geometric," often attempted it, but without conspicuous success.

In Germany it was customary to use geometric diaper work long after it had gone out of use in France. In fact, it is there more likely a sign of the second period. The cross lines in the diaper from Regensburg (opposite) would have been in lead, not paint, if the work had been executed in the thirteenth century; again, the diaper below it would not at that period have been painted in the likeness of oak-leaves. Diaper of this kind was not used merely to fill up between medallions, but as background, for example, to canopy work. Frequently it was very small in scale, as well as elaborate in pattern. It can hardly

125. 14TH CENTURY GERMAN.

126. Freiburg.

be said that it was always worth the pains spent upon it —often it was not; but the Germans avoided, as a rule, the dangerous red and blue combination, and preferred, as did also the Italians, less stereotyped arrangements of green and yellow, or of red and green, or of red and green and yellow; if they ventured upon red and blue, it was with a difference very much to their credit. For example, they would enclose diamonds of ruby in bands of purple-brown, with just a point of blue at the interstices; again, they would make a diaper of purple, purple-brown, and grey; and in many another way show that they deliberately aimed at colour in such work—whereas many of the Early diapers suggest that the glazier was thinking more of pattern. An instance of heraldic diaper is given on page 169.

In Italy also you find sometimes, as at Florence and Assisi, medallion windows with mosaic diaper between, or mosaic diaper used as background to figures which certainly cannot be described as Early.

The Germans differed from the rest of us in their frank use of geometric pattern. We habitually disguised it more or less, clothing it most likely with foliation; they used it quite nakedly, and were not ashamed. Instances of this innocent use of geometric form are here given. At Freiburg are quite a number of windows entirely of geometric

127. Freiburg.

pattern work. There is a good deal of white glass in them, but they count rather for colour than for grisaille. It would not be quite unfair to say they fall between the two stools. These designs are much more pleasing in the glass than in black and white (where they have rather too much the appearance of floor-cloth), but they are by no means the happiest work of the Germans of that day. Where they were really most successful, more successful than their contemporaries, was in foliated or floral pattern windows, and those of a kind also standing dangerously near midway between colour and grisaille. The method of execution employed in them was to a large extent strictly mosaic; but there is quite a refreshing variety and novelty, as well as very considerable ingenuity, in their design.

The window from Regensburg on page 389 sets out very much as if it

128. FROM REGENSBURG, MUNICH MUSEUM.

were going to be a grisaille window; but it has, in the first place, more colour than is usual in grisaille, and, in the second, it will be seen that the little triangular ground spaces next the border are filled with pot-metal. The contrast of the set pattern and the four coloured leaves crossing each circle with the flowing undergrowth of grisaille is unusual, and so is the cunning alternation of cross-hatching and plain white ground. The designs from Munich Museum on pages 171 to 174 have nothing in common with grisaille. The design consists of natural foliage chiefly in white, growing tree-like upon a coloured ground up the centre of the light. In the one the stem is waved, in the other it takes a spiral form, in the third it is more naturalistic. But nature is not very consistently followed.

129. IVY—MUNICH MUSEUM.

What appears like a vine on page 171 has husks or flowers which it is not easy to recognise; and the ivy here is endowed with tendrils. The border of convolvulus leaves and the hop scroll, opposite, are unmistakable, though there is some inconsistency between the naturalness of the leaves and the stiffness of their growth. The ivy pattern differs from the others inasmuch as the leaves show light against the yellow ground, whilst the green stem and stalks tell dark upon it, and there is a band of red within the outer border which holds the rather spiky leaves together. The most interesting window of this kind illustrated is that on page 174, in which the stem is ingeniously twisted into quatrefoil medallion shapes, so as to allow a change in the colour of the ground, and the leaves are designed to go beyond the filling and form a pattern upon the border. The rose is a hackneyed theme enough, but this at least is a new way of working it out. Fourteenth century German windows are altogether more varied in design than contemporary French

130. GERMAN ORNAMENTAL GLASS

or English work. The glass is not so much all of one pattern. There are more surprises in it. The Germans treated grisaille in a way very much their own. At the risk of a certain coarseness of execution, they would paint out the background to their natural foliage in solid pigment, or in brown just hatched with lines scratched through to the clear glass. That is very effectively done, for example, at the Church of S. Thomas at Strassburg. It is not contended that this is at all a better plan than that practised in France or England: it is on the whole less happy; but there are positions in which it is more to the purpose; and it has at least the merit of being different: it suggests something better than it accomplishes, and it is a timely reminder that the best methods we know of cannot be accepted as final.

Again at Regensburg there is some distant ornamental work, so simple in execution that it is little more than glazing in colours; in fact just what distant work should be—effective in its place without any waste of labour.

A word or two remains to be said about borders. The narrower decorated light implied, as was said, a narrower border. It was, as a rule, only when a wide Early window had to be glazed that there was room for a broad one. In that case it showed of course the new naturalism, with perhaps

131. 14TH CENTURY GLASS.

13TH CENTURY
GERMAN.

the added interest of animal life, as here
illustrated; but there lingers in German borders such as this and the one on page 338,
something of early tradition. It looks as if
it would not be difficult to accept glazing
lines like these and fill them in with painted
detail *à la Romanesque*. In one of the windows in York Minster there is a border of
alternate leaves and monkeys, both much of
a size, which broadens out at the base,
affording space for the representation of a
hunt, men, dogs, grass and all complete.

There was another reason for the adoption
of a narrower border. Not only were windows
narrower now, but their arched heads were
cusped, which made it exceedingly difficult to
carry any but the narrowest possible border
round them satisfactorily. It will be seen how
awkwardly the border fits
(or does not fit) the window head on page 155.
Even the simplest border
had to be very much dis-
torted in order to make it follow the line of
the masonry; and, in any case, it gave a very
ugly shape within the border, and one again
difficult to fill. Already, at the beginning of
the fourteenth century, the designer found it
convenient to run his border straight up into
the cusped head of the light and let the stonework cut it abruptly short; that occurs at
Carcassonne. Sometimes, as at Tewkesbury,
the inconvenient border is allowed to end just
above the springing line of the arch, against
a pinnacle of the canopy, beyond which point
there is only a line or two of white or colour,
by way of frame or finish to the background.
An unusual but quite satisfactory way of
getting over the difficulty of carrying the
border round the window head is, to accept
the springing line of the arch as the end of

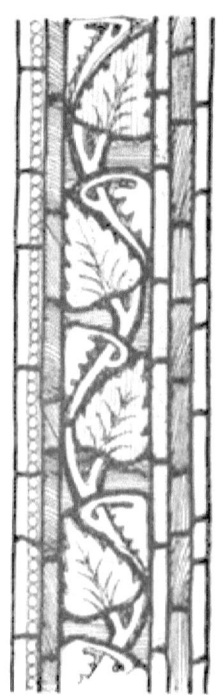

13TH CENTURY
GERMAN.

the central design, and to make the foliated border spread and fill the entire window head above. Some quarry lights in the triforium at Evreux are effectively treated in that manner.

Types of ordinary Decorated borders, English, French, and German, are shown in this and the preceding chapter. The leafage springs from one side or the other or from a central stem, or from either side of a waving stem, or from two stems intertwined (page 158). Sometimes the ground on one side is of a different colour from that on the other; in any case the glazing is usually simple. One of the leaf borders at Rouen

133. 14TH CENTURY GERMAN.

Cathedral includes a series of little green birds; another, an oak pattern, is inhabited at intervals by squirrels and wild men of the woods. Rather interesting variations upon the ordinary type of border are given on this and the preceding pages. The broader one above is of distinctly unusual character, inasmuch as it has no background except the painting-out, and the colour of the leafage varies quasi-accidentally.

The use of the rosette borders on pages 171, 172 is sufficiently accounted for by the desire to get contrast to the foliated filling, but it occurs at all periods more or less. So does the "block border"; but for all that it is almost as characteristic of Decorated work as the leaf border. It is seen in its simplest form on page 144. On page 389 it is associated with foliage and rosettes. A typical form of it is where the blocks are charged with heraldic devices, which may serve to indicate the date, or to confuse one. In the design from Evreux on page 160 there occur, for example, the Fleurs-de-Lys of France alternating with the Castle of Castille. These

134. STRASS-
BURG.

particular charges occur frequently in the windows of the S. Chapelle at Paris, and in the lights from that source now in the South Kensington Museum; and they go perhaps to show that Blanche of Castille (who married Louis VIII.) gave them to the chapel, or that they were in her memory. She died in 1252. It is most improbable that the Evreux glass should belong to so early a date as that. Were it so, the occurrence of this kind of thing in such early work would only go to show that heraldic devices are as old as heraldry, and that when the glazier had a narrow light to fill he treated it as a narrow light, with a border in proportion to its width: he certainly did that at the S. Chapelle. The fact remains that this particular form of "block" border marks, as a rule, the approach of the fourteenth century.

It may be as well to remind the reader that dates and periods are only mentioned in order to save circumlocution. When the thirteenth century is mentioned, it is not meant to convey the year 1201, nor yet 1299, but the century in its prime. And, what is more, it is not meant to say that the work ascribed to that period was quite certainly and indisputably done after the year 1200 or before the year 1300, but only that it bears the mark of the century—which, from the present point of view, is the important thing. The precise and certain year in which this or that device was by exception for the first time employed, or until which by chance a practically obsolete practice survived, is interesting (if it can be ascertained) only as a question of archæology. Anyway, a workman would rather believe the evidence of his eyes, which he can trust, than of documents, which, even if authentic, may not be trustworthy, and which are perhaps open to misinterpretation.

Typically Decorated glass, apart from the ornamental windows just referred to, is the least interesting of Gothic. There is in it a straying from Early tradition without reaching the later freedom and attainment. In colour it has neither the strength of the Early work nor the delicacy of the Late. It marks some progress in technique, but little in design, and none in taste.

CHAPTER XVI.

LATE GOTHIC WINDOWS.

THE subdivision of art into periods is in reality the veriest makeshift. To be on quite safe ground we should have, as a matter of fact, to reduce our periods to not more than half their supposed duration, and to class all the rest of the time as belonging to intervals of transition.

The truth is, it is always a period of transition. The stream moves perpetually on; there are only moments in its course when it seems to move more slowly, and we have time to fix its characteristics. It follows that, if we divide our periods according to time, we have to include within them work of very various character; and if we divide them according to style, our dates get hopelessly confused.

Some sort of classification is necessary in order to emphasise changes which actually took place only by degrees, and are perceptible only to the expert. But no sooner do we begin to classify, than we find so many exceptions, that we are inclined almost to wonder if they do not form the rule. All that has been said, therefore, and may yet be said, about the periods of design, must be taken with more than a grain of suspicion. For example, what shall be said about the great East window at Gloucester Cathedral, which Winston instances as a typical example of Decorated glass? Doubtless the technique is that of soon after the middle of the fourteenth century, and the detail of the canopies, when you come to examine them, is more nearly Decorated than anything else; but the first impression of the glass is quite that of Perpendicular work. This may come partly of the circumstances that the masonry of the window follows already distinctly Perpendicular lines; but it comes much more from the colour of the glass and its distribution. It is not merely that blue and ruby backgrounds are carried straight up through the long lengths of each alternate light, or that the blue is lighter and greyer than in Decorated glass, but that the figures, and especially the canopies, are for the first time, practically speaking, altogether in white, only very slightly relieved with yellow stain. The student who accepted this as typical Decorated work, would be quite at sea when he came to Perpendicular glass, in which this paler colour, this preponderance of white, and especially this framing of the figures in white canopy work, is a most distinctive, if not the most distinctive, feature. After all, the window is Perpendicular; and, though the glass in it may have many characteristics of Decorated work, it cannot well be said that the glass is Decorated, true though it be that glass did, as a rule, follow rather in the wake of architectural progress.

Many windows are almost equally difficult to classify. In the Decorated glass at Wells there are both earlier and later features.

136. PEDESTAL, WELLS.

The heads glazed in pinkish glass, with eyes and beards leaded up in white, strike an Early note, whilst the broadly treated bases or pedestals of certain canopies in the Lady Chapel, one of which is here shown (the canopies themselves are strictly Decorated), prelude the coming style.

These bases remind one of those in the ante-chapel at New College, Oxford, dating from the last quarter of the fourteenth century, which, though it is not difficult to trace in them the lingering influence of Decorated tradition, must undoubtedly be put down as early examples of the later style. In these fine windows (upon which the tourist turns his back whilst he admires the poor attempt of Sir Joshua Reynolds in the West window) there is not yet the accomplishment of full-fledged Perpendicular work. The figures, though full of fine feeling, are not well drawn, and the painting is not delicate; but the design of the glass, its setting out, the balance and arrangement of colour, the tone of the windows, and the breadth of effect, are admirable; and it is precisely in these respects that it proclaims itself of the later school of Gothic. Indeed, we may assume that it was in order

137. CANOPY, NEW COLLEGE, OXFORD.

to include such work as this that the line was drawn at the year 1380. To class it with Decorated glass would have been too absurd. Compare the New College canopy on page 180 with the Decorated canopy on page 155 and the more orthodox Perpendicular canopies below and on pages 185, 340, and there is no possible hesitation as to which it most resembles. The only thing in which it shows any leaning towards Decorated work is in the very occasional introduction of pot-metal colour; and the main thing in which it differs from later Perpendicular design is that its shafts are round instead of square, and that it is more solidly built up, larger, more nobly conceived.

A parallel French instance is at the S. Chapelle at Riom, in which canopies, having at first sight all the appearance of typically Late Gothic work, prove to have details which one would rather describe as Decorated. The German canopy work at Shrewsbury (pages 183, 186) is not very far removed from Decorated. The later Perpendicular canopies run to finikin pinnacles.

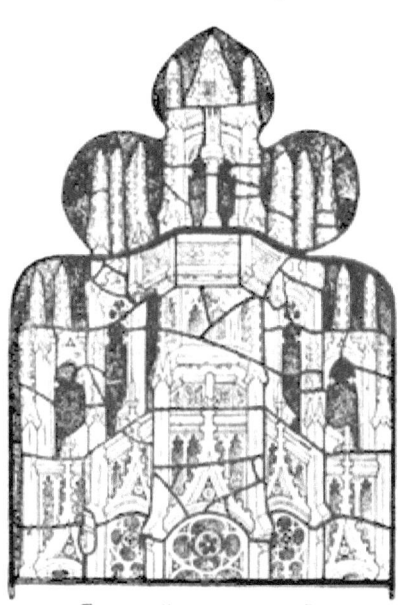

138. TYPICAL PERPENDICULAR CANOPY.

The New College canopies have none of the brassy-yellow colour characteristic of Decorated work, but are absolutely silvery in effect. The gradual dilution, as one may say, of the deep, rich, Early colour is noticeable throughout the fourteenth century. Towards its close the glass painter halts no longer between two opinions, between light and colour. He has quite made up his mind in favour of white glass. He has come pretty generally to conceive his window as a field of white, into which to introduce a certain amount of rich colour, not often a very large amount. As a rule, perhaps not more than one-fourth of the area of a fifteenth-century window was colour; for, in addition to the white of the canopy, there was commonly a fair amount of white in the draperies, and the flesh was now always represented by white. The typical Perpendicular window, then, is filled with shrinework in white, enclosing figures, or figure subjects, into which white enters largely (the flesh and some of the drapery, often a good deal, is sure to be white), upon a background of colour. Not much of this coloured background, most often in blue or ruby, and sometimes deep in colour, was ordinarily shown, so fully was the space occupied by figure work. Sometimes there would be represented, behind the figure, a screen of white, so that only the head and shoulders would stand revealed against dark colour. Sometimes this screen would be in colour, contrasting with the background, richly diapered in imitation of damask (page 342). Sometimes the background would be white, leaded perhaps in quarries; but in any case the prevalent scheme of design was to frame up pictures, more or less in colour, in architectural canopy work of white and stain. Yellow stain, it should be said, was freely used in connection with all this white; and its invariable association therewith is one of the marked characteristics of Later Gothic glass; but as a rule the yellow was not only delicate in tint but delicately introduced, so that it did not much disturb the effect of white. There were significant passages of yellow in it, but the effect of the mass was cool and silvery.

In canopies yellow stain was used as gold might be in stonework, which the canopies imitated; crockets and pinnacles would be tipped with yellow, as with gilding (see opposite), and the reveal of the arch, shown in false perspective above the figure, would be similarly stained, so as to soften the transition from the dark colour of the background to the white of the canopy mass.

One comes upon windows, probably of about the beginning of the end of the fourteenth century, in which the colour scheme is practically limited to red, white, and blue, the yellow being, comparatively speaking, lost in the white. Again, one finds windows in which the colours are much lighter than in earlier glass. But as a rule the lighter colours now introduced (the glazier's palette was by this time quite extensive) were used to support, and not to the exclusion of, the richer and deeper colour, which is the glory of glass, seldom to be dispensed with even in grisaille. You may do without colour altogether, but pale colours always have a poor effect.

139. FIGURE AND CANOPY, S. MARY'S, SHREWSBURY.

The typical Perpendicular canopies illustrated and already referred to are quite favourable specimens of the kind of thing in vogue throughout the fifteenth century. In France much the same forms were adopted (page 342). Some exceptionally delicate figure-and-canopy windows (or parts of them) are to be found in the cathedral at Toulouse—the figure in colour, or in white and colour, against a background of white, richly diapered with damask pattern, which quite sufficiently distinguishes it from the architecture only just touched with yellow. An instance of later German work is given below. The German designer indulged temperamentally in the interpenetration of shafting and other vagaries of the kind, which we find in German stone carving. Sometimes in German work, and occasionally also in French, Late Gothic canopies were all in yellow, framing the picture, as it were, in gold. As a rule, however, they were, as with us, silvery in tone, and framed the coloured glass in a way most absolutely satisfactory, so far as effect is concerned.

140. GERMAN LATE GOTHIC CANOPY.

In itself, however, this canopy work is rarely of any great interest; occasionally, as already in the preceding century, the designer has enriched in the shafts little figures of saints or angels (there is just the indication of such introduction of little statuettes in the very simple and restrained example of canopy work from Cologne, on page 191), redeeming it from dulness: but as a rule it is trite and commonplace to a degree. The white, as frame, is perfect. It is none the more so that it simulates misplaced stonework. What a strange thing it is in the history of ornament that the natural bias of the designer seems to be so irresistibly towards imitation! The man's first

136. ALL SOULS' COLLEGE, OXFORD.

thought seems to be to make the thing he is doing look like something it is not. Why, having designed openings in the wall of his building, he should proceed forthwith to fill them up with something in poor imitation of masonry, is a mystery. Economy had then, perhaps, as now, more to do with it than art, for it is a very cheap expedient.

Not only in the matter of colour, but in that of proportion, the later Gothic canopies were a great improvement upon what had gone before. They were distributed still very much upon the horizontal principle so noticeable in Decorated work; but by this time the architect had come to the tardy conclusion that the long lights of his window wanted holding together, and he tied them together, if they were of any length, by means of transoms, in which case the glass-worker had to deal with lights of manageable length. The light from All Souls' College, here given, is an example of a very usual Perpendicular arrangement. About one half its entire length is occupied by a figure enshrined, as it were, in an architectural niche. The base of the canopy is about equal in height to the width of the light. The shafts are broad enough to emphasise the independence of the light. The pinnacles of the canopy extend into the window head. A point or two of background colour, as though one could see through, are ingeniously introduced into the canopy and its base. It would be difficult to better

142. TWO WINDOWS. S. MARY'S, SHREWSBURY.

such an arrangement of white and colour, except that one feels the urgent want of a margin of white, to separate the coloured background from the masonry round the window head.

143. FAIRFORD.

The idea is, no doubt, that the shrine work should appear to stand in the opening, and the figure be sheltered under that. The illusion aimed at, it is scarcely necessary to say, is not produced, and in any case would not have been worth producing. On the contrary, the desirable thing to be done was, to acknowledge the window opening, which, except for this pretence, the colour of the design effectually does.

A frequent and equally typical arrangement was, where the light was long enough, to make the base itself take the form of a low canopy over a more or less square-proportioned subject, possibly a scene in the life of the Saint pourtrayed above. This gave opportunity of introducing figures on two different scales, without in any way endangering the significance of the more important figure, which, by its size and breadth of colour, asserted itself at a distance from which the smaller subject appeared only a mass of broken colour. The proportions and outline of such a subject are indicated by the Nativity on page 54, the jagged line at the top of the picture marking the inner line of the canopy work. In German work very commonly the base canopy encloses, as, for example, at Cologne Cathedral, a panel of heraldic blazonry.

The height of the canopy was, with us, more or less in accordance with the length of the window; but sometimes more space was allowed for the figure than at All Souls', and the vacant space about the head of the saint was occupied with a label in white and stain bearing an inscription. There are some admirable figure-and-canopy windows of this description on the north side of the choir of York Minster, which seem to have inspired a great deal of our modern mock-Perpendicular figure-and-canopy glass. The label occurs, on a background of white architecture, behind the Prophets from Fairford on pages 187, 391. A more important example of it occurs round the figure of Edward the Confessor, from S. Mary's, Ross (opposite), and again in the group from the same source on page 339. Extremely clever ornamental use is made of the label—a typically Perpendicular form of enrichment—in the German glass on page 186. The extraordinary breadth of the phylacteries held by the Prophets in the early fifteenth century windows in the S. Chapelle at Riom, gives them quite a character of their own, and an admirable one.

144. THE QUEEN OF SHEBA BEFORE SOLOMON. FAIRFORD.

At Great Malvern we find the lights above the transom of a window occupied each by a figure and its canopy, whilst

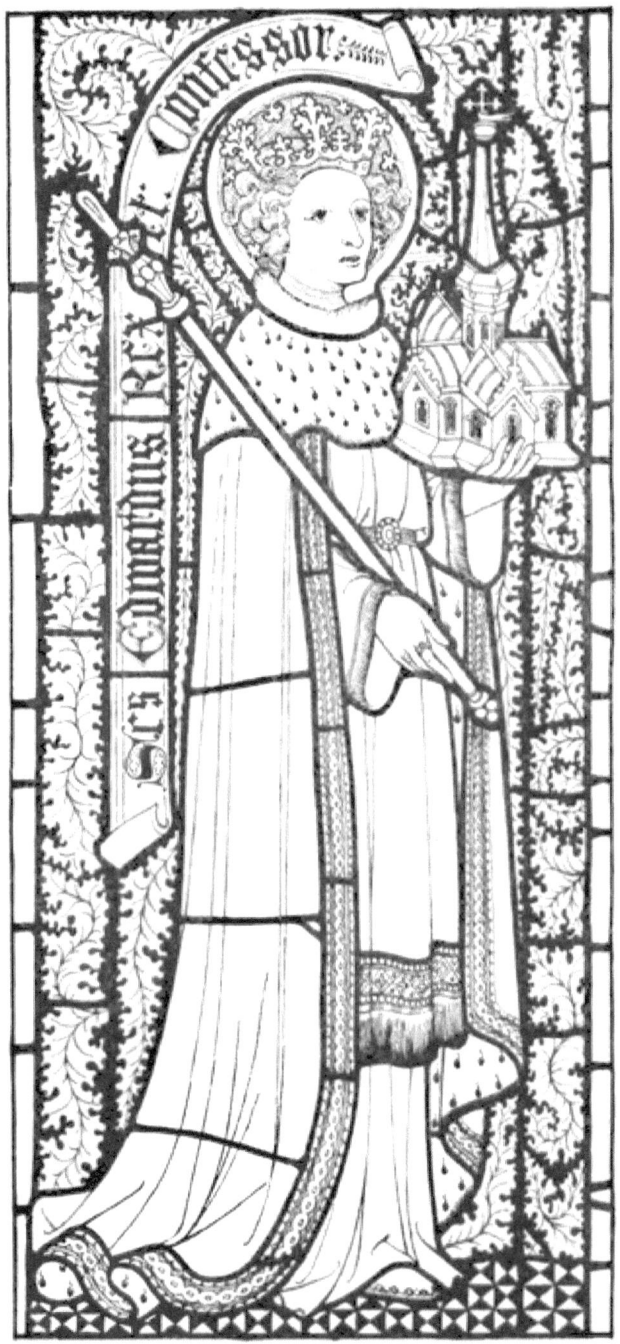

145. KING EDWARD, S. MARY'S, ROSS.

the lower lights contain each three tiers of small subjects, separated only by bands of inscription. In the four-light window at Malvern illustrating the Days of Creation, each light contains three little subjects, one of which is given on page 252. Sometimes, as in the windows from Fairford on pages 188, 372,

146. YORK MINSTER.

subjects under a canopy are drawn to a scale as large as the size of the window will allow.

In some shape or another the canopy almost invariably appears in connection with figure work; it is the rarest thing to find, in place of the familiar shafting, a border, such as that opposite.

Of the gradual improvement in drawing in the fifteenth century work it is not necessary to say much. It belongs to the period rather than to glass painting, and it is shown in the examples illustrated. It is of no particular country, though our English work was possibly more constrained than contemporary continental work. Particularly characteristic of English work was the delicate tracing of the faces, which were pencilled, in fine lines, the treatment altogether rather flat, and this at a period when foreign glass was much more solidly modelled. It is not possible, on the scale of illustration determined by a book of this size, to illustrate this English peculiarity as clearly as one would wish, but it will be apparent to the seeing eye even here. It is within the bounds of possibility that the Fairford glass may have been executed in England; if so, Flemish or German painters certainly had a hand in it. To compare it with the neighbouring Perpendicular glass at Cirencester, with its delicate tracing and fine stain (in which matter the Fairford glass does not by any means excel), is to see how very different it is from typical English work. Whether we

look at the detail
of the canopies, or
the drawing of the
drapery, or the
painting of the
glass, we see little
to connect this with
English work,
though it falls at
once into its place
as excellent Late
Gothic glass. In
the windows of the
nave of Cologne
Cathedral, a figure
from one of which
is here given, Ger-
man Gothic glass
reaches its limit.
There is already a
trace, if only in the
broad shaft of the
canopy, of Renais-
sance influence in
the design. In
others of these win-
dows there are no
single figures. En-
tire lights are filled
with biblical or le-
gendary scenes, one
above the other,
under dwarf cano-
pies, which do not
very clearly define
the horizontal divi-
sions of the win-
dow; for all that,
the horizontal divi-
sions are for the
most part there.
Except where the

147. COLOGNE CATHEDRAL.

canopies are so insignificant as not to count, a Perpendicular window presents, as a rule, a screen of silvery white, on which the pictures form so many panels of more or less jewelled colour.

The enormous East window at York Minster, which belongs to the very early years of the fifteenth century, contains, apart from its tracery, no less than a hundred and seventeen subjects in its twenty-seven lights; but the canopies dividing them are so narrow that they scarcely answer the purpose of frames to the separate subjects. The design is inextricably confused, and the subjects are very difficult to read; but the effect is still as of a mass of jewels caught in a network of white. In fact, the progress towards light is such that, whereas in the last century the problem was how to get more and more white glass into a coloured window, it seems now more often to be how to get colour into a white one.

White and stain enter so largely into Late Gothic glass that there remains little to be said about grisaille. The glass of the period is, for the most part, in grisaille and colour, the difference between it and earlier grisaille being, that it consists so largely of figure-and-canopy work. Windows, however, do occur all in white or all in white and stain. Figures, for example, in white and stain, occur, as in the South transept at York, on a ground of delicately painted quarries. Again, a common arrangement is that of figures in white and colour against a background of quarry work, a band of inscription separating the pavement upon which they stand from quarries below them. Such figures form a belt across many moderate-sized windows in parish churches. Mere quarry lights also occur, with a border in which perhaps some colour occurs. But the subject of quarries and quarry windows is reserved for consideration in a chapter by itself.

It must not be supposed that the drift of Later Gothic in the direction of white glass was uninterrupted. That was by no means so. At certain places, and at certain periods, and especially by certain artists, there seems to have been a reaction against this tendency, if ever there was any yielding to it. For example, notwithstanding all that has been said about the lighter tone of Decorated glass, some of the very finest fourteenth century German work, at S. Sebald's Church, Nuremberg, is as intensely and beautifully rich as anything in Early work. There rows of small subjects are framed in little canopies as deep in colour as the pictures, and white glass is conspicuous by its absence. The nearest approach to it is an opaque-looking horn colour, and that is used only very sparingly. Possibly, however, it is not quite fair to call these windows rich, for the upper part of them is light. So light is it, and so little has it to do with the stained glass, that one scarcely accepts it as part of the window, and therefore speaks of it as if it ended with the colour.

The unfortunate plan has been adopted here, as in the cathedral at Munich and elsewhere in Germany, of filling only about half the window, from the sill upwards, with strong stained glass. This ends abruptly at an arbitrary and very unsatisfactory canopy arch, which, in a way, frames it; and above it the window is filled with plain white rounds. At Freiburg there is yet a further band of plain rounds next the sill of the windows. The object of this is, doubtless, to get light into the church: but the effect is as if the builders had run short of coloured glass, and had only finished off the window temporarily. As a means of combining white and colour this German shift is not, of course, to be compared to the plan current elsewhere of distributing them in alternating bands. It does not attempt to combine them, but cuts the window deliberately in two. Not until you have shaded off from your eyes the distracting rays of white light, can you properly appreciate or enjoy the coloured glass.

But, if these windows must be considered, as in a sense they must be, as conforming to the demand for more light, there are others in which strong colour is carried consistently through, not only in the fourteenth but in the fifteenth century. (It is irritating and annoying to have to hark back in this way to periods supposed to have been long since left behind, but any arbitrary line of division between the styles must, as it were, cut off points which project from one into the other, sometimes very far indeed across the boundary line; and hence the absolute necessity, at times, of seeming to retrace our steps, if we would really trace the progress of design.) There are shown opposite four lights out of a large window in the clerestory of the cathedral at Troyes, in which the history of the Prodigal Son is pictured in little upright subjects, framed in canopies of quite modest proportions and of colour which in no wise keeps them separate from the richly coloured figures

148. THE PRODIGAL SON, TROYES.

underneath. One of them, for example, is of green, very much the colour of an emerald, on an inky-purple ground. The result is a very rich window, full of quaintly dramatic interest when you come to examine it; but there are no broadly marked divisions of colour in the glass to affect the architecture of the building one way or the other, nor does it tell its tale very plainly. It is more easily read on page 194 than from the floor of the church.

In the windows so far discussed the figure subjects, however small and however close together, have always been marked off one from the other, slightly as it might be, at first by the marginal lines round the early subject medallions, and then by canopies. It is shown in another fifteenth century window from Troyes (opposite) how even that amount of framework was now sometimes abandoned.

Progress in glass design, it was said, was in the direction of light and of picture. Moved by the double impulse, the designer of the Later Gothic period framed his coloured pictures in white. But where he happened not to care so much about light, or had not to consider it, he omitted even the narrow shaft of white or colour (which, so long as he used a canopy, usually divided the picture from the stonework) and left it to the mullions to separate them vertically. Horizontally he divided them slightly by a band of ornament, as at Troyes, of about the width of the mullions, or more frequently, and more plainly, by lines of inscription on white or yellow bands. If the subjects were arranged across the window in tiers alternately on ruby and blue grounds, that, of course, separated each somewhat from the one next above and below it, but it banded those on the same level together. This helped the architectural effect, but confused the story-telling.

If the pictures were arranged, throughout the width as well as the length of the window, alternately in panels on red and blue grounds, that kept the pictures rather more apart, but made the distribution of the colour all-overish. That mere change of ground could not keep pictures effectively separate will be clear when it is seen (opposite) how little of the background extends to the mullion. The greater part of the figures come quite up to the stonework, and the subjects consequently run together. It is difficult to realise, except by experience, how little the stonework can be depended upon to frame stained glass. It

149. THE STORY OF TOBIT, TROYES

seems when you see it all upon paper that the mullions, with their strongly marked mouldings, must effectually frame the glass between them. They do nothing of the kind. They go for so much shadow: what you see is the glass. This the glass painters realised at length, and took to carrying their pictures across them. And it has to be confessed that so long as they schemed them cleverly the interference of the mullion was not much felt.

The distinction drawn so far between "single figures" and "subjects" has answered its obvious purpose; but that also is, in a manner, arbitrary. Figures standing separately, each in a light by itself, form very often a series—such as the four Evangelists, the twelve Apostles, the Prophets, the Doctors of the Church, or a succession of kings, bishops, or other ecclesiastics. More than that, they form perhaps a group. When we discover that facing the figure of the Virgin Mary is that of the Angel Gabriel, we see at once that, though each figure occupies a separate light of the window, and each stands in its own separate niche, we have in reality here a subject extending through two lights—the Annunciation. So in a four-light window—if in one light stands the Virgin with the Infant Christ, and in the others a series of richly garbed figures with crowns and gifts in their hands, it is clear that this represents the Adoration of the Magi—a subject in four lights ; and the canopies over them may be taken to be one canopy with four niches. A yet more familiar instance of continuity between the single figures in the lights of a window occurs where the central light contains the Christ upon the cross, and in the sidelights stand the Virgin and S. John. We have in such cases the beginning of the subject extending through several lights. It is only a short step from the Annunciation, or the Adoration, or the Crucifixion described, to the same subject, under one canopy, extending boldly across the window, with shafts only to frame the picture at its sides. That is what was done—especially in Germany. It occurs already in Early Decorated glass, where the upper part of a big geometric window is sometimes occupied by brassy pinnacle work, which asserts itself, perhaps, upon a ground of mosaic diaper, in the most unpleasant way. In the white glass of a later period the effect was happier.

At first the designer did not, as a rule, aspire to carry his subjects right across a big window. Accepting the transom as a natural division, he would perhaps divide a four-light window vertically into two, so as to get four subjects, each under a canopy extending across two lights; or, in a five-light window, he would probably separate these by other narrow subjects in the central lights. Divisions of this kind often occur already in the stonework of the window, the lights being architecturally divided by stronger mullions into groups. In that case all the glass painter does is to emphasise the grouping of the lights schemed by the architect. Where the architect has not provided for such grouping he does it, perhaps, for himself. It enables him to design his figures on a larger scale, and to get a much broader effect in his glass than he could do so long as he kept each picture rigorously within the limits of a single light. Consideration for his picture had probably more to do with his reticence than respect for its architectural framework; and so soon as ever he realised how little even a strong mullion would really interfere with his work, he made no scruple to take all the space he wanted for his purpose. Infinite variety of composition is the result. The upper half of the window is perhaps devoted to a single subject, or to two important pictures, whilst below the transom the lights are broken up into quite little pictures; or in place of these smaller pictures may be found little panels of heraldry, as occurs often in Flemish work. These or the smaller pictures may be continued in the sidelights of a broad window, flanking, and in a way framing, a large central picture. Sometimes, as in the nave of Cologne Cathedral, the upper half of the window may contain one imposing composition; below that may be a series of important single figures, each provided with its separate canopy; and below that again, at the base of the window, may be a series, or several series, of small heraldic panels.

The canopy extending across a broad window (page 200) may be so schemed that there is obvious recognition of the lights into which it is divided, or it may sprawl across the window space with as little regard to intervening mullions as possible. There is now, in short, full scope for the fancy of the artist, were he never so fanciful; and it would be a hopeless task to try and catalogue the lines on which the design of a large window might now be set out.

We do not in the fifteenth century arrive yet at the most remarkable achievements in glass painting. But you have only to compare such pictures as those on pages 194, 196, with that on page 127 to see what a complete revolution has come over the spirit of design. It is not only that the draughtsman has learnt to draw, and the painter to paint; they work on quite a different system. It was explained (page 44) how in early days the glazier conceived his design as mosaic, how he first thought it out in lead lines, and only relied on paint to help him out in details which glazing could not give him. Now, it is easy to see that the painter begins at the other end. He thinks out his picture as a painting, and relies upon glazing only for the colour which he cannot get without it.

In the beginning, it was said, the glazier might often have fixed his lead lines, and trusted to his ingenuity to fill them in with painted detail. Now, it would seem, the painter might almost have sketched his picture, and then bethought him how to glaze it. But that is not yet really so. He did not even conceive his design as a picture and then translate it into glass. His work runs so smoothly it cannot be translation. The ingenuity with which he leads up little bits of colour in the midst of white, is no mere feat of engineering: it is spontaneous. It is clear that he had the thought of glazing in his mind all along—that he designed for it, in fact. The difference between the thirteenth century and the fifteenth century designer is, that one thinks first of glazing, is primarily a glazier, the other thinks first of painting, is primarily a painter.

150. LAMFORD.

151 RENAISSANCE WINDOW, TROYES CATHEDRAL

CHAPTER XVII.

SIXTEENTH CENTURY WINDOWS.

THE customary line between Gothic and Renaissance glass is drawn at about A.D. 1530. That is to say, that there are to be found examples, presumably of that date, which are still undoubtedly Gothic in character. But he would be a bold man, even for an archæologist, who dared to say precisely when the Gothic era came to an end.

Quite early in the sixteenth century the new Italian movement began to make itself felt in France, Germany, Flanders; in due course it spread to this country. Eventually it supplanted the older style; but it was only by degrees that it insinuated itself into the affections of cis-alpine craftsmen. And in stained glass, even more plainly than in wood or stone carving, is seen how gradually the new style was assimilated by the mediæval craftsmen—more quickly, of course, by the younger generation than the older—so that, concurrently with design in the quasi-Italian manner, Gothic work was still being done. Much of the earlier Renaissance work shows lingering Gothic influence. In the first quarter of the sixteenth century a great deal of glass was designed and executed by men hesitating between the old love and the new, only partially emancipated from mediæval tradition, or only imperfectly versed in the foreign style.

There is a window at S. Nizier, at Troyes, for example, in which the details are Renaissance, but the feeling is quite Gothic. The subjects are even explained by elaborate yellow scrolls or labels inscribed in black, very much after the manner of those which form such a feature in the German Gothic work at Shrewsbury (page 186). Renaissance forms are traced with a hand which betrays long training in the more rigid mediæval school; and Gothic and Italian details are put together in the same composition with a *naïveté* which is sometimes quite charming.

You can see that the designer of the window on page 203 was not untouched by Renaissance influence. Possibly

S.G. N

he thought the hybrid ornament in his canopy was quite up to date.

In the glass in the nave of Cologne Cathedral the suspicion aroused by the side columns of the otherwise quite Gothic canopy on page 191 is confirmed by definitely Renaissance forms in the ornament in the window head. Again, at the Church of S. Peter, at Cologne, is a sort of pointed canopy with ornament which looks at first like Gothic crockets, but on nearer view it is just Italian arabesque in white and stain. Apart from architectural accessories and detail of costume or ornament, to justify the attribution of the work to this or that period, it is very often difficult to give a name to early Renaissance work: the only safe refuge is in the convenient word transitional.

But for the nimbus in perspective, and the shield of arms and its little amorino supporter, it would have seemed safe to describe the "Charge to S. Peter" from S. Vincent at Rouen on page 207 as "Gothic."

In French glass a lingering Gothic element is noticeable at a period when Italian forms had firmly established themselves in contemporary plastic art; but, then, glass painting was not an Italian art; and, whilst wood carvers and sculptors were imported from Italy, and directly influenced the Frenchmen working with them, glass painting remained in the hands of native artists.

Before very long the Renaissance did, of course, assert itself, in glass painting as in all art, and we arrive at windows absolutely different from anything that was done in the Middle Ages. The change was in some places much more rapid than in others. Wherever there was a strong man his influence would make for or against it. But meanwhile much intermediate work was done, belonging more or less to the new school, whilst retaining very much of the character of Gothic glass.

That Gothic character was something well worth keeping: for it is the character which belongs inherently to the material.

The Gothic glass painters did, in fact, so thoroughly develop the resources of the material, that a Renaissance window treated really like glass inevitably suggests the lingering of Gothic tradition. This is no slight praise of Gothic work; and, by implication, it tells against the later Renaissance glass painters, whose triumphs were in a direction somewhat apart from their

152. St. Mary's, Shrewsbury.

craft. The great windows at Brussels, for example (page 71), illustrate a new departure. They seem to have nothing in common with mediæval art. On the other hand, one traces the descent of such masterpieces of translucent glass painting as are to be found at Arezzo (page 397), through those same intermediate efforts, directly to Gothic sources.

To trace the steps by which the new encroached upon the old, as one may do, for example, at Rouen, is almost to come to the conclusion that the short but brilliant period of Renaissance glass painting is really the after-fruit of Gothic tradition, fertilised only by the great flood of Renaissance feeling which swept over sixteenth century art. Nowhere is this

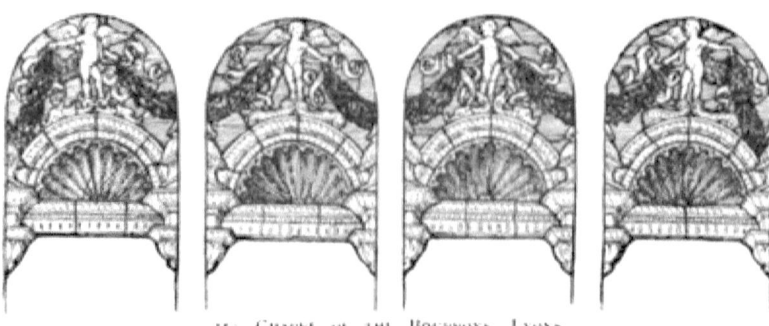

151. CHAPEL OF THE BOURBONS, LYONS.

more clearly argued than in the windows at Auch, completed, according to all accounts, as early as 1513. A strain of Gothic is betrayed by the cusping which here and there fringes a semicircular canopy arch; but no less mistakably mediæval is the technique throughout, and equally so the setting out of the windows. For the somewhat imposing canopies are not, for once, devised as frames to correspondingly important pictures: but are simply shrines adorned with figures each confined to its separate light: it is only the small subsidiary predella or other such pictures which extend beyond the mullions. No doubt there is doctrinal intention in the juxtaposition of Prophets, Sibyls, and the rest—one of whom may even be supposed to be addressing the other—but to all intents and purposes decorative, they are just a row of standing figures, as distinct one from the other as the usual series of figures under quite separate canopies. It is only the canopy which connects them. This kind of composition (which is seen again at Troyes, page 200) would never have occurred to a man altogether cut off from Gothic tradition.

It is worth remarking that, even when Gothic and Renaissance canopies alternate at Auch in a single window, or where Gothic niches are built, as it were, into or on to larger Renaissance structures, there is no appearance of incongruity. Truth to tell, the Gothic is not so purely Gothic, nor the Renaissance so purely Renaissance, as that they should clash one with the other. Both are seen through the temperament of the artist. He mixed them in his mind; and the result is quite one, *his* style in short.

Early Renaissance glass submitted itself, one can hardly say duly, but almost as readily as late Gothic design, to the restraint of Gothic mullions. The windows in which, as it happens, some of the best Early French Renaissance work is found (and it is in France that the best is to be found) are often smaller than the great Perpendicular windows referred to, and do not lend themselves to such elaborate subdivision. But the lines on which they are subdivided are very much as heretofore. The canopy still extends through several lights, and covers a single subject. Only now it is Renaissance in design. That does not mean to say merely that round arched architecture takes the place of pointed. The round arch occurs indeed, as in the windows in the Chapel of the Bourbons, in Lyons Cathedral (on pages 204 and 349), supplemented by amorini and festoons of fruit. But more often the canopy takes the form of a frieze of Renaissance ornament, painted in white and stain, as at S. Godard, Rouen (opposite), or glazed in white on colour, as in the cathedral of the same city (pages 75, 350), supported at each end by a pilaster. Not seldom it resolves itself into arabesque only very remotely connected with architecture at all. Indeed, if it simulate anything, it is goldsmith's work rather than masonry. Executed, as at Rouen (pages 75, 206), in brilliant yellow on a dark coloured ground, it has very much the appearance and value of beaten gold. That, rather than sculpture, must have been in the mind of the designer. One form of imitation is not much better than another; but here, at all events, there is nothing which in the least competes with the surrounding architecture; and it will scarcely be denied by any one who takes the least interest in ornament, that design of this kind is vastly more amusing than the dull array of misplaced pinnacles which often did duty for ornamental detail in Gothic shrine work. A German version of a canopy which ceases almost to be a canopy and becomes more like arabesque, is given on page 350. That is supported by columns (the caps are shown in the illustration) rather out of keeping with the ornament they support, which makes very little pretence of being architectural. The canopies on pages 204, 350, are supported only on little brackets at each side, and have no shafts at all. This marks a new departure. The picture has now no frame at its sides, only the stone mullion.

It was explained, in reference to glazing, what confusion of detail resulted from the use of leads of which some were intended to form part of the design and some not. Similar confusion is inevitable when certain of the mullions are meant to be accepted

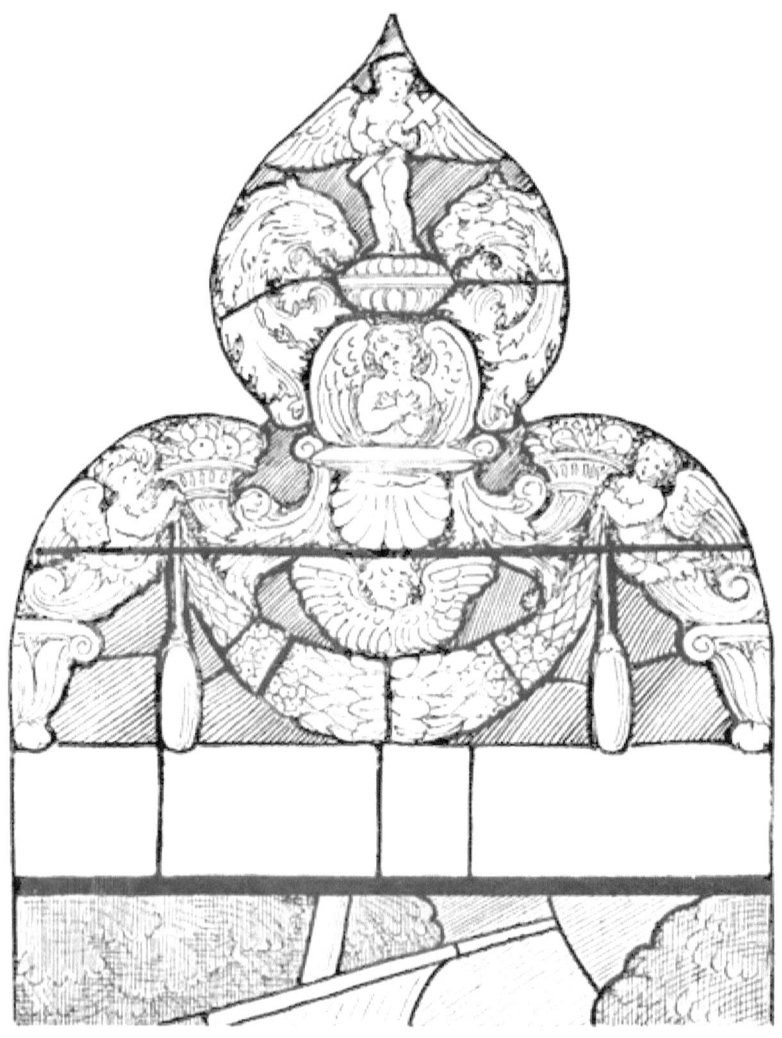

133. S. PATRICE, ROUEN.

as frame to the picture and others to be ignored. The perhaps not very conspicuous canopy is often the only hint as to which of the stone divisions you are to accept as such, and which not. Even that was not always there to serve as a guide. Already,

156. SUBJECT, S. VINCENT, ROUEN, 1525.

as early as 1525, the date given to the window illustrating the life of S. Peter (page 207), the canopy was sometimes annulled, and the window given over entirely to picture, either one complete subject or a series of smaller ones. The window dedicated to S. Peter contains in its four lights eight equal subjects, a plan adopted in several others of the windows at S. Vincent, Rouen. In a series of unframed subjects, such as these, there is much less danger of confusion should some one prominent figure recur throughout always in the same costume. That is the case here, and again at Châlons, where the figure of Our Lord, robed in purple, is conspicuous throughout: the mind grasps at a glance that this is not one picture but a series.

A change of period is indicated by the departure from the disc-shaped nimbus. On pages 207, 210, 234, 397, the nimbus is shown in perspective; an attempt is even made to make it hover above the head, an effect not possible to produce in leaded glass; even at Arezzo it is not achieved. Neither is the use of a mere ring of light, whether in flat or in perspective, a happy substitution for the Gothic colour disc, as may be seen, for example, at Cologne. The idea of the nimbus only keeps within the border line which separates the sublime from the ridiculous, so long as the thing is frankly accepted as a symbol, not as an effect. But, were it otherwise, the use of the strongly marked disc of colour about the head of prominent personages has an enormous value as a means of distinguishing them from the background or from surrounding figures. Its decorative importance is no less than its symbolic. Very especially is this so in glass; and the glass painter who wantonly departs from its use, reduces it to a mere ring (which does not separate it at all from the background) or poises it in the air, is beginning to wander from the way, narrow if you please, which leads to success in glass. This is said with some reluctance in face of the all but perfect little panel from S. Bonnet, at Bourges, on page 210. It is true that there the nimbus of the boy saint, though in perspective, does by its dark tone separate the head from the light ground, as the face is separated from the darker drapery of his teacher; and, in so far, little of definition is sacrificed; but, after all, admirably as the design is schemed, the oval nimbus is not a whit less conventional than the round disc of mediæval times, and it does lack something of distinction and dignity which that conveyed.

The date inscribed (1544) serves to remind us that we are nearing the middle of the century, at which period glass painting may safely be said to have reached its zenith and to be nearing the verge of decline.

It will have been seen in the examples lately instanced how story is gradually more and more naturally set forth in glass. There is now no vestige of flat treatment left. Even the standing figure (page 191) stands forth from his niche, and though he may be backed by a curtain of damask, there is shown above that a background of receding architecture. So in the S. Bernard windows at Shrewsbury (pages 56, 203) there is architectural distance shown in perspective, and again in the subjects from Fairford, whether it be the portcullised gate of Jerusalem that is represented (page 251), or the very inadequate palace of King Solomon (page 188), or the Garden of Eden, in which the scene of the Temptation is primitively pourtrayed (page 372), there is some attempt to render the scene. Even in the fifteenth century work at Troyes (page 194) the Prodigal is not merely shown among the swine, joining them in a dinner of gigantic acorns, but he leans against an oak tree, and in the distance is a little forest of trees. In Renaissance glass the scene is much more naturally rendered, and forms almost invariably an important part of the composition. Witness the palace of Herod (page 74) when Salome dances before him, which is a great advance upon the Gothic throne-room of King Solomon (page 188).

The scene takes one of three forms: either it is architectural, or it is landscape, or it is of architecture and landscape combined. A very favourite plan of the French was to show distant architecture (glazed in deep purple) through which were seen glimpses of grey sky, and perhaps a peep of landscape; and it resulted invariably in a beautiful effect of colour. In fact, a scheme of colour which recurs again and again at Rouen, and in other French glass of the first part of the sixteenth century, consists in the introduction of figures in rich colour and white upon a background where white, green, purple, and pale blue predominate to such an extent as to give quite a distinctive character to the glass. The more distant landscape was painted very delicately upon the pale grey-blue glass which served for sky, as shown on page 255, and in the same way architecture was also painted upon it. In the view through

157 SUBJECT. S BONNET, BOURGES

the arches above the screen in a window at Montmorency (page 213), both trees and buildings are represented in that way upon pale grey glass, the green of the trees and hills stained upon it. Sometimes the distance is painted upon white, as at King's College, Cambridge; but in France the pale grey-blue background is so usual as to be quite characteristic of the period. All this is a long way from the mere diaper of clouds which in the early fifteenth century sometimes took the place of damask pattern upon the blue which formed a background to the Crucifixion, or other scene out of doors. It is now no longer a case of symbolising, but of representing, the sky, and it is wonderful what atmospheric quality is obtained by the judicious use of pale blue painted with the requisite delicacy. The beauty of this kind of work, especially on a small scale, is beyond dispute. Together with the rendering of the flesh, it implies consummate skill in painting. The painter comes quite to the front; but he justifies himself inasmuch as he is able to hold the place. He does what his Gothic predecessors could not have done, and does it perfectly. Could the Gothic artist have painted like this, he also might have been tempted so far in the pictorial direction as to have sacrificed some of the sterner qualities of his design.

The architectural environment of the figures on page 213 fulfils somewhat the function of the Perpendicular canopy; it forms a kind of setting of white for the colour; but, in the first place, it does not pretend to frame them at the side, and, in the second, the attempt at actual perspective necessitates an amount of shading upon the white glass which detracts at once from its purity and from its value as setting to the colour. The idea is there that you see through the window into space; and, though that effect is never obtained, it is wonderful how far some of the glass painters later in the century went towards illusion. A certain false air of truth was sometimes given to the would-be deception by an acknowledgment of the window-shape—that is, by making the foremost arch or arches follow the shape of the windowhead, and form, as it were, a canopy losing itself in perspective. Architecture proper to the subject, or not too inappropriate to it, is sometimes schemed so far to accommodate itself to the window-shape as to form, with the white pavement, a more or less canopy-like setting for the figures. It may be a sort of proscenium, the sides of which recede into the picture, and form what may be called the scenery. At King's College, Cambridge, Esau is seen bargaining away his birthright at a table where stands the coveted pottage, in the midst of spacious halls going back into distant vistas, seen through a sort of canopy next the actual stonework. That concession to the framework of the window does mend matters somewhat. The base of the picture opposite, for example, is much more satisfactory than it would have been had it not acknowledged the window-sill; but the architecture in the top part of the lights is not a frame to the picture at all, nor yet a finish to the glass: it is part of the picture, which thus, you may say, occupies the window as a picture its canvas. In reality that is not quite so. There is some acknowledgment, though inadequate, of the spring of the arch by a horizontal cornice parallel with the bar; and the arcading, though interrupted by the mullion and by the marble columns, steadies the design; and altogether the architecture is planned with ingenuity, though without frank enough acceptance of the window-shape. One would be more tolerant to such misguided freedom of design were it not for the kind of thing it led to. It must be admitted that both French and Flemings, until they began to force their perspective, and to paint shadow heavily, did very beautiful and effective work in this way.

A multitude of figures, as, for example, in the Judgment of Solomon at S. Gervais, Paris, more or less in rich colour, could be held together by distant architecture and foreground pavement largely consisting of white glass, in a way which left little to be desired, except fuller acknowledgment of the stonework. But it took a master of design to do it, and one with a fine sense of breadth and architectural fitness.

When such architecture was kept so light as to have the full value of white, and when the figures against it were also to a large extent in white, and the colour was introduced only in little patches and jewels skilfully designed to form, here the sleeves of a white-robed figure, there a headdress, there again the glimpse of an underskirt, and so on—all ingeniously designed for the express purpose of introducing rich colour, the whole shot through with golden stain—the effect is sometimes very beautiful.

Admirable Flemish work, Renaissance in detail, but carrying on the traditions of Gothic art, is to be found in plenty at

158 SAINTS, CH. OF S. MARTIN, MONTMORENCY.

Liège, both in the cathedral (1530 to 1557) and at S. Martin. This is excellent in drawing and composition, most highly finished in painting, fine in colour, and silvery as to its white glass, which last is splendidly stained. In the same city there is beautiful work also at S. Jacques, with admirable treatment of the canopy on a large scale. It differs from French work inasmuch as it is Flemish, just as the glass at the church of Brou differs in that there is a characteristic Burgundian flavour about it; but those are details of locality, which do not especially affect the course of glass-painting, and which it would be out of place here to discuss.

In England we are not rich in Renaissance glass. The best we have is Flemish, from Herkenrode, now in the cathedral at Lichfield. The greater part of this is collected in seven windows of the Lady Chapel—no need to explain which; the miserable shields of arms in the remaining two convict themselves of modernity. In the tracery, too, there is some old glass, but it is lost in the glare of new glazing adjacent. Otherwise this glass is not much hurt by restoration. Four of the windows are treated much alike; that is, they have each three subjects, extending each across the three lights of which they are composed, some with enclosing canopy, and some without. A fifth three-light window is broken up into six tiers of subjects, each of which appears at first sight as if it were confined to the limits of a single light, but there is in fact connection between the figures; for example, of three figures the central one proves to be the Patron Saint of the Donor, himself occupying one of the side lights, and his wife the other. If the Saint is seated the Donors stand. If he is represented standing they kneel before him. The two larger six-light windows at Lichfield are divided each into four; that is to say, the four quarters of the window have each a separate subject which extends laterally through three lights, and in depth occupies with its canopy about half the entire height of the window.

The Lichfield glass has very much the character of that at Liège. So has the Flemish glass now at the east end of S. George's, Hanover Square, a church famous for its fashionable weddings. This is some of the best glass in London, well worthy the attention of the guests pending the arrival of the bride. The design, however, is calculated to mystify the student, until he becomes aware that the lights form part of a "Tree of Jesse," adapted, not very intelligently, to their present position, and marred by hideous restoration, such as the patch of excruciating blue in the robe of the Virgin. The vine, executed in stain upon white, with grapes in pot-metal purples, is not nearly strong enough to support the figures; this may be in part due to the decay of the paint, which has proceeded apace.

Again, at Chantilly (page 218) may be seen how lead-lines quarrel with delicate painting. The more delicate the painting, the greater the danger of that—a danger seldom altogether overcome.

The most important series of Renaissance windows in this country is in King's College Chapel, Cambridge. "Indentures" still remain to tell us that these were contracted for in 1516 and 1526. Apart from some strikingly English-looking figures in white and stain upon quarry backgrounds in a side chapel, and other remains of similar character, and from a very beautiful window almost opposite the door by which one enters —differing in type, in scale, in colour, altogether from the other windows—the glass throughout the huge chapel was obviously planned at the time of the first contract, and there is a certain symmetry of arrangement throughout which bespeaks the period of transition. The windows consist each of two tiers of five lights. A five-light window offers some difficulty to the designer if he desire (as in the sixteenth century he naturally did) to introduce subjects extending across more than one light. A subject in two lights does not symmetrically balance with a subject in three. He might carry his subject right across the window, but that might give him very likely a larger space to fill than he wanted; and besides, the time was hardly come for him to think of that. He might carry it across the central group of three; but that would leave him a single light on each side to dispose of. Remains the idea of a subject in two lights at each side of the window, and a central composition occupying only one light. That was not a very usual plan, although it was adopted, at Fairford for example, where the side subjects in two lights under a canopy are effectually separated by a central subject which has none. At King's the side-lights have no canopies further than such as may be accepted as part of the architecture proper to the subject,

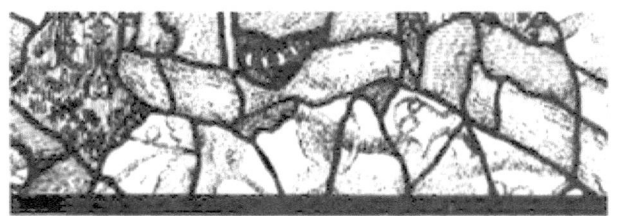

159. S. GEORGE'S, HANOVER SQUARE, LONDON

schemed more or less to frame the picture (as in the case of the
window at Montmorency, page 213); it is only in the centre
lights that the figures (two in each light, one above the other)
are enclosed in canopy work. These figures (described as
"messengers"), with elaborately flowing scrolls about them
inscribed with texts of Scripture, are many of them quite
Gothic in character, even though they have Renaissance
canopies over them. The designs of these mostly do duty
many times over, as if this merely decorative or descriptive
work were not of much account; and the same figure occurs,
here well painted, there ill done, or painted perhaps in a
late, loose way, quite out of keeping with the drawing: there
is no sort of sequence in them. The notion of these intermediate figures, at once distinguishing the subjects one from
the other, and throwing light upon their meaning, is good.
But in effect it fails of its object, thanks to the independent
spirit of the later painters, who thought more of their pictures
than of architectural restraint.

The subjects on each side of the window are very large
in scale, very pictorially and very freely treated, very finely
designed at times, and very splendid in effect; but they are
most unequal, and they are all more or less of a tangle. Their
confusion is the greater inasmuch as there is no attempt to
balance one picture with another. A landscape background
on one side of the window answers to an architectural background on the other. On one side the interest of the subject
is towards the top of the lights, on the other to the bottom,
and so on. Either subject or both may be so merged with the
"messengers" that a casual observer would hardly be aware of
the existence of such personages.

All this makes it difficult to trace the subject; and yet the
windows are in a certain pictorial way the more effective. In
fact the unity of the *window* has been preserved: the white
landscape on one side, and the white architecture on the other,
make equally a setting for the colour, and form, with the
"messengers" and their little canopies, *one* framing, not several
frames. Right or wrong, the artist has done what he meant
to do, and done it oftentimes very cleverly, though not with
uniform success. The inequality spoken of is not only in workmanship but in design. Some of these pictures have characteristics, such as the needless evasion of leading, which one

160   THE STORY OF PSYCHE, CHANTILLY.

associates rather with quite the end of the century than with anything like the date of the second contract: possibly the execution of the work extended over a longer period of time than is generally supposed. However that may be, the windows generally, remarkable as they are, are not markedly enough of a period to serve as an object-lesson in glass design. They are neither quite late enough to illustrate the decline of art, nor workmanlike enough to show the culmination of sixteenth century design—painter-like and pictorial, but in which the designer knew how to make the most of the glass in which it was to be wrought.

That is best seen in some of the French and Flemish work above referred to, in the work, for example, at Ecouen and Montmorency, so fully illustrated in Monsieur Magne's most admirable monograph. The figure, for example, of William of Montmorency (page 66), the father of the great Anne, might serve for a votive picture of the period; but it is designed, nevertheless, as only a man careful of the conditions under which glass-painting was done could design. Careful of conditions! That is just what the designers of the King's College glass were not, or not enough. And so begins the end.

CHAPTER XVIII.

LATER RENAISSANCE WINDOWS.

THE magnificent windows of Van Orley at S. Gudule, Brussels, mark in a sense the summit of design, as well as of painting, in stained glass. But it is design of a kind not strictly proper to the material, for which reason the discussion of his work, though it was done well within the first half of the sixteenth century, has been reserved by way of introduction to the period which it inaugurated, the period when the glass painter not merely put painting first of all, but sacrificed to it qualities peculiar to glass.

The heavy painting of this work and much that followed it has already been discussed. But something of that was perhaps implied in the very ideal of the painter; the execution only follows out the scheme of the design. The scope as well as the power of the designer is better illustrated in the two great transept windows, than in those of the chapel of the Holy Sacrament. Even in the very inadequate rendering of the one of them on page 71 may be seen how large and dignified the man's conception was. The effect is gorgeous; but it is produced as simply, for all the unsurpassed elaboration of ornamental detail, as a Goth could wish. An unsophisticated designer of the thirteenth century could scarcely have gone more directly to work. He would not have grouped his figures with such art, but he would have separated each from the other and from the ground in much such a straightforward way. Yet the *motif* of the design, the idea of making figures and architecture stand as it were in strong and round relief against the light, went far to bring about excessive use of paint; and the design is therefore in a measure at fault, as was the later Netherlandish work, founded upon it, of which it may be taken as the nobler type.

It is a far cry from the slender Perpendicular canopy to this triumphal arch. The architecture is here no frame to the picture, but the backbone of the picture itself, and it is disposed in the most masterly way. It takes the place of a magnificent high altar. Sometimes in compositions of this kind the altar-like canopy enshrines a rich picture, just as veritable stonework might frame a painted altarpiece, whilst in the foreground kneel the Donors. In this case Charles the Fifth and his wife Isabella and their attendant saints are the picture, the object of their adoration, the Almighty, being relegated to one of the side arches. Similarly in a three-light window (of much more glassy character, however) at Montmorency, Guy de Laval has the central position, and the crucifix before which he kneels is put on one side. This is rather characteristic of the period. In the sixteenth century windows were erected, not so much to the glory of God, as to the glorification of the Donor, who claimed a foremost, if not the very central, place for himself.

The donor was no doubt always, as to this day, an important person in connection with the putting up of a stained glass window. But in early days he was content to efface himself, or if he appeared upon the scene at all it was in miniature, modestly presenting the little image of his gift in a lower corner of the window. In the fourteenth century he is still content with the space of a small panel, bearing his effigy or his arms, at the base of the window. Even in the fifteenth he is content at times to be represented by his patron saint, as in the beautiful window in the chapel of Jacques Cœur, at Bourges. In the sixteenth he is very much in evidence. No scruple of modesty, or suspicion of unworthiness, restrains him from putting in an appearance in the midst of the most serious and sacred scenes, very much sometimes to the confusion of the story. Eventually the donor, his wife, and perhaps his family, with their patron saints, who literally back them up in their obtrusiveness, claim, if they do not absorb, all our attention, and the sacred subject takes quite a back place. In the foreground of the scene of the Last Judgment which occupies the great west window at S. Gudule, Brussels, kneels the donor, with attendant angels, on a scale much larger than the rest of the world, competing in fact in importance with the figure of Our Lord in Majesty above.

However, the vain-glory of princes and seigneurs resulted in the production of works of such consummate art that, as artists, we can but be grateful to them. In the presence of the splendid achievement of Van Orley, who shall say that the artist does not justify himself? Nothing equal to it *in its way* was ever done.

It may not be according to the strict rules of the game: it is not; but that it is magnificent, no fair-minded artist can deny. Our just cause of quarrel is, not with that, but with what that led to, what that became in less competent hands. It is the price we pay for strong men that they induce weak ones to follow them in a direction where they are bound to fail. Van Orley's triumphant answer to any carping of ours would be, to point to the great west window of the cathedral, designed on earlier and more orthodox lines, and say: "Compare!" We have no right to limit art to what small folk can do.

The further development of the Gouda glass above.

164. THE PARABLE OF THE PHARISEE AND THE PUBLICAN, GOUDA.

Netherlandish canopy is shown in the Here is still considerable skill in the way in which the window is set out, and the patches of colour are introduced (for example, in the two figures leaning on the balcony and the wreath of leaves and fruit above them) amidst the predominant white,—if only the white glass had been whiter in effect. But there is altogether too much of this architectural work, even though it is used, in the pictured parable at least, to dramatic purpose. The notion of the Pharisee gesticulating away in the far distance, whilst the Publican modestly fills the foreground, is cleverly conceived and skilfully carried out; but the picture is overpowered by its ponderous frame.

It is in the wonderful series of late sixteenth century windows at Gouda, in Holland, that the fullest and furthest development of pictorial design is shown. The period of their execution extends from 1555 to 1603; and, as they are admittedly the finest works of their day, they may be taken to represent the best work of the latter half of the sixteenth century. They are, in fact, typical of the period, only at its best: it is not often that work of that date was designed with such power or painted with such skill. The diagrams given here and on pages 79, 244, 258, do no manner of justice to the glass; but they will help the reader better to understand what is said concerning it. They indicate at least the lines on which these daring designers planned their huge windows, the main lines which pictorial design on a large scale is destined henceforth to take.

162. GOUDA. 1596.

In the clerestory of S. Eustache, Paris, are some large two-light windows which somewhat recall the Gouda work; but the design is rather original. One vast architectural composition in white, not very heavily painted, fills the window, against which stand a series of giant Apostles in colour, one in each light, occupying about one-third of the height of the

FIG. S. SEBALD'S, NUREMBERG.

window. This much recognition of the separate openings is something to be thankful for towards the middle of the seventeenth century.

A striking feature, we have seen, about the later Renaissance canopy as shown at Gouda, and already at Brussels, is its vast dimensions. It no longer frames the picture: it is a prominent, sometimes the most prominent, feature in its design.

Even earlier than that the canopy was already sometimes of very considerable extent. At S. Sebald's, Nuremberg, there is a great altar-like canopy ending in a pediment about two-thirds of the way up the window, with plain white glass above, in which the shafting at the side takes up practically the entire width of the two outer lights, as here shown in the diagram of a portion of the glass. Yet this window is as early as the year 1515, and before the period when masses of deep shadow were represented by paint. Accordingly the canopy in this instance is glazed in pot-metal of steely grey-blue, which, with the little figures, mainly in steely grey armour against a white ground, and the heraldic shields at the side, mainly in red and white, all very slightly shaded, has a singularly fresh, bright, and delicate effect.

Another instance of preponderating architectural work occurs also at Nuremberg in the choir of the church of S. Lorenz, and though it belongs to the beginning of the seventeenth century, that too is leaded up much as it might have been in the fifteenth. But the great clumsy column, opposite, with its clumsier figure of Fame, against a ruby background extending right up to the stonework of the window, is not a satisfactory filling to the outer light of a big window.

The last thing to expect of late Renaissance work is modesty in the use of architectural accessories, whether in the form of frame or background. Frame and background they are not; they claim to be all or nothing. Just as ornamental design was gradually pushed out of use by figure-work, so the picture was in time overpowered by its frame. And the frame was in the end such that, when it came to be discarded, it was not much loss.

In the latter half of the sixteenth century and thenceforward design continued to travel in the direction of what was meant for a sort of realism. If the more or less altar-like canopy was retained, it was meant to appear as if it stood bodily under the arch of the window; if it was abandoned, you were supposed to see more or less *through* the window, perhaps into distant country, perhaps into receding aisles of the church.

It formed part of the canopy scheme, that the structure should end before it reached the top of the window, so that you could see beyond it into space. The designers would have been only too happy if they could have done away with the glass above that. If they had had big sheets of plate glass, they would certainly have used them to produce the effect of out of doors—there was already a *plein air* school in the eighteenth century—as they had not, they were obliged to accept the inevitable, and lead up their white glass; but they went as far as they could to doing away with its effect, using thin, transparent material, which was not meant to appear as though it formed part of the composition. Occasionally they would use pale blue glass, or tint it in a blue enamel, further to suggest the sky beyond. This (page 222) would commonly be glazed in squares. The pure white glass also was often glazed in square or, as at Brussels, diamond quarries (page 71).

Subjects themselves, it has been explained, came to be glazed as much as possible in rectangular panes; but it marks, it may here be mentioned, a decline of design, as well as of technique, when these came to interfere in any way, as they did, with the drawing. Having made up his mind that his design is to be glazed in rigid square lines, the artist should logically have designed accordingly. He had

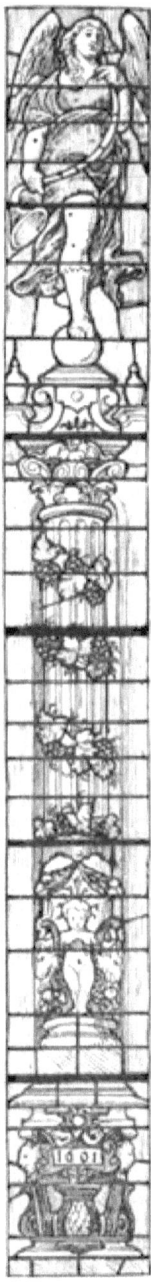

164. S. LORENZ, NUREMBERG.

only to mark off the glazing lines on his cartoon, and scheme his composition so that it was not hurt by them. Towards the seventeenth century the plain glass, the extra part beyond the canopy or beyond the picture, would often be glazed in some simple pattern. That, you might imagine, stood for the window *behind* the picture or the monument. At the church of S. Jacques, Antwerp, above a picture of the Circumcision, is a canopy leaded in squares and painted to look like falsehood, beyond which clear glass is glazed in a pattern.

Occasionally an attempt is made to merge the picture into the plain glazing above, as at S. Paul's, Antwerp, where the yellow sky, against which is shown the distant city, and so on, is glazed in squares, which further off become gradually white, and then at their interstices have smaller diamond-shaped pieces of glass let in.

Where a subject glazed in quarries is represented against a background of plain glazing of more elaborate design, there is difficulty in joining the two, except by means of a strong lead outline to the figures, or whatever may come next to the plain glass, which outline the seventeenth century designer was anxious before all things to avoid. Accordingly, as the plain pattern work approached the margin of the painted work, he replaced the leads by paint, which sham leads, of course, could be made to disappear as seemed good to him. But these little games of his, to judge by results, were hardly worth the candle.

It will be seen how, in the French glass on page 200, the canopy came to be backed and surrounded by unpainted glass, quarries in that case. There the canopy sufficiently occupies the window space not to strike one unpleasantly; but that is sixteenth century work; later, and especially in Flanders, canopies are represented, as in the cathedral at Antwerp (1615), adrift, as it were, in a sea of plain glazing. Even when the glass has some quality of glass the effect of that is not happy. When the glass is thin and transparent it is disastrous.

At S. Jacques, Antwerp, again, coats of arms hover unsupported in mid air, the mere lines of the glazing being quite inadequate to their apparent support. It is different, of course, where the heraldic device, as opposite, is itself little more than plain glazing. That is a very mild form of art; but, in its way, it is satisfactory enough.

Perhaps least fortunate of all in effect are the landscapes at S. Jacques, which float, without even a canopy to frame them, in an atmosphere of leaded glass. Antwerp is rich in glass, much of it very cleverly executed, which would serve very well to illustrate how *not* to design a window.

The place of the canopy was supplied sometimes, especially in later Netherlandish work, by the cartouche so dear to the Dutch. It fulfilled very much the office of the canopy, framing

165. GOUDA, 1688.

166. PLAIN GLAZING, S. GERVAIS, PARIS

the design; and, had it been kept white, it would have framed it well, affording circular and other shapes which form a welcome variation upon the usual arched opening. But it was not white at all; very much the reverse. Indeed the idea of the Dutch cartouche, with its interpenetration of parts, and curling and projecting straps and bolts, tempts the painter to a heavy method of painting, destructive of the very quality of white. The device depends for its effect far too much upon force of shadow to be of any great use in white glass. The comparatively early cartouche in the lower half of the window at Gouda, given on page 223, is of the simplest kind, and has none of that too-seductive bolt work : but it is dull and heavy in effect, being painted in heavy brown, with the idea of giving atmospheric effect to the picture supposed to be seen through it.

A great cartouche is often used as a kind of base to a canopy extending across the whole width of a wide window, or the base of the canopy may include a very important cartouche, occupied in either case by a long inscription. Here again the oblong patch of white or yellow may have value, in proportion as it is allowed to preserve the quality of glass. There is, however, something poor and mean about large areas of small lettering, and it is a pity to see the opportunity which bold inscriptions give quite thrown away. Moreover, the inscriptions are invariably too long. The framers of inscriptions do not realise the multitude of readers they scare away by the volume of their wording. The design of a window at

S. Jacques, Antwerp, consists merely of an inscription label, with a helmet above and mantling in black and white (the black, of course, paint) set in plain glazing.

Up to the very last whole windows were glazed very often in plain patterns, usually all in clear white glass. A couple of designs, into which a little colour is introduced, are given below and opposite. In spite of the increased facility for cutting glass, afforded from the beginning of the century by the use of the diamond, patterns were seldom very elaborate; but, by way of illustrating what can be done by means of the diamond, there is shown overleaf quite a conjuring feat of glazing. The thick black lines in the drawing represent the leads; the white spaces enclosed are plain white glass, rather poor in quality; the thinner lines stand for cracks, possibly not, or not all of them, of the glazier's doing, for it would be almost impossible to handle such work without breaking it. It is well-nigh incredible that each of these *fleurs-de-lys* should have been cut out of a single piece of glass, the marginal band to it out of a second, and so with the background spaces. Glaziers may be inclined to question the possibility of such a *tour de force*, even in poor thin glass. Certainly one would not have thought it possible; but there it is, in the museum at Angers, close to the eye, where you can see and examine it. This is glazing with a vengeance. It is not the sort of thing that any one would undertake, except as a trial piece, to show his skill; but if ever a glazier deserved his diploma of mastership here is the man.

The composition of some of the windows belonging to the first half of the seventeenth century at Troyes does not follow the general tendency of the period. The better part of this, if not the greater, is attributed to Linard Gontier (1606—1648). But the design of these

167. PLAIN GLAZING, LISIEUX.

168. A TOUR DE FORCE IN GLAZING, ANGERS MUSEUM.

windows, and the style of them, is so varied, and sometimes so little of the period, that one is disposed to think, either that he was a painter only and did not design them at all, or that he borrowed his designs freely from Italian and other sources. The panel on page 400, the Virgin girt with clouds and cherubs, distinctly recalls the work of the Della Robbia School; and again the figures opposite remind one of late sixteenth century paintings. An unusual thing, however, about some of these windows is the way they are set out. The disposition of the design of the three-light window from S. Martin es Vignes is as simple and severe as though it had been Gothic. The glazing, too, is not in squares, but follows the design. Except for the rather robustious drawing of the figures, and the futile kind of detail which does duty for canopy work, the glass might belong to the first half of the sixteenth century.

169. THREE LIGHTS, S. MARTIN-ES-VIGNES, TROYES

Again, in the subject of the marriage of SS. Joachim and Anna on page 234, it is rather by the types of feature and the cast of draperies, than by the composition, that the date of the work proclaims itself. It is proclaimed, of course, unmistakably by the use of enamel, not only in the warm-coloured flesh, but throughout, to support, and sometimes to supply the place of, pot-metal glass. Nevertheless, the effect of much of this glass is brilliant to a degree almost unprecedented in the first half of the seventeenth century. The painter had skill enough to get the maximum of modelling with the minimum of paint. He could afford, therefore, to use paint sparingly, leaving plenty of glass clear, and seldom sacrificing its translucency, as was done in the group of donors on page 81, whose black mantles are rendered in solid paint. Those heavily painted figures recall a couple of Donors in a window at Antwerp (1626), equally black robed, against a nearly black screen, all in paint; they would have made a capital votive picture; but they are about as unlike glass as anything one can conceive.

Exceptionally good seventeenth century work is to be found also at Auch. It seems that it was proposed (towards 1650) to complete the windows in a way worthy of the splendid beginning in the choir; but the art was not forthcoming; and the Chapter of that day was wise enough to fall back upon comparatively unimportant quarry windows, with borders and tracery in white and stain and blue enamel, which is at least brilliant in colour, and pleasing in effect. That may be said also of the Western Rose. In the Roses of the transepts, the artist goes further, and produces, by means of arabesque in white and stain, upon a ground mainly of blue and ruby, occasionally varied by green, each light defined by a simple border of white and stain, a couple of flamboyant Rose windows with glass which would do credit to the period of the stonework. They might well (at the distance they are placed from the eye) be taken at first sight for Early Renaissance work. In fact they are really mosaic glass—so rare a thing by this time that the windows are probably of their kind unique.

Even at its best enamelled glass is less effective than the earlier work. In proportion as the place of pot-metal is supplied by enamel, the colour is inevitably diluted, and at times it is quite thin. Indeed, it is pretty well proved, by the work of men who are masters in their way, that, in painted as distinguished from mosaic glass, the choice lies between weak colour and opacity. At Auch and at Troyes we have weak but still often pure and brilliant colour.

The opposite defect of opacity reaches probably its greatest depth in the four great Rubens-like windows at S. Gudule in the chapel of Our Lady immediately opposite that of the Holy Sacrament, where Van Orley's windows are. The design is there absolutely regardless of any consideration of glass or architecture. Each window is treated as a vast oil picture, without so much as a frame. Here is no vista of distant architecture, nor any such relief of lighter colour as you find at Gouda. Force of colour is sought by masses of deep shadow, into which the figures merge. This shadow being obtained by paint, and the glazing being in the now usual squares, there are literally yards of painted quarries, which, except when the sun is at its fiercest, are all but black. And withal the effect is not rich as compared with even the common Gothic glass, though it is not without a certain picturesqueness when perchance the sun struggles through. A painter might find it an admirable background to his picture; no architect would choose it for his building. Three of these windows were designed, it seems, by a pupil of Rubens, Van Thulden, who worked under him at the Luxembourg, and they have all the character of his work—except that the colour is dull.

At New College, Oxford, are some smaller windows with figures, also recalling the manner of the master, and said to be by pupils of his. They, too, are dull and heavy in effect. The canopies over the figures are terrible caricatures of the Gothic shrines in the antechapel. Better seventeenth century glass is to be found at Oxford in the work of the Van Lingen, a family of Dutchmen settled in England, who executed windows in Wadham and Balliol Colleges and elsewhere. Some of these are rich in colour. Apart from the rather interesting use of enamel made in them, they are not of great value; but they show as well as more important examples the kind of thing which did duty for design.

The windows in Lincoln's Inn Chapel, London, illustrate not unfairly the dreary level of dulness as to colour and design to which seventeenth century glass declined. That it could fall still lower was shown, for example, by Peckitt, of York, who is responsible for the glass on the north side of New

170. ST MARTIN ÈS VIGNES, TROYES.

College Chapel, Oxford, facing the work of the Dutchmen. These date from 1765 to 1774.

The history of eighteenth century windows may, if one may plagiarise a famous bull, be put into the fewest possible words: there were none—worth looking at. To find pleasure even in Sir Joshua's design at New College, you must consider it as anything but glass.

CHAPTER XIX.

PICTURE-WINDOWS.

THE course of glass design was picture-ward. Picture design, however, did not stand still, and hence arises some confusion in the use of the word "pictorial." It is time to try and clear that up. Stained glass, it may be truly said, has been from the very first pictorial. The earliest glass, therefore, and the latest, the best and the worst, may alike be termed pictorial. The difference is in the conception as to what constituted a picture, say, in the thirteenth century and the seventeenth. It all depends upon the kind of picture attempted.

Archaic art aims already at nature. We probably do not give the early painter credit enough for his intention of rendering natural things naturally. In part at least the stiffness of his design comes from lack of skill, and often where we find him quaint he meant no doubt to be perfectly serious and matter-of-fact. But it was not alone incompetence that held his hand. He was restrained always by a decorative purpose in his work. Here again he was not conscious of sacrificing to any higher rule of art; he bothered himself as little about that as a bee about the way it shall fashion its cell; he worked in the way to which he was born; but the idea had not yet developed itself that a picture could be painted quite apart from the decoration of something, and it never entered his mind to do anything but adapt himself to the decorative situation.

A picture, then, in mediæval times was a work of decorative art, designed to fit a place, to fulfil part of a scheme of decoration, in which it might more often than not take the first place, but no more: it had no claim to independence.

In glass the picture obeyed two conditions which more or less pulled together: as art it subserved to decorative and architectural effect; as craftsmanship it acknowledged and accepted the limitations of glass painting. In the course of years the ideal of architectural fitness underwent successive changes, and the limitations of the glass painter grew less; his scope, that is to say, was widened, and his art took what we call more pictorial shape. Still, so long as the pictorial ideal itself was restrained within the limits of mediæval ambition, glass painting might safely approach the pictorial. It was not until painting broke loose from traditional decorative trammels and set up, so to speak, on its own account, until pictorial came to mean something widely different from decorative, that the term became in any way distinctive of one kind of art or another. It is in that later sense that the word pictorial is here used.

Artists still differ, and will continue to differ, as to the precise use of the term. There are artists still who contend that, since in old time art was decorative, and since in their opinion all art should be decorative, therefore the picture which is not decorative is not art. Arguing thus in a circle, they would say (the pictorial including in their estimation the perfection of decorative fitness, and all art which overshot the mark ceasing to count with them) that art was always at its best when it was most pictorial. But that is a species of quibbling about words which not only leads us no farther, but hinders mutual understanding. It is wiser to accept words in the sense in which they are generally understood, and to try and see where the real difference of opinion is.

Difficult it may be, impossible even, to draw the line between a picture which is decorative and decoration which is pictorial; but there is no difficulty in drawing a band on one side of which is decoration and on the other picture. You have only to draw it wide enough. If we can succeed in defining a picture as distinguished from a work of decorative art, and can then show how a stained glass window, in attempting to conform to conditions which we have agreed to call pictorial, fails of its decorative function, it will then not be so difficult to see how, in proportion as glass aims at the pictorial, it falls short of making good windows. Granted, then, that a picture may fulfil all decorative conditions, and that a decoration may sometimes rightly be pictorial, that the two go, as historically they did, a long way hand in hand, it is contended that there is a point at which decoration and picture part company and take distinctly different ways; thenceforth, if either is led away by the other, it is at the cost of possible success in the direction more peculiarly its own.

Now, the first point at which picture definitely parts company with decoration is where the painter begins to consider his work apart from its surroundings. The problems the artist may set himself to solve are two. "How shall I adorn this church, this clerestory, this chancel, this window, with stained glass?"—that is distinctly a problem of the decorator; "How shall I realise, on canvas or what not, this thought of mine, this fact in nature, this effect seen or imagined?"—that is distinctly a problem of the painter. Each, it is granted, may be swayed more or less by the other consideration also, but according as a man starts with the one problem or the other, and seeks primarily to solve that, he is painter or decorator. Suppose him seriously to endeavour to combine pictorial and decorative qualities in his work, there will come times when he has perforce to choose between the two. Upon the choice he makes will hang the final character of his work, decorative or pictorial.

We are too much in the habit of laying down laws as to what a man may or may not do in art. He may do what he can. He may introduce as much decorative intention into his picture, as much pictorial effect into his decoration, as it will stand; it is not till he overweights one with the other, attempts more than his means or his power allow him, and fails to do the thing that was to be done, that we can say he has gone wrong.

When the two ideals of decoration and painting were more nearly one, and in proportion as that was so, success in the two directions was possible; when painting aimed at effects of painting—in proportion, that is, as it became pictorial—it was impossible. It is safe to say, since masters attempted it and failed—since, for example, the finest work in glass which aims at the pictorial and depends upon painting ends always in being either thin or opaque in effect—that the happy medium was not found. The fact is, the time came when a painter, in order to design successfully for glass, was called upon to relinquish some of the effects he had come greatly to value in painting: effects of light and shade, atmosphere, reflected light, relief, perspective, violent foreshortening. To seek these at the expense of qualities proper to decoration and to glass, was to attempt picture; to sacrifice such pictorial qualities to considerations of architectural fitness, to the quality of

S.G.   P

the glass, its translucency, its colour, its consistent treatment, was to attempt decoration; and in proportion as the sacrifice is not made, the work of the glass painter may be characterised as "pictorial." There should now be no possible misunderstanding as to what is meant by the word. It implies something of reproach, but only as applied to glass. Let the pictorial flourish, in its place—that is, in picture. All it is here meant to assert is that, pictures being what they are, what they were already by the end of the sixteenth century, the pictorial element in stained glass is bound to spoil the window.

There are two respects in which a stained glass window differs from a picture: first, in that it is a window; second, in that it is glass. Suppose we take these two points separately. It scarcely needs showing that the designing of a window is a very different thing from the painting of a picture. In the first place, the architectural frame of the window is there, arbitrarily fixed, whereas the painter chooses his frame to suit his picture. The designer of a window has not only to accept the window-shape, but to respect both it and the architecture of the building. The scale of his work, the main lines of its composition, if not more, are practically determined for him by architectural considerations, just as the depth of colour in his scheme is determined by the position of his window and the amount of light he desires "or is allowed" to shut out. Moreover, he has to accept the window plane, to acknowledge it as part of the building, to let you feel, whatever he does, that it is a window you see, and not something through the window or standing in it. That was tried, as we have seen, at Gouda and S. Gudule; but, even if the illusion had been achieved, it would have been destructive of architectural effect. The idea of a picture seen through the mullions of a window is one of the will-o'-the-wisps which led glass painters astray. They did not succeed; and, had they done so, they would have given a very false, and to some of us a very uncomfortable, impression of not being protected from the outer air.

Mullions are in any case a very serious consideration. It has been shown already (page 197) how the artist sought continuity of subject through the lights of his window, and gradually extended his picture across them. And if he is at liberty to occupy a four-light window with the Virgin and

Child and the Three Kings, and if it is lawful to introduce more than one figure into a light, why may not each king be accompanied by an attendant, holding his horse or bearing gifts; why should not the Kings kneel in adoration; why should not Joseph be there, the manger, and the cattle; why should there not be one landscape stretching behind the Magi, binding the whole into one picture? So with the Crucifixion. If the Virgin and S. John may occupy side-lights, why not introduce as well in a larger window the two thieves, the Magdalene at the foot of the cross, the good centurion, the soldiers, the crowd? Obviously there is no reason why the subject should not be carried across a window; and from the time that windows were divided into lights it was done, at all events in the case of certain subjects, such as the Tree of Jesse, which spread throughout the window, or the Last Judgment, for which the available space was yet never enough.

But there is a wide difference between designing a subject which extends through the whole width of a window and designing it so that it appears to be seen through the window. In the one case the mullions are seriously taken into account; in the other they are ignored. If you were looking at a scene through a window, of course the mullions would interfere. Why, therefore, consider them if you wish to produce the effect of something seen through? Naturally you would not allow the stonework to cut across the face of a principal personage, or anything of that kind; but, apart from that, its intervention would only add to the air of reality. The problem of dealing with the mullions is thus rather shirked than solved. Its solution is not really so difficult as would seem. Mullions count for much less in the window than one would suppose. The eye, for example, follows naturally the branches of a Tree of Jesse from one light into another, and it is not felt that the stonework interferes with it at all seriously, whilst the scheming of the figures, each within a single light, is a very distinct acknowledgment of its individuality. So in the case of a subject. If the design is so planned that the important figures are grouped in separate lights, the landscape or other continuous background helps to hold the picture together, and is not hurt by the mullions.

The important thing is that mullions should be considered; only on that condition do they cease to interfere with the design. There is no reason always to put a border round each light, or even to keep every figure within the bounds of a single light. A reclining figure, such as that of Jesse at the base of the window (below), Jacob asleep and dreaming, or the widow's son upon the bier, may safely cross two or three lights, if it be designed with reference to the intervening stonework.

Further, it seems desirable that the shape of each separate window opening should be acknowledged by at least a narrow fillet of white or pale colour next the masonry, broken, it may be, here and there by some feature designed to hold the lights together, but practically clearing the colour from the stonework, and giving to the division of the window the slight emphasis it deserves. It is not worth while dividing a window into lights and then effacing the divisions in the glass. Given a window of four or five lights, the decorator has no choice but to design a four or five-light window. He must render his subject so that the constructional divisions of the window keep their proper architectural place; if his subject will not allow that, he must abandon his subject, or give very good reason why not. The reason of mere pictorial ambition will not hold good. The test of a good picture-window is, how the mullions affect the design. If to take them away would make it look foolish, then it has probably been designed as a window, decoratively; if to take them away would improve it, then it has been designed pictorially; and, however good a picture it might have been, it is a bad window design.

It is quite possible, nay, probable, that in connection with any given window, or series of windows, there will be archi-

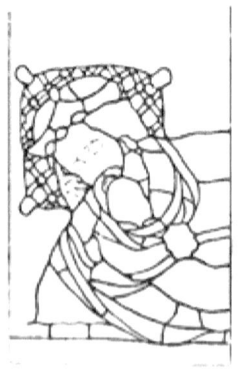 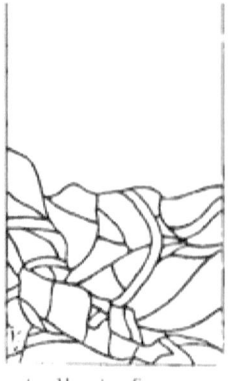 

171 — S. Mary's, Shrewsbury.

tectural features which deserve to be emphasised. It may be the springing of the arch which calls for accentuation; it may be a string-course in the walls that asks for recognition; it may be that the proportion of the window wants correction. Whatever it be, it is the part of the decorator to feel the want and to meet it, to grasp the situation and to accept it. In not doing so, he shows perhaps pictorial, certainly not decorative, instinct. So with regard to the plane of a glass picture. It is not necessary to restrict one's design to silhouette, to make one's picture as flat as the first glass painters or the Greek vase painters made theirs. How much of distance and relief a man may indulge in is partly his own affair. It depends upon what he can manage to do without destroying the surface of his window. So long as he preserve that, he may do as he pleases, and yet not lay himself open to the charge of being unduly pictorial; only it is as well to remember that on the simplest and severest lines grand work has been done, and may still be done, without falling into archaism; whilst the Crabeths, and the rest of the astoundingly clever glass painters of Gouda fail to reconcile us to the attempt to render the sky beyond (page 258) or distant architectural vistas in glass.

It has sometimes been contended that all lines of perspective (which in the sixteenth century begin to take a very important place in design) are amiss in glass, inasmuch as they destroy its flatness. That is surely to go too far. So long as no effect of relief is sought, no effect of distance attempted, no illusion aimed at, one can hardly find fault with lines indicating the perspective necessary perhaps to the expression of the design —assuming, of course, that the lines of perspective take their place in the decorative scheme, and help the composition of the window. They do that very cleverly in Crabeth's picture of "Christ Purifying the Temple" (page 244). Our complaint is rather with the strong relief attempted, the abuse of shadow, and especially of painted shadow. The case is far worse where, as at S. Eustache, Paris, the architectural background is shown obliquely. In that case, no uncommon one in the seventeenth century, when the painter would just as likely as not choose his point of view as best suited his picture, without any reference whatever to its architectural setting, the painter shows himself, as glass painter, at his most pictorial and worst.

So much for the window as an architectural feature, now let us look at it as glass.

It becomes here very much a question of craftsmanship. To a workman it seems so natural, and so obvious, that the material he is working in, and the tools he is using, must from beginning to end affect the treatment of his design, that it appears almost unnecessary to insist upon such a truism. Experience, however, goes to show that only the workman and here and there a man who ought, perhaps, to have been one, have any appreciation of what artists call treatment. The rest of the world have heard tell that there is such a thing as technique, to which they think far too much importance is attached. That is so, indeed, when artists think technique is enough; but not when they look upon it as indispensable, the beginning of all performance, not when they insist that a man shall know the grammar of his art before he breaks out into poetry.

Now the A, B, C, of workmanship is to treat each material after its kind. It is a truism, therefore, to say that glass should be treated as glass. Yet we find that a man may be enthusiastic to a degree about an art, learned above most men in its history, and yet end in entirely misconceiving its scope. " What is to be condemned on canvas," said Winston, " ought not to be admitted on glass." As well might he have said, that what would be condemned on glass should not be allowed on canvas, or that language and behaviour which would be unbecoming in church should not be tolerated on the platform, or at the dinner-table.

The fallacy that one rule applies to all forms of art is responsible alike for the muddiness of seventeenth and eighteenth century windows and for the thin transparent tinting of nineteenth century Munich glass.

That " art is one " is a fine saying, rightly understood. So is humanity one, and it is well to remind ourselves of the fact; but race, climate, country, count for something; and to speak with effect we must speak the language of the land. Each separate craft included in the all-embracing title of art, and making for its good and its glory, works under conditions as definite as those of climate, has characteristics as marked as those of nationality, and speaks also a language of its own. And, to express itself to full purpose, it must speak in its own tongue. The only pictures, then, which prove satisfactory in glass are the pictures of the glass painter; and by glass painter is not meant any one who may choose to try his hand at glass painting, but the man who has learnt his trade and knows it from end to end, to whom use has become second nature, who thinks in glass, as we say. Now and again, perhaps, where a draughtsman and a glass painter are in unusual sympathy, it may be possible for the one to translate the design of the other into the language of his craft; but good translators are rare, and translation is at best second-hand. Success in glass is achieved mainly by the man to whom ideas come in the form of glass, who sees them first in his mind's eye as windows. Even such a man may lack taste, insight, discretion; he may be led away by a misplaced ambition— it is not merely on the stage that the low comedian aspires to play Hamlet—but only the man who knows so well the dangers ahead that he insensibly avoids them, who knows so surely what can be got out of his material that he makes straight for that, who does, in short, the best that can be done in glass, can dare to be "pictorial" without danger of being false to his trade.

172. CHRIST PURGING THE TEMPLE, GOUDA.

A painter without experience of glass might, of course, be coached in the technique of the material; but he would never get the most out of it. Conditions which to the glass painter would be as easy as an old coat, would be a restraint to him, and the greater his position the more impatient he would be of such restraint, the more surely his will would override the better judgment of the subordinate who happened to know.

It was unfortunate that at a critical period in the history of glass, just when great painters from the outside began to be called in to design for it, knowledge was in rather an uncertain state. The use of enamel had been discovered; it offered undoubted facilities to the painter; it was believed in; it was the fashion. Any one who had protested the superiority of the old method would possibly have been set down as an old fogey, even by glass painters. At that moment, very likely, a glass painter, anxious of course to conciliate the great man, but flushed also with faith in his new-found method, would have said to Van Orley, in reply to any question about technique :— " Never you mind about glazing and all that; give us a design, and we will execute it in glass." And he did execute it in a masterly and quite wonderful way. Still the success of it is less than it would have been had the designer known all about glass : in that case his artistic instinct would have led him surely to trust more to qualities inherent in glass, and less to painting upon it. Van Orley's picture scheme depended too much upon relief to be really well adapted to glass, but it was splendidly monumental in design, and to that extent admirably decorative. Something of decorative restraint we find almost to the end in sixteenth century work; the picture had not yet emancipated itself entirely, and the pictorial ideal did not therefore necessarily go beyond what glass could do ; in any case, it did not take quite a different direction.

It may be as well to define more precisely the ideal glass picture. The ideal glass picture is. the picture which gives full scope for the qualities of glass, and does not depend in any way upon effects which cannot be obtained in glass, or which are to be attained only at the sacrifice of qualities peculiar to it.

And what are those qualities ? The qualities of glass are light and colour, a quality of light and a quality of colour to be obtained no other way than by the transmission of light through pot-metal glass.

Compare these qualities with those of oil painting, and see how far they are compatible. Something depends upon the conception of oil painting. The qualities of glass are compatible enough with the pictorial ideal of the oil (or more likely tempera) painters whom we designate by the name of " primitives"; and, indeed, fifteenth century Italian windows often take the form of circular pictures which one of the masters might have designed. A painting by Botticelli, Filippo Lippi, Mantegna, or Crivelli, might almost be put into the hands of a glass painter to translate. It is quite possible that some of the

Florentine windows were executed in Germany from paintings by Italian masters; the odd thing is that they are attributed sometimes to sculptors. Ghiberti and Donatello may, for all one knows, have been great colourists; but it is so universal a foible to ascribe works of decorative art to famous painters or sculptors who could never by any possibility have had a hand in them, that one never has much faith in such reputed authorship.

The severity of the "primitive" painters' design, the firm outline, the comparatively flat treatment, the brilliant, not yet degraded, colour—all these were qualities which the glass painter could turn to account. Without firm and definite outline, of course, a design does not lend itself to mosaic. But it is especially the early painter's ideal of colour which was so sympathetic to the glass painter. A designer for glass must be a colourist; but the colour he seeks is *sui generis*. Not every colourist would make a glass designer. Van Thulden may not have been a colourist of his master's stamp, but Peter Paul Rubens himself could not have made a complete success of those windows in the Chapel of Our Lady in S. Gudule. Reynolds was a colourist, but he came conspicuously to grief in glass. Velasquez was a colourist, but one fails to see how by any possibility the quality of his work could be expressed in glass.

On the other hand, colour in which the simple artist delighted, as in light and sunshine, in the sparkle of the sea, in the purity of the sky, in the brilliancy of flowers, in the flash of jewels, in the deep verdure of moss, in the lusciousness of fruit or wine, colour as the early Florentine painters saw it and sought it— this is what glass can give, and gives better than oil, tempera, or fresco, on an opaque surface. How far these early painters deliberately sacrificed to pure bright colour qualities of light and shade, aerial perspective, and so on, may be open to question. The certain thing is that, if we want the quality of glass in all its purity and translucency, we have to sacrifice to it something of the light and shade, the relief, the atmospheric effect, the subtlety of realistic colour, which we are accustomed nowadays to look for in a picture. Happy the men who could contentedly pursue their work undisturbed by the thought that there were effects to be obtained in art beyond what it was possible for them to get.

Even the Italian painters soon travelled beyond the limits of what could possibly be done in glass. Flesh-painting, as Titian understood it, or Correggio, or Bonifacio, is hopelessly beyond its range. But it was the Dutch who formed for themselves the idea most widely and hopelessly beyond realisation in glass. The Crabeths, like good glass painters, struggled more or less against it: but they could not keep out of the current altogether; and in proportion as their work aims at anything like chiaroscuro it loses its quality of glass. Rembrandt, to have realised his ideal in glass, would have had to paint out of it every quality which distinguishes it and gives it value. In proportion, as the painter's aim was light and shade rather than colour, and especially as it was shade rather than light (or perhaps it would be fairer to say, as it was light intensified by obscuring light around it) it was diametrically opposed to that of the glass painter. His pursuit of it was a sort of artistic suicide. It led by quick and sure degrees to what was to all intents and purposes the collapse of glass painting. Realism of a kind was inevitable when once the painter gained the strength to realise what he saw, but when the glass painter, seeking the strength of actual light and shade, began to rely upon painted shadow for his effects, the case was hopeless. Glass asks to be translucent.

The point of perfection in glass design is not easily to be fixed. Glass painting, it must be confessed, as it approaches perfection of technique, is always dangerously near the border line: the painter is so often tempted to carry his handiwork a little further than is consistent with the translucency of glass. It happens, therefore, that one expects almost to find consummate drawing and painting marred by some obscuration of the glass. If on the other hand we travel back to the time when the evil does not exist, we find ourselves at a period when neither drawing nor painting were at their best. It is by no means surprising that this should be the outcome of the association of glazier and painter. According as one cares more for glass or for painting one will be disposed to shift, backwards or forwards, the date at which glass painting began to decline. It may safely be said, however, that pictorial glass painting was at its best during the first half of the sixteenth century. That is the period during which you may expect to find masterly drawing, consummate painting, and yet sufficient recognition of the character of glass to satisfy all but the staunch partisan of pure mosaic glass—who, by the way, stands upon very firm ground.

In Flanders, as has been said, and in France, are to be found exquisite pictures in glass, admirably decorative in design, glowing with jewel-like brilliancy of colour, not seriously obscured by paint, the figures modelled with a delicacy reminding one rather of sculpture in very low relief than of more realistic painting and carving, the colour delicate and yet not thin, the effect strong without brutality.

But it is in Italy that are to be seen probably the finest glass pictures that have ever been painted; the work, nevertheless, of a Frenchman—William of Marseilles—who established himself at Arezzo, and painted, amongst other glass, five windows for the cathedral there, which go about as far as glass can go in the direction of picture. The man was a realist in his way—realist, that is, so far as suited his artistic purpose. Not merely are his figures studied obviously from the life, but they are conceived in the realistic spirit, as when, in the scene of the Baptism, he draws a man getting into his clothes with the difficulty we have all experienced after bathing, or when, in the Raising of Lazarus (page 397), he makes more than one onlooker hold his nose as the grave-clothes are unwrapped from the body. In design the artist is quite up to the high level of his day (1525 or thereabouts); but you see all through his work that it was colour, always colour, that made his heart beat (we have here nothing to do with the religious sentiment which may or may not be embodied in his work), colour that prompted his design, as in the case of so many a great Italian master.

This man possibly did in glass much what *he* would have done on canvas; but he could never have got such pure, intense, and at the same time luminous, effects of colour in anything but glass, and he knew it, never lost sight of it, and tried to get the most out of what it could best give him —that is to say, purity of colour, and translucency and brilliancy of glass. Whatever amount of pigment he employed (probably more than it seems, the light is so strong in Italy) it seldom appears to do more than just give the needful modelling. Now and again, in the architectural parts of his composition, the white is lowered by means of a matt of paint, where a tint of deeper-coloured glass had better have been employed; but even there the effect is neither dirty nor in the least heavy. And in the main, for all his pictorial bias, the system of the artist is distinctly mosaic; his colour is pot-metal always or purest stain. The sky and the landscape, for example, in which the scene of the Baptism is laid, are leaded up in tints of blue and green. In the scene where Christ purges the Temple the pavement is of clear aquamarine-tinted glass, against which the scales, moneybags, overturned bench, and so on, stand out in quite full enough relief of red and yellow, without any aid of heavy shading, or cast shadow, such as a Netherlander would have used.

And, for all that, the difficulty even of foreshortening is boldly faced. Not even in the most violently shaded Flemish glass would it be easy to find a figure more successfully foreshortened than the kneeling money-changer, scooping up his money into a bag. That a designer could do this without strong shading, means that he was careful to choose the pose or point of view which allowed itself to be expressed in lightly painted glass. There is no riotous indulgence in perspective, but distance is sufficiently indicated; and the personages in the background, drawn to a smaller scale than the chief actors in the scene, keep their place in the picture. Everywhere it is apparent that the figures have been composed with a cunning eye to glazing.

These are not pictures which have been done into glass; they are no translations, but the creations of a glass painter—one who knew all about glass, and instinctively designed only what could be done in it, and best done. This man makes full use of all the resources of his art. His window is constructed as only a glazier could do it. He does not shirk his leads. He uses abrasion freely, not so much to save glazing, as to get effects not otherwise possible. Thus the deep red skirt or petticoat of the woman taken in adultery is dotted with white in a way that bespeaks at a glance the woman of the people, whilst more sumptuous draperies of red and green are, as it were, embroidered with gold, or sewn with pearls. These are the effects he aims at, not the mere texture of silk or velvet. He delights in delicate stain on white, and revels in most gorgeous stain upon stain. In short, these are pictures indeed, but the pictures of a glass painter.

Work like this disarms criticism. One may have a strong personal bias towards strictly mosaic glass, and yet acknowledge that success justifies departure from what one thought the likelier way. Things of beauty decline to be put away always in the nice little pigeon-holes we have carefully provided for them. Shall we be such pedants as to reject them because they do not fit in with our preconceived ideas of fitness?

Alas!—or happily?—alas for what might have been, happily for our wavering allegiance to sterner principles of design, it is seldom that the glass painter so perfectly tunes his work to the key of glass. In particular, he finds it difficult to harmonise his painting with the glazing which goes with it. He is incapable in the early sixteenth century of the brutalities of his successors, who carry harsh lines of lead across flesh painting recklessly; but the very association of ultra-delicate painting with lead-lines at all demands infinite tact. An idea of the point to which painting is eventually carried may be gathered from the representation of little nude boys blowing bubbles in which are reflected the windows of the room where they are supposed to be playing. That is an extreme instance, and a late one. Short, however, of such frivolity, and in work of the good period, painting is often so delicate that bars and leads unquestionably hurt it. It is so even in the very fine Jesse window at Beauvais (page 368).

Occur where it may it is a false note which stops our admiration short; and, after all our enthusiasm, we come back heart-whole to our delight in the earlier, bolder, more monumental, and more workmanlike mosaic glass. The beautiful sixteenth century work at Montmorency or at Conches does not shake the conviction of the glass lover, that the painter is there a little too much in evidence, that something of simple, dignified decoration is sacrificed to the display of his skill. The balance between glass decoration and picture is perhaps never more nearly adjusted than in some of the rather earlier Italian windows.

CHAPTER XX.

LANDSCAPE IN GLASS.

175. FROM THE ENTRY INTO JERUSALEM, FAIRFORD.

At once a distinguishing feature of picture-glass, and a characteristic of later work generally, is the *mise-en-scène* of the subject.

In quite the earliest glass the figures, it was shown, were cut out against a ground of plain colour (pages 33, 127), or diapered perhaps with a painted pattern, or leaded up in squares, or broken by spots of pot-metal (page 37), which, by the way, being usually of too strongly contrasting colour, assert themselves instead of qualifying its tone. Sometimes the ground was leaded up in the form of a more or less elaborate geometric diaper (page 336). Occasionally it was broken by the simplest possible conventional foliage. The figure stood on a cloud, an inscribed label, a disc or band of earth. In the fourteenth century spots breaking the ground took very often the form of badges, *fleurs-de-lys*, heraldic animals, cyphers, and so on (page 156), and even in the fifteenth it was quite common to find figures against a flat ground, broken only by inscription, either on white or yellow labels (pages 186, 339), or leaded in bold letters of white or yellow into the background itself (page 196). But simultaneously with this the figure was frequently represented against a screen of damask (page 191), above which showed the further background, usually more or less architectural in character. In the Fairford windows (page 187) is

174 FROM THE CREATION. MALVERN ABBEY

shown this treatment together with the label which helps to break the formality of the horizontal line. Sometimes the line is curved, as though the figure stood in a semi-circular niche, or broken, as though the recess were three-sided. Sometimes the figure stood upon a pedestal (page 391), but more usually, as time went on, upon a pavement. Certain subjects were bound to include accessory architecture, but at first it was as simple as the scenery in the immortal play of *Pyramus and Thisbe*. But even in the fifteenth century it was rendered, one may judge how naïvely, from the little Nativity on page 54, a subject hardly to be rendered without the stable. Again, the quite conventional vinework, also from Malvern, shown in the upper part of page 345 (a jumble of odds and ends), forms really part of the scene depicting Noah in his vineyard—see the hand holding the spade handle. The Fairford scenery (pages 251, 372), quaint as it is, goes much nearer to realism than that; and towards the sixteenth century, and during its first years, there was a good deal of landscape in which trees were leaded in vivid green against blue, with gleaming white stems suggestive of birch-bark, always effective, and refreshingly cool in colour. There is something of that kind in the window facing the entrance to King's College, Cambridge; but the more usual English practice in the fifteenth century was to execute the landscape in white and stain against a coloured ground. That is the system adopted in the scene of the Creation at Malvern (page 252), where trees, water, birds, fishes, are all very delicately painted and stained. In the left-hand corner it will be seen that solid or nearly solid brown is used for foliage in order to throw up the white and yellow leafage in front of it. There is some considerably later work very much in this manner at S. Nizier, Troyes. But that kind of thing was not usual in French glass.

The sky had of course from the first been indicated by a blue background; but, the blue ground being used, in alternation with ruby, for all backgrounds, except a few in white, it was not distinctive enough to suggest the heavens, without some indication of clouds, which accordingly were leaded up upon it, sometimes in mere streaks of colour, sometimes in fantastically ornamental shapes. It was a later thought, which came with the use of paler glass, to paint the blue with clouds, indicating them, that is to say, more or less in the form of diaper. As with the sky so with the sea. It was at first glazed in wave pattern; eventually the wave lines were painted on the blue.

The blue background, which had gradually become paler and paler, became soon in the sixteenth century pale enough to stand approximately for a grey-blue sky, on which was painted, with marvellous delicacy, distant landscape, architecture, or what not, always in the brown tint used generally for shading, although a tint of green was given to grass and trees by the use of yellow stain. This distant view painted upon blue was a beautiful and most characteristic feature of sixteenth century glass. The French painters adopted it, and made it peculiarly their own, though it occurs also in German and Flemish glass. Backgrounds of this kind, which in themselves suffice to mark the departure from Gothic use, are shown on pages 207, 213, and on a larger scale opposite. The wintry landscape there with the bare tree trunks against the cold grey sky, forms the upper portion of the subject shown on page 207, in which Our Lord gives His charge to Peter; the paler grey behind the heads of the group stands for the sea. The wintry effect of the scene is not suggestive of the Holy Land, but it brings the subject innocently home to us. The leads, it will be seen, take the lines of the larger limbs of the trees, whilst the lesser branches and small twigs are painted on the glass. There is ingenuity in the glazing as well as delicacy in the painting. This is a very different thing from the landscape painted in enamel colours. The propriety, the beauty, the decorative quality of such work as this, comes of the acceptance of the necessary convention of treating the painted background, of rendering it, that is, always more or less in monochrome, and not attempting anything like realism in colour.

The painted landscapes illustrated are of the simplest. The French painters went much further than that, associating with their painting broad masses of pot-metal colour, but still keeping distinctly within the convention of deliberately simple colour. By the use of silvery-white and shades of pot-metal blue and purple and green, they produced the most pleasing and harmonious effects. There was no great variety in the tune they played, but the variations upon it were infinite. Let us picture here a few of them.

RENAISSANCE LANDSCAPE.

1. *Ecouen.*—A distant city, in white, and beyond that more distant architecture, painted on the pale blue of the sky.

2. *Conches.*—Against a pale blue sky, broken by cumulous white clouds, a grey-blue tower.

3. *Conches.*—A grey-blue sea and deeper sky beyond: from the waves rises a castle, in white, breaking the sky-line, the

175. Background to the Charge of S. Peter, S. Vincent, Rouen. (Comp. 156.)

pointed roofs of its turrets painted in black upon the background.

4. *Freiburg*, 1528.—A smoke-grey sea, fading away towards the horizon into pale silver, the sky beyond dark blue, its outline broken by a range of deeper blue mountains.

5. *Conches.*—Beyond the foreground landscape in rich green, a pale blue sea, with slightly deeper grey-blue sky beyond,

a tower in darker blue against it; a strip of deep blue shore divides the sky and sea, and gives support to the dark tower; against that a smaller tower catches the light, and stands out in glittering white.

6. *Montmorency.*—A canopied figure-subject in gorgeous colour: the foreground a landscape with rich green herbage, separated by a belt of white cliffs from buildings of pale grey, amidst trees stained greenish, backed by purple hills; further a pale blue sky: against the sky, overshadowed beneath the canopy arch by a mass of purple cloud, the stained and painted foliage of a tree, growing from this side the hill.

7. *Montmorency.*—S. Christopher crossing the stream; blue water painted with waves and water plants, the foliage stained.

8. *S. Nizier, Troyes.*—A vineyard, very prettily managed; the vines painted on the blue, their leaves stained to green, the grapes grey-blue, whilst grey stakes are leaded in pot-metal.

Sometimes, as at Ecouen, far-off architecture would be painted not upon blue but upon a pale purple hill. At Laigle figures and animals are painted upon green, but they do not hold their own. On the other hand, at Alençon, some distant figures appearing in very pale grey against a delicate greenish landscape (stained upon the grey), are charming in effect.

White backgrounds painted as delicately as the blue are not rare. At Groslay, for example, steely-white architecture is separated from white sky beyond by grey-blue hills, a church with blue steeple breaking the sky. But white does not lend itself so readily to combination with colour as blue; and, as a rule, such backgrounds are grisaille in character, relieved, of course, with stain.

The great sea-scape at Gouda (page 223), representing the taking of Dalmatia in Egypt (a very Dutch Dalmatia), is nearly all in grisaille, against quarries of clear white, with only a little stain in the flags and costumes, and one single touch of poor ruby (about two inches square), which looks as if it might be modern. The port in perspective, the ships, the whole scene, in fact, is realistically rendered, and comes as near to success as is possible in glass.

Delightful peeps of landscape are sometimes seen through the columns and arches of an architectural background. Whether the architecture be in purple of divers shades, or in white with only shadows in purple, or whether the nearer architecture be in white and the more distant in purple, in any case a distance beyond is commonly painted upon the greyblue sky seen through it. Possibly, as at Conches, further vistas of architecture may be stained greenish upon it—any colour almost, for a change. But whatever it may be, and wherever it may be, in the best work it is colour; and it is always more effective than where the shadow is represented by paint, even though the brown be not laid on with a heavy hand, infinitely more effective than when blue or other coloured enamels are relied upon, as in some instances at Montmorency. Enamel may, for all one can tell, have been used in some of the landscapes here commended—it is impossible to say without minute examination of the glass, which is rarely feasible—but it never asserts its presence; and in any case it has not been used in sufficient quantity to damage the effect.

It will be gathered from the descriptions of early sixteenth century glazed and painted distances, that they were as carefully schemed with a view to glazing (though in a very different way) as a Gothic picture. Sometimes, as at Conches, they are rather elaborately leaded; and where that is the case there is not so much danger of incongruity between the delicacy of the painting and the strength of the leads—which assert themselves less than where they occur singly. It stands to reason also that the more mosaic the glass the less fragile it is. Painting alone upon the blue is best employed for small peeps of distance. It adapts itself to smaller windows; and it must be done (as for a while it was done) so well, that it seems as if the designer must himself have painted it. Were the artist always the glass painter, and the glass painter always an artist, who knows what case pictorial glass might not make out for itself?

It is a coarser kind of distance than the French that we find at King's College, Cambridge. There the landscape backgrounds are in white and stain, grey-blue being reserved for the sky beyond, broken more or less by white clouds, or, occasionally, by the white trunks of trees, the foliage of which is sometimes glazed in green glass, sometimes painted upon the blue and stained. Here and there a distant tree is painted entirely upon the blue. This treatment is not ill adapted to subjects on the large scale of the work at King's College, but one does not feel that the painters made anything like the most of their opportunity. The inexperience of the designers is shown in their fear of using leads, a most unnecessary fear, seeing that, at the distance the work is from the eye, the bars themselves have only about the value of ordinary lead lines.

Stronger and more workmanlike, but not quite satisfactory, is the much later landscape (1557) of Dirk Crabeth at Gouda. There the sky is blue, leaded in quarries, on which are trees, painted and stained, and some rather florid clouds. In the later work generally the lead lines are no longer either frankly acknowledged or skilfully disguised. The outline of a green hill against the sky will be feebly softened with trivial little twigs and scraps of painted leafage. The decline of landscape is amply illustrated at Troyes. At Antwerp again there is a window bearing date 1626, in which the landscape background of a quite incomprehensible subject extends to a distant horizon, above which the sky is glazed in white quarries, with clouds painted upon it. This is an attempt to repeat the famous feat of glass painting which had been done some twenty years before at Gouda. The Relief of Leyden, of which a diagram is here given, is in its way a most remarkable glass picture. In the foreground is a crowd of soldiers and citizens, upon the quay,

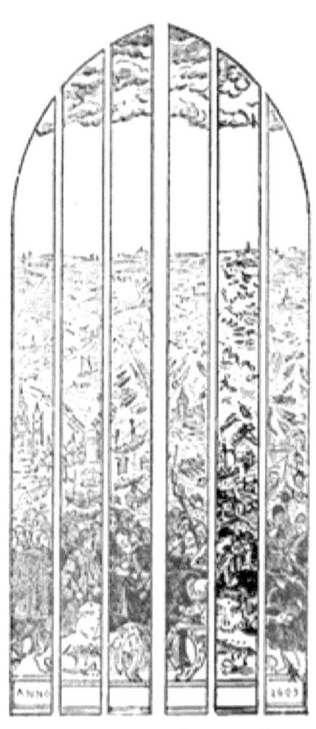

176. THE RELIEF OF LEYDEN, GOUDA.

about lifesize. They form a band of rich colour at the base of the composition; but the design is confused by the introduction of shields of arms and their supporters immediately in front of the scene. Beyond are the walls and towers of the city of Delft, and the adjacent towns and villages, and the river dwindling into the far distance where Leyden lies—in the glass a really marvellous bird's-eye view over characteristically flat country. The horizon extends almost to the springing line of the window arch, and above that rises a sky of plain blue quarries, broken only towards the top by a few bolster-like and rather dirty white clouds. Absolute realism is of course not reached, but it is approached near enough to startle us into admiration. It is astonishing what has here been done. But the painter has not done what he meant to do. That was not possible, even with the aid of enamel.

CHAPTER XXI.

ITALIAN GLASS.

IN the course of the preceding chapters the reader has been rather unceremoniously carried from country to country, in a way which may have seemed to him erratic. But there was a reason in the zig-zag course taken. The progress of the glass painter's art was not by any means a straight line. Nor did it develop itself on parallel lines in the various countries in which it throve. It advanced in one place whilst it was almost at a standstill in another.

That is easily understood. It was inevitable that glass painting, though it arose in France, should languish there during the troublous times when English troops overran it under Edward III, and throughout the Hundred Years' War, that it should revive in all its glory under Francis the First, and that during the disturbances of the Fronde it should again decline. The extremity of France was England's opportunity; and our greatest wealth of stained glass windows dates from the reign of the later Plantagenets. The Wars of the Roses do not appear greatly to have affected art; but after the Reformation we were more busy smashing glass than painting it.

In Germany the course of art ran smoother. Glass throve under the Holy Roman Empire, and it was not until the Reformation that it suffered any very severe check. Mediæval Swiss glass may be classed with German.

In the Netherlands glass painting blossomed out suddenly under the Imperial favour of Charles V. It continued to bear fruit under the Dutch Republic, until it ran to seed at the end of the seventeenth century.

So it happens that, in following the development of glass painting, it has been necessary to seek the best and most characteristic illustrations first in one country and then in another, to travel from France to England, from England to Germany and back to France, thence to Flanders, to France again, and finally once more to the Netherlands, to say nothing of shorter excursions from one place to another, as occasion might demand. In each separate locality there was naturally some sort of progress, but we cannot take any one country as all-sufficient type of the rest; and to have traversed each in turn would have been tedious. There were everywhere differences of practice and design; in each country, for that matter, there were local schools with marked characteristics of their own. Some of the characteristic national differences have been pointed out in passing. To describe them at length would be to write a comparative history of glass, of which there is here no thought. What concerns us is the broadly marked progress of glass painting, not the minor local differences in style.

Something more, however, remains to be said of Italian glass than was possible in any general survey. The mere facts, that the Renaissance arose in Italy so long before it reached this side the Alps, and that glass painting was never really quite at home in Italy (any more than the Gothic architecture which mothered it), sufficiently account for the difficulty, nay, the impossibility, of classing it according to the Gothic periods. Indeed, one is reminded in Italian glass less often of other windows of the period, English, French, or German, than of contemporary Italian painting.

The comparative fitness of the works of the "Primitive" painters for models of glass design has already been pointed out. It is so evident that the Italian sense of colour could find more adequate expression than ever in glass, that one is inclined to wonder, until it is remembered that Italian churches were at the same time picture galleries, that it did not more commonly find vent in that medium. Even as it is, Italian painters did found a school of glass painting, comparatively uninfluenced by the traditional Gothic types of design, whilst observing the best traditions of glazier-like technique. Hence it is that we find in Italy windows such as are nowhere else to be seen, windows which at their best are of the very best.

There are resemblances in Italian glass to German work; and some of it is said to have been executed by Germans. It is none the less Italian. Though it were executed in Germany, glazier and painter must have worked under the direct influence of the Italian master, and in complete accord with him, putting at his service all their experience in their craft, and all their skill. So well did they work together, that it seems more likely that the executant not only worked under the eye of the master, but was at his elbow whilst he designed. That alone would account satisfactorily for the absolutely harmonious co-operation of designer and glass-worker. One thing is clear, that the artist, whatever his experience in glass, great or little, had absolute sympathy with his new material, felt what it could do, saw the opportunities it offered him, and seized them.

An Englishman, or a Frenchman, who found himself for the first time in Italy, would be puzzled to give a date to the windows at Pisa or Milan, or in either of the churches of S. Francis at Assisi. Even an expert in the glass of other countries has to speak guardedly as to Italian work, or he may have to retract his words. Italian Gothic is so Italian and so little Gothic, it is of no use attempting to compare it with Northern work. To those, moreover, who have been in the habit of associating the Renaissance with the sixteenth century, the forms of Quattro-Cento ornament will persist at first in suggesting the later date—just as the first time one goes to Germany the survival of the old form of lettering in inscriptions throws a suspicion of lingering Gothic influence over even full-blown Renaissance design. It takes some time to get over the perplexity arising from the unaccustomed association of an absolutely mosaic treatment of glass (which with us would mean emphatically Gothic work) with distinctly Renaissance detail, such as one finds at the churches already mentioned, at the Certosa of Pavia, or at Florence.

At Assisi the glass means, for the most part, to be Gothic. One is reminded there sometimes of German work, both by the colour of the glass and by the design of some of the medallion and other windows. The ornament generally inclines to the naturalistic rather than to the Quattro-Cento arabesque, or to the geometric kind shown on page 96; and though it includes a fair amount of interlacing bandwork of distinctly Italian type, and is sometimes as deep in colour as quite Early glass, it is approximately Decorated in character. That is so equally with the brilliant remains in the tracery lights of Or San Michele at Florence. But it is characteristic of Italian glass of the fourteenth and fifteenth centuries that, both by the depth of its colour and the very quality of the material, it should continually recall the thirteenth century. Sometimes, as at Milan, for example, you find even sixteenth century glass in which there is practically no white at all except what is used for the flesh tint.

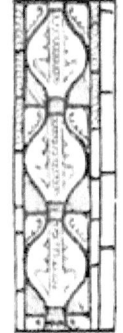

177. Assisi.

In the cathedral at Pisa are some windows with little subjects, framed in ornament, all in richest and most brilliant colour, which are at first sight extremely perplexing. The leading is elaborately minute, and there is no modelling in the figures, which yet have nothing of archaic or very early character. It turns out that the paint upon the glass has perished, and there is hardly a vestige of it left to show that this was not intended for mere mosaic. The effect, nevertheless, is such as to prove how much can be done in pot-metal glass, and how little it depends upon the painting on it.

Elsewhere, as at Arezzo (in work earlier than that of William of Marseilles), the paint has often peeled off to a very considerable extent, revealing sometimes patches of quite crude green and purple, which go to show that the Italians habitually used glass of a raw colour, where it suited their convenience, and just toned it down with brown enamel. The result proves that it was a dangerous practice; but, where the paint has held, the effect is not dull or dirty, as with us it would be. The Italian sun accounts probably both for the use of this scum of paint and for its not injuring the effect of colour.

The same quality of deep rich pot-metal colour associated with Renaissance design, is the first thing that strikes one in the windows at Bologna, in the cathedral at Milan, and in Florence everywhere. At Milan in particular there are compositions, in which blue and red predominate, magnificently rich and deep, in spite of recent cleaning. The cunning way in which green is occasionally used to prevent any flowing together of red and blue into purple, is a lesson in colour. Two schemes of design prevail in the nave windows (the old glass in the choir is so mixed up with new that it does not count), both equally simple. In the one the rectangular divisions formed by the mullions and the stouter bars are accepted, without further framing, as separate picture spaces; in the other the main form of the window is taken as frame to a single picture, the mullions being only so far taken into account that the prominent figures are designed within them. Some of these windows are late enough in the century to show a falling off in treatment. In the Apostle window (attributed to Michel Angelo?) the white glass is all reduced to a granular tint of umber; and in the one illustrating the Life of the Virgin there is a most aggressively foreshortened figure, which may have been effective in the cartoon, but is absurd in the glass. It is not, therefore, at Milan that typically Italian glass is best to be studied, though there is enough of it to startle the student of glass whose experience had not hitherto extended so far as Italy. Neither is Italian glass at its best at Bologna, though the city was noted for glass painting, which was practised there by no less a person than the Blessed James of Ulm. But, truth to tell, the best windows at Bologna (they are most of them fairly good) are not those of the Saint but of Pellegrino Tibaldi and Lorenzo Costa. It is at Florence that the distinctive quality of Italian glass is best appreciated. There is a vast quantity of it, varying in date from the early part of the fifteenth to the latter part of the sixteenth century, but it is uniformly Italian, and, with few exceptions, it is extremely good.

Figures under canopies are of common occurrence in Florentine windows; but the canopies differ in several respects, both from the ordinary Gothic canopy and from the shrine-like structure of the later Renaissance. In the first place, the canopy returns in Italy to its primitive dimensions. It may or may not be architecturally interesting, but there is in no case very much of it. The Italians never went canopy-mad; and they kept the framework of their pictures within moderate dimensions. The Italian canopy of the fifteenth and sixteenth centuries, then, was just a niche, sometimes of Renaissance design, sometimes affecting a more Gothic form with pointed or cusped arch and so on, under which, or in front of which, the figures stood. It bore definite relation to the figures, and it was neither impossible of construction nor absurd in perspective. Occasionally, in later work, as at the Certosa at Pavia, it was delicate in colour, but, as a rule, it was strong and rich. It was not merely that the shadowed portions were glazed in pot-metal, as when, at Santa Croce, the coffered soffits of the

178. S. MARIA NOVELLA, FLORENCE.

arches are one mosaic of jewellery, but that the canopy throughout was in colour.

That is the most striking characteristic of Italian canopy-work, and indeed of other ornamental setting—that it is as rich as the picture, a part of it, not a frame to it. Constructionally, of course, it is a frame; but the colour does away with the effect of framework. It serves rather to connect the patches of contrasting colour in the figures, than to separate one picture from another. Occasionally this results in too much all-overishness, more commonly it results in breadth, making you feel that the window is one. It was explained what use was made of white canopy work in Gothic glass, judiciously to break up the surface of the window. In Italy the surface is judiciously left unbroken, and in that case also the result is most admirable.

With the exception of an occasional brassy-yellow canopy, recalling German colour, the same system of connecting canopy and subject together by colour is adopted alike at S. Croce, at S. Maria Novella, and at the Duomo at Florence. The composition of the windows is simple: within a border of foliage or other ornament, two or three tiers of figures, under modest canopies, separated perhaps by little medallions containing busts or demi-figures. That occurs at S. Domenico, Perugia, as well as at Florence.

A modification of the canopy occurs in the nave

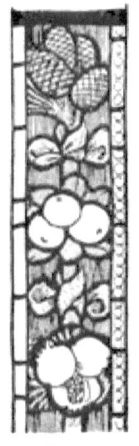

179. FLORENCE.

180. S. GIOVANNI IN MONTE, BOLOGNA.

windows of the Duomo. The space within a narrow border which frames the broad lancet, is divided into two by a strong upright bar, and the divisions thus formed are treated as separate trefoil-arched lancets, each with another border of its own, the space above being treated much as though it were tracery. (Something like this occurs, it will be remembered, already in the thirteenth century, at Bourges.) In the tall spaces within the borders are the usual tiers of figures under canopies. Again, in the chapel of the Certosa in Val d'Ema, near Florence, there is a window with double-niched canopies and pronounced central shaft dividing the broad lancet into two narrow ones.

The Italian canopy is not of so stereotyped a character as in Decorated or Perpendicular design; and generally it may be said that there is, both in the design and colour of Italian glass, more variety than one finds out of Italy. The plan is less obvious, the scheme less cut and dried; you know much less what to expect than in Northern Gothic, and enjoy more often the pleasure of surprise.

Elaborately pictorial schemes of design are less common in Italian glass than might have been expected. There is a famous window in the church of SS. Giovanni e Paolo, at Venice (1473), in which the four lights below the bands of tracery which here takes the place of transom are given over to subject. There green trees and pale blue water against a deep blue sky and deeper blue hills, anticipate a favourite sixteenth century colour scheme; but the glass is a mere wreck of what was once probably a fine window.

Figure groups on a considerable scale are chiefly to be found in the great "bull's-eye" windows, which are a striking feature in Italian Gothic churches, occupying a position where in France would have been a rose—over the West door, for example.

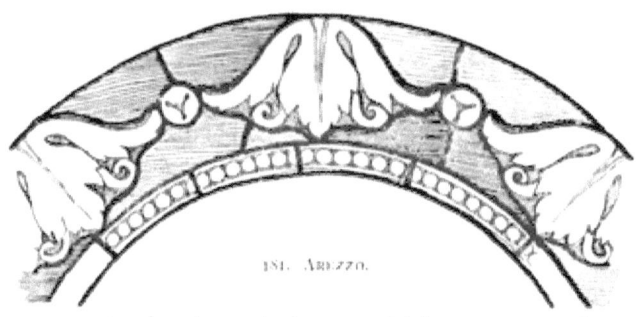

181. Arezzo.

These great circular windows, which occur at Arezzo, at Bologna, at Siena, and especially at Florence, are usually surrounded by an arabesque border. Occasionally the border consists of a medley of cherubic wings and faces; occasionally, as at Siena, it is in white, more in the form of mouldings; in one case, at least, it disappears, as it were, behind the figure group in the lower part of the window; but, as a rule, it consists of Renaissance pattern, such as are shown here and on page 70, large in scale, simple in design, and as mosaic in execution as though it had been twelfth century work. The centre of these circular lights may have, as at the Duomo at Florence, a single upright figure, enthroned, occupying a sort of tall central panel, supported by angels in the spandrils at the sides; or it may have a subject running across it, as in the case of Perino del Vaga's "Last Supper" (1549) at the West end of the cathedral at Siena. But very often it enclosed one big figure subject, such as the "Descent from the Cross" at Santa Croce, attributed to Ghiberti. An earlier manner of occupying a bull's-eye is shown in the East window at Siena, dating probably from about the beginning of the fourteenth century. This is subdivided by four huge cross-bars (two horizontal and two vertical) into nine compartments, or a cross consisting of one central square, four squarish arms, and four triangular spandrils. Each of these divisions is taken as though it were a separate light, and has its own border, enclosing a separate subject. The bars, it is true, are of great size, wide enough almost to have been of stone; but the scheme rather suggests that the designer was not quite aware, when he designed it, how much less significant they would appear in the glass than they did in his drawing.

Unquestionably the finest windows in Florence are the great lancets in the apse and south apsidal transept of the Duomo, finer than the three lights at the East end of S. Maria Novella, which are so much more often spoken of, possibly because they are seen to so much more advantage in the dark-walled Lady Chapel. It is difficult to trace in these Duomo windows the hand of Ghiberti or Donatello (1434), their reputed designers. They are planned on the simplest lines. In the upper series, the space within a narrowish border is divided, by a band of ornament or inscription, into two fairly equal parts, in each of which stand two figures facing one another (opposite) under the simplest form of canopy, if canopy it can be called. It is a mere frame, at the back of which is a two-arched arcade, with shafts disappearing behind the figures. They stand, that is to say, not under but in front of it.

In the lower series the arrangement is the same, except that the upper compartment contains a single figure, larger in scale, and seated, under a canopy of rather more architectural pretensions. Some of the canopies have cusped arches, and some of the borders are foliated in a more or less Gothic way; but obviously the Gothicism throughout is only in deference to prevailing fashion. In feeling and effect the work is Renaissance.

The design here given shows about one half of a window; but it gives, unfortunately, no hint of the colour. The depth of it may be imagined when it is told that the only approach to white in it is in the beaded line round the nimbus of the figure to the right, and that is of the horniest character. The flesh is of a rich brownish tint.

The head on page 270 goes nearer to suggesting colour. There again the face is brown, the hair and beard dark and bluish; against it the band round the head, which is ruby, tells light. The orange-yellow nimbus, rayed, is rather lighter still, the beaded fillet edging it bone-white. The drapery is of brightest yellow diapered with occasional blue trefoils, each of which has in its centre a touch of red. The background is of very dark blue, the architecture nearest it bright green, beyond that it is dark red.

This short explanation will serve to indicate the key in which the colour is pitched. The glass itself, it has been said, is as rich as French work of the twelfth century, as deep as German of the fourteenth, but more vivid than either; there are no low-toned greens or inky blues. The blue is sapphire, the green has the

182 FIGURES, DUOMO, FLORENCE.

quality of an emerald. In this palette of pure colour the artist revelled. Nowhere as in the Duomo at Florence is one so impressed with the feeling that the designer was dealing deliberately always with colour. Plainly that, and no other, was his impulse, colour—broad, large, beautiful, impressive, solemn colour masses. Elsewhere the storyteller speaks, or the draughtsman, here the colourist confesses himself. The grand scale of his figures allows him to treat his colour largely, and its breadth is no less notable than its brilliancy. There is infinite variety in it; but the general impression is of great masses of red, blue, yellow, green, purple, brown, and so on, held together by the same colours distributed in smaller threads and spots, as in diapers on drapery. The broad mass of any one colour is itself made up of many various tints of glass. The accidental fusion of colour, as of red and blue into purple, is guarded against by framing, say, the blue with green, or the ruby with brownish-yellow. At other times neutral tones are deliberately produced by the combination of, for example, red and green lines.

183. FLORENCE.

The event proves that in this way, and by the choice of deep rather than low tones, not only mellowness but sobriety of colour is to be obtained. The artist would certainly have chosen rather to be crude than dull; but it is very rarely that a false note occurs, and then most likely it is due to the decay of the brown paint upon which he relied to bring it into tone.

At Arezzo one was disposed to think nothing could be finer than the glass of William of Marseilles; at Florence one is quite certain that nothing could be more beautiful than the glass in the Duomo. Each is, after its kind, perfect. But at Florence, at all events (*les absents ont toujours tort*), one finds that this is not only the more decorative kind, but the more dignified. One is disposed to ask, whether it is not better that in glass there should be no deceptive pictures, no perspective to speak of, only simple and severely disposed figures, which never in any way disturb the architectural effect, which give to the least attractive interior—the Duomo is as bare as a barn and as drab as a meeting-house—something of architectural dignity.

Pl. Prato.

CHAPTER XXII.

TRACERY LIGHTS AND ROSE WINDOWS.

GLASS in tracery lights and Rose windows cannot consistently be planned on the lines suitable to lancets or other upright shapes; and it is interesting to observe the modifications of design necessitated by its adaptation to circumstances so different. This applies not only to Gothic glass but to Renaissance, the best of which, as it happens, is in Gothic windows. Happily it never occurred to sixteenth century artists to hamper themselves by any affectation of archaism, and their work is deliberately in the new manner. One can understand, too, a certain "up-to-date" contempt on their part for the "old-fashioned" stonework; but it is rather surprising that so few of them seem to have realised how greatly their own work would have gained by a little more consideration of (if not for) the stonework.

Where, as at Gouda, by way of exception, Gothic windows were built to receive later glass, tracery is to all intents and purposes abandoned: the builders would have done away with mullions had they known how otherwise to support such huge glass pictures. It has been explained already, in reference to the influence of the window shape, and especially of the mullions, upon glass design, how much more formidable these divisions appear upon paper than in the window. That is very plainly seen in many a window where the designer has relied upon them to frame his subjects. The pictures have a way of running together in the most perplexing way, and one has to pick them out for oneself again. The practical conclusion from that is, that the designer is under no obligation to confine himself too strictly within the separate lights of a large window. What he is bound to do is to take care that the mullions never hurt his picture; if they do, it is his picture which is to blame. He may urge with reason that the upright shafts of stone are there merely for the support of the window, and that it is not his business to emphasise them, enough if he acknowledge them. In tracery, however, it is his bounden duty to take much more heed of the stonework. It was designed, in intricate and often very beautiful lines, with deliberately ornamental intent; it was meant to be seen, and it is his function to show it off. The question he has to put to himself is now no longer: does the stonework hurt my design? but: does my design hurt the stonework? And he should not be satisfied unless it helps it. The artist who, at Bourges, having *fleur-de-lys*-shaped tracery to deal with, carried across it a design quite contrary to the lines of the stonework, was guilty of a blank absurdity.

The Early Rose windows, which were habitually filled with rich coloured glass, consisted either of simple piercings, as at Lincoln, or they were made up of piercings very definitely divided by massive stonework. In proportion as mullions become narrow, and form in themselves a design, it seems doubtful how far deep-coloured glass can do them justice. Only strong tracery lines will stand strong colour. At Châlons-sur-Marne, for example, the foils of certain cusped lights surrounding a central circular picture are successfully ornamented with arabesque of deep yellow upon paler yellow ground: and again at Or San Michele, Florence, certain gorgeous wheels of ruby and yellow, or of blue, green, and yellow, and so on, are unusually satisfactory. In such cases not only breadth of effect but definition of the tracery forms is gained by keeping them (more especially in their outer circumference) much of one tone, whilst contrast of colour between one light and another helps still further to assist definition. But this applies only to stonework strong enough to take care of itself. There is a sort of perverse brutality in putting into delicate and graceful tracery deep rich glass which hides its lines. Such lines want sharply defining against the light.

Early windows had, of course, no tracery properly so called. The great Rose windows, and the smaller Roses surmounting a pair of lancets, were rather piercings than tracery; and it was not difficult to adapt the design of a medallion window to suit them. A small piercing was ready designed for a medallion subject: nothing was wanted but a border round it, narrower, of course, than would have been used for a broad lancet light, but of the same foliated character. The individual quatrefoils or other principal openings, which went to make up a great Rose window, were filled in the same way. If the opening were wedge-shaped, as it often was, the obvious thing to do was to introduce into it a medallion (probably circular) of the full width of the opening, at about its widest, and to fill up the space about it with foliated ornament or geometric mosaic, with which also the smaller and less important piercings would naturally be filled. Sometimes the recurring figure medallions were set alternately in foliated ornament and geometric diaper; or the lights might be grouped in pairs, two with foliage and two with diaper. Similar alternation of the two common kinds of Early filling, naturally occurred in minor openings which contained no medallion. Something of this kind occurs at Reims.

When the shape of the great Rose permitted it—if, that is to say, the circular outline was strongly pronounced—it was possibly further acknowledged by a fairly broad border, following it and disappearing, as it were, behind the stonework; otherwise, except in the case of smaller medallion-shaped openings, it was not usual to mark them by even so much as a border line. Small Roses had sometimes, as at Auxerre, a central figure medallion round which were secondary foliage medallions set in diaper. A certain waywardness of design, already remarked in medallion windows, was sometimes shown by filling the central medallion with ornament and grouping the pictures round it.

As the lights of a Rose window radiated from the centre, features which recurred throughout the series arranged themselves inevitably in rings; and according to the disposition of the emphatic features of the design, the rays or the rings pronounced themselves. This is partly the affair of the architect who sets out the stonework, but it lies with the glazier whether he choose to subdue or to emphasise either feature. It is hard to say why one or other of these schemes of glass design, in rays or in rings, should be preferred; but, as a matter of experience, the sun and star patterns are not among the most happy. Perhaps the stone spokes of a wheel window assert themselves quite enough any way, and the eye wants leading, not vaguely away from the centre, but definitely round the window.

The circular belts of pattern formed by medallions or other features answer to, and fulfil the part of, the horizontal bands in upright windows (page 153), and bind the lights together. The band has it all its own way in a mere "bull's-eye," such as you find in Italy, where there are no radiating lines of masonry. It is strongly pronounced in some circular medallion windows at Assisi, in which an extraordinarily wide border (a quarter of their diameter in width) is divided into eight equal panels, each enclosed in its own series of border lines, within which is a medallion set in foliated ornament. This is fourteenth century work; but, as in thirteenth century Roses, the bars follow and accentuate the main divisions of the window.

Even when it came to the glazing of a Rose window in a later Gothic style, it is not uncommon to find a series or two of medallions running round the window, as occurs at Angers. They hold the design together; but in the nature of the case they are on too small a scale for the pictures to count for more than broken colour. Indeed you may see here the relative value in such a position of small figure subjects and bold ornament. The scroll work is as effective as the medallions are insignificant. In fact, compared to them, the illegible medallion subjects in the lancet lights below are readable by him who runs. It has to be confessed that quite some of the most beautiful and impressive Rose windows are perfectly unintelligible, even with a good field-glass. This is so with the West Rose at Reims. In the centre it is ablaze with red and orange, towards the rim it shades off into deliciously cool greens and greenish-yellows. It may mean what it may: the colour is enough.

Room for figure work on an intelligible scale is only to be found by a device which verges on the ridiculous. In the beautiful North Rose at S. Ouen, Rouen, figures which should be upright are arranged in a circle like herrings in a barrel. Similar figures on a smaller scale occur in certain tracery lights at Lincoln, two of which are here given. Again in the North Rose at Le Mans there are twenty-four radiating figures. In fact, they were customarily so arranged, even down to the sixteenth century, a period at which one does not credit the designer with mediaeval artlessness.

It is obvious that out of a series of twenty or more figures, radiating like the spokes of a wheel, only a very few can stand anything like upright. The designer of the South Rose at S. Ouen has endeavoured to get over the difficulty, as well as

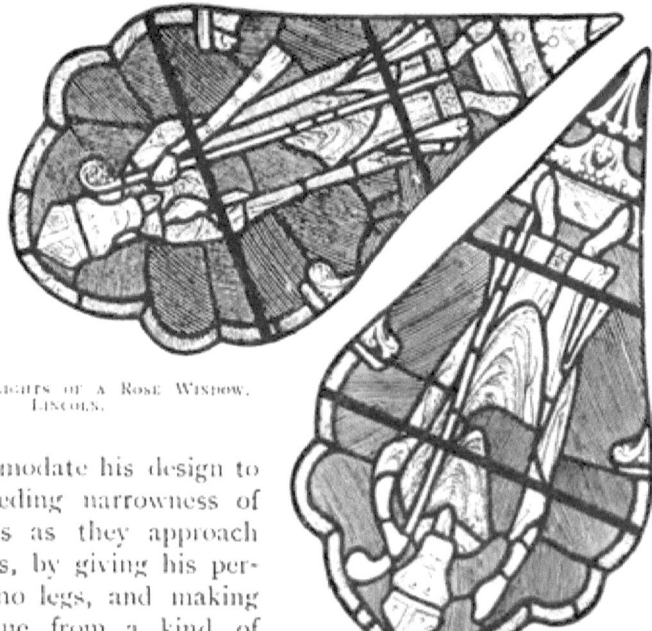

TWO LIGHTS OF A ROSE WINDOW,
LINCOLN.

to accommodate his design to
the exceeding narrowness of
the lights as they approach
their axis, by giving his personages no legs, and making
them issue from a kind of
sheath or bouquet-holder. A
number of the figures pretend-
ing to stand in the radiating lights by a Rose or wheel window
must be ridiculously placed. And then there occurs the question
as to whether they shall all stand with their feet towards the
hub. Where the figures have space to float, it is different.
The angels in the Late Gothic Rose window at Angers, with
swirling drapery which hides their feet, and makes them by so
much the less obviously human, if not more actually angelic,
solve the difficulty of full-length figures (on any appreciable
scale) in the only possible way.

A portion of a simple and rather striking wheel window of
the Decorated period, in which concentric bands of ornament
form a conspicuous feature, is shown overleaf. In the small
Rose from Assisi (page 278) the glazier has very successfully
supplemented the design of the architect, completing the four
circles, and accentuating them further by glazing the central
spandrils in much darker colour than the rest of the glass,
which is mainly white.

In the elaborate tracery of the Decorated or geometric period
the mullions, as was said, ask to be pronounced. This was

usually done in the Second Gothic period by framing each light with a border, separated from the stonework always by a fillet of white glass. The exception to this was in the case of trefoiled or other many-foiled openings, in which a central medallion or boss, usually circular, extended to the points of the cusps, and the border round the cuspings stopped short against the border to that. Or again in triangular openings a central boss would sometimes extend to its margin, and the borders would stop against that, or pass seemingly behind it.

A typical form of Decorated tracery occurs in the West window at York Minster, by far the most beautiful part of it. There, every important opening has within its white marginal line a broader band of ruby or green, broken at intervals by yellow spots, within which border is foliage of white and yellow on a green or ruby ground. Some of the smaller openings show white and yellow foliage only, without any coloured ground. A plan equally characteristic of the period is illustrated at Tewkesbury. There again occurs similar white foliage, its stem encircling a central spot of yellow. This also is on green and ruby backgrounds, the former reserved for the more prominent openings; but the border is in white, painted with a pattern. This broader white border more effectively relieves the dark lines of the masonry than the border of colour, which sometimes confuses the shapes of the smaller tracery openings: it does so, for example, in the Late glass on page 200.

186. PART OF A ROSE WINDOW, GERMAN 14TH CENTURY.

For what was said of the difficulty of carrying a broad border round the heads of Decorated lights applies more forcibly still to tracery. The merest fillet of colour is often as much as can safely be carried round the opening, if even that. On the other hand, a broad border of white and stain, even though it contain a fair amount of black in it, may safely be used—as at Châlons, where it frames small subjects in rich colour. Some admirable Decorated tracery occurs at Wells, much on the usual lines, and containing a good deal of pleasant green; but there the white and yellow foliage in the centre part of the lights is sometimes so closely designed that very little of the coloured ground shows through it, and it looks at first as if what little ground there is had all been painted-out. At S. Denis Walmgate, York, the background to the foliage in white and yellow (which last predominates) is painted solid; the only pot-metal colour (except in the central medallion head) is in a rosette or two of colour leaded into it; the border is white. Another expedient there employed is to introduce figures in white and stain upon a ground of green or ruby, diapered. At Wells there occur little figures of saints in pot-metal colour, planted upon the white foliated filling of the tracery lights. Decorated circular medallions occupying the centre of ornamental tracery lights are usually framed in coloured lines; occasionally the inner margin of the medallion is cusped, in imitation of stonework.

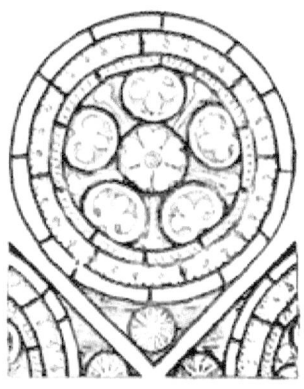

137. Assisi.

An effective plan, adopted at Evreux, is to gather the lights into groups, by means of the colour introduced into them, which grouping may or may not be indicated by the stonework. In any case, it is a means of obtaining at once variety and breadth of colour.

Perpendicular tracery lights are themselves, in most cases, only copies in miniature of the larger lights below, and the glass is designed on the same plan. A good illustration of this is at Great Malvern, where the design consists of the orthodox canopy work in white and stain, with little figures also nearly all in white, colour occurring only in the lower skirts of their drapery, in the background about their heads, and behind the pinnacles above. The effect is beautifully silvery. Often such figures under the canopies are angels, all in white and stain.

Sometimes seraphim, in stain upon a white ground, quarried perhaps, fill the lights, without canopies. These are all typical ways of filling the tracery of a Perpendicular window.

It was quite a common thing to fill it with glass wholly of white and stain. In the centre there might be a medallion head in grisaille, or an inscribed label, the rest of the space being occupied by conventional foliage having just a line of clear white next the stonework. Beautiful examples of this treatment occur at Great Malvern; occasionally the foliage is all in yellow with white flowers. Small openings are thus often glazed in a single piece of glass, or in any case with the fewest possible leads. At S. Serge, Angers, there is larger work of a similar kind, a bold scroll in white and stain on a ground of solid pigment, out of which is scratched a smaller pattern, not so bold as in the least to interfere with the scroll, but enough to prevent anything like heaviness in the painted ground. Similar treatment is adopted in the cathedral at Beauvais. Once in a while one comes, in English work, upon figures in white and stain on a solid black ground extending to the stonework, without any line of white to show where the glass ends and the stonework begins. It would be impossible more emphatically than that to show one's contempt for the architecture.

Some disregard, if not actually contempt, is shown for architecture in the practice, common no less in Late Gothic than in Renaissance design, of carrying a coloured ground right up to the stone, without so much as a line of light to separate the two. Comparatively light though the colour may be, it is usually dark enough, unless it be yellow, to confuse the forms of any but the boldest tracery. Something of the kind occurred by way of exception even in fourteenth century glass, as at S. Radegonde, Poitiers, and at Toulouse, where the tracery of the windows is one field of blue, irregularly sprinkled with white stars. The lines of the tracery are lost, and one sees only spots of white.

The Later Gothic plan was to keep tracery light, even though the window below it were altogether in rich colour, and the effect was good; as at Alençon, where a distinctly blue window has in the tracery only angels in white and yellow on a white ground; or, again, at Conches, where white-robed angels, on a ground of rich stain, contrast pleasantly with the cool blue of the lights below.

Unusual treatment of the tracery occurs at Auch (1513). In the main the tracery lights contain figures in colour upon a ruby or paler-coloured ground, which, as in so many a Renaissance window, runs out to the stonework; but occasionally here and there a light is distinguished by a border of white. Moreover, the ground is, as a rule, not of one colour throughout, nor even throughout a single light, but varied; and that not symmetrically or patternwise, but so as artfully to carry the colour through. In fact, the artist has taken his tracery much more seriously than usual, and has carefully studied how best he could balance by the colour in it the not quite so easily-to-be-controlled colour of his figure composition below. The result is that the windows are all of one piece—each a complete and well-considered colour composition: the tracery is not merely the top part of the frame to the coloured picture below.

188. LYONS.

In Renaissance glass the tracery was more often in comparatively full colour, even though the lights below were pale. A grisaille window at Évreux, with practically blue tracery, has a very pleasant effect.

It was not often that the Renaissance glass painters gave very serious attention to the tracery which they had to fill. They were, for the most part, content to conceive each separate opening as a blue field upon which to place an angel (as above), a crown, a *fleur-de-lys*, or other emblem, as best might fit. In very many sixteenth century windows the design consists merely of angels, emblems, labels, or even clouds, dotted about, as suited the convenience of the designer. Sometimes, as at S. Alpin, at Troyes, there occurs in a tracery light a tablet bearing a date,—presumably, but not always positively, that of the window. Such devices were very often in white upon a ground of blue, purple, or ruby. Angels of course adapted themselves to irregular shapes in the most angelic way; and they are introduced in every conceivable attitude—standing, kneeling, flying, swinging censers, singing, playing on musical instruments, bearing scrolls or shields; angels all in white, angels in white with coloured wings, angels in gorgeous array of colour: and more accommodating still, is the bodiless cherub, beloved of Luca della Robbia.

There is a quite charming effect of colour in a Jesse window at S. Maclou, Rouen, where the tracery lights are inhabited by little cherubs, in ruby on a grey-blue ground, in grey on deeper grey-blue, and in emerald-like green upon the same.

The scroll without the angel was a very convenient filling for smaller openings. Some elaborately twisted scrolls, in white and stain on purple, occur at Moulins.

Larger and more prominent lights often contain a separate picture, or one picture runs through several lights, or perhaps all through the tracery. Worse than that is, where the picture runs through from the lights below: as at Alençon, where the trees grow up into the blue of the tracery, broken otherwise only by white clouds; or at Conches, where the architecture from the subject below aspires so high. It is almost worse still where, as at Alençon again, and at the chapel at Vincennes, it is the canopy which so encroaches. In the exceptional case of a Jesse window there seems less objection to accepting the whole window as a field through which the tree may grow: yet the tracery is not the happiest part of the Beauvais window (page 368). Sometimes the heads of the lower lights are made to appear as though they were part of the tracery.

A happier form of Renaissance tracery design is where medallion heads in white and stain are introduced upon a ground of plain colour—blue at Châlons, purple-brown at Montmorency. These are sometimes most beautifully painted, as are the Raffaellesque little cherubs amidst white clouds, also at Montmorency; but they are much more delicately done than they need have been, and less effective than they might.

Very delicate painting upon white does produce an effect even at a distance: at least it gives quality; but there should be some relation between effort and effect; and here the effect is weak as compared with the expenditure of art. In the tracery on page 213, fairly effective though monotonous, the birds are glazed in with such unnecessary avoidance of lead, that the cutting of the ground must have been a work of great difficulty. In glass of every period it has been the custom to put too much into tracery; in Early work too much detail, in Later too much finish. What is wanted is breadth.

CHAPTER XXIII.

QUARRY WINDOWS.

THE very simplest form of window glazing, the easiest and the thriftiest thing for the cutter to do, and the most straightforward for the glazier, is to frame together parallel-sided pieces of glass in the form of a lead lattice.

Quarries, as all such little square or rhomboid shaped panes of glass came to be called, were used from the first. Ordinarily they were set on end, so as to form diamonds; which as time went on, were generally not rectangular, but long in proportion to their breadth.

For the most part they were painted with patterns traced in brown; and, on the discovery of silver stain, they were in parts tinted yellow. From the fourteenth century onwards, quarry lights, framed in borders, and enlivened with colour, form a very important variety of grisaille.

Many a grisaille pattern was not far removed from quarry glazing, as may be seen opposite. It was natural that, for clerestory and triforium windows in particular, the glazier should do all he could to simplify his work. Clerestory windows are placed too high to be fairly seen in a narrow church, and triforium lights are often half shut off from view by projecting shafts of open arcading in front of them. It is only when, by rare chance, they happen to front you squarely at the end of an aisle or transept, that they are properly seen. There is no occasion, therefore, to indulge in subtleties of design; the one thing needful is that the effect of the windows as a whole, should be pleasant, since all study of detail is out of the question, except from the triforium galleries opposite, or by the aid of a field-glass; and light arrangements of grisaille and colour are in most cases all that is wanted. The colour may be more or less, according as it is desired to exclude light or to admit it; but some very simple, unpretending, and perhaps even rude treatment, is indicated by the conditions of the case, which to contradict, is wasteful and unworkmanlike.

189. LINCOLN.

The effect, for example, of the band of figures across the grisaille in the triforium of the transepts at Evreux is admirable; but the way in which seven saints out of the eight are cut vertically in two by the pillars of the architectural screen in front of them, is nothing less than exasperating. These figures tell only as the patches of colour; and that could so easily have been obtained by much simpler means. In such a position, quarries may well take the place, not only of figures, but of more interesting grisaille; and, even though they be not painted at all (as is again the case at Evreux), but merely broken by occasional sun-discs in white and stain crossing them, and framed in a simple block-border of white and colour, the effect may be entirely adequate. It is not meant to deny that figures in rich colour embedded in carefully designed grisaille are more attractive; but, for its purpose, quarry work, with borders and bosses of colour, is in the majority of such cases, enough.

Figures or figure subjects in formal bands across tall quarry lights are always effective; so are figures planted more casually upon the quarries — kneeling donors, flying angels, or whatever they may be. So again, are figure panels alternating with bosses of ornament; but, if the

190. EVREUX.

window occupy a position where the figures can be appreciated, a surrounding of quarries seems hardly of interest enough, and if not, the figures seem rather thrown away. One is tempted to make exception in favour of figures in grisaille, which, if very delicately painted (as for example at S. Martin-cum-Gregory, York), show to advantage on a quarry ground, which has the modesty not to compete with them in interest. The quarries keep their place perfectly as a background; and the slight painting upon them is just enough to give the glass quality, and to indicate that, however subordinate, it is yet part of the picture.

A quarry window, no less than any other, wants a border, if only to prevent the strongly marked straight lines of lead from appearing to run into the stone work. A simple line of colour with another of white next the mullions is enough for that. Even this is occasionally omitted, more especially in tracery lights, but in that case the glass seems to lack finish. The most satisfactory border to quarry lights into which otherwise no colour is introduced, is a broadish border of white, painted with pattern and in part stained. A coloured border seems to imply other colour breaking the field of quarries. By itself it is too much or not enough. Its proportion is a thing to be determined in each case on the spot : but even in narrow lights, if they contain bosses of colour (as do those in the transepts at Le Mans) a broad border about one fifth the width of the window, with a broad white line next the stone, is very effective.

The monotony of any great surface of quarry work, has led to the introduction of medallions and the like, even where it is not desired to introduce pot-metal colour. In the window from Evreux, illustrated opposite, the effect of the delicately painted little angel medallions, in white on a ground of stain, is all that could be wished. Any little surprise of that kind is always welcome; but, should it occur too frequently, it becomes itself monotonous.

There is no end to the variety of forms in which colour may be introduced into quarry work. It is best in the form of patches, and not in the form of lines between the quarries as occurs occasionally, at Poitiers, for example, at Rouen cathedral, and at Châlons (page 167).

Big rosettes, discs, wreaths, rings of colour, and the like,

191. QUARRY WINDOW, EVREUX.

are more effective than small spots. They need not be heavy, there may be any amount of white in them. In narrow lights, they may sometimes with advantage come in front of the border; that admits of the biggest possible medallion, and it is best to have such features large and few. Mean little rosettes are too suggestive of the contractor; in the church of S. Ouen, at Rouen, one is uncomfortably reminded of him—it would be so easy to estimate for glass of that kind at so much the foot! Heraldic shields form often peculiarly effective colour-patches in quarry windows, more especially because of the accidental arrangement of colour they compel. There is a point at which symmetry of colour palls upon the eye.

192. LINCOLN.

The even surface of quarry lights all in white and stain is broken sometimes by an occasional band of inscription, which may either take the line of the quarries, or cross them in the form of a label. At Evreux some quarry lights are most pleasingly interrupted by square patches of inscription in yellow, or, which is still more satisfactory, in white. In the same cathedral there is a very

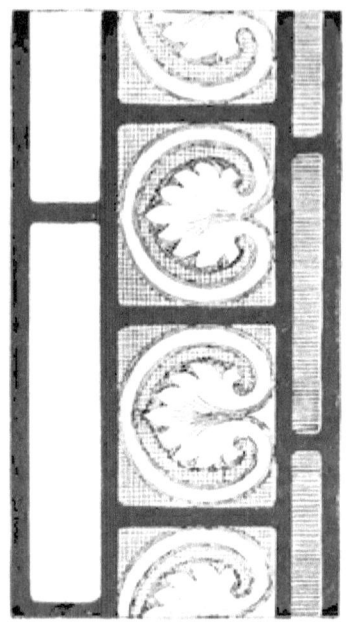

195. GERMAN QUARRY BORDER.

interesting instance of inscription, in letters some five or six inches high, leaded in blue upon a quarry ground.

The patterns with which quarries are painted naturally followed the ordinary course of grisaille. In the thirteenth century the designs were strongly outlined, and showed clear against a cross-hatched ground; which, however, did not, as a rule, extend to the lead, but a margin of clear glass was left next to it, in acknowledgment of the quarry shape. The combination of quarries and strap ornament in the example at Lincoln (page 287) is unusual, but the quarries themselves are, but for the absence of a clear line next the leads, characteristically of the thirteenth century. The quarry border from Nuremberg (above) is rather later in character. In that case also, as it happens, there is no marginal line of clear glass. The typical treatment is shown below. Later, as in other grisaille, the cross-hatched ground was omitted; and the foliage took, of course, more natural form. It was presently more delicately traced (page 290), and more often than not tinted in yellow stain. Consistently with the more natural form of leafage the design in fourteenth century work was often one continuous growth trailing through the window, and passing behind the marginal band of stain which now usually emphasised the top sides of the quarries. Often a futile attempt was made (page 286) to give the appearance of interlacing to these bands, but that was nullified by the stronger lead lines. True, interlacing was only possible where, as in some earlier work, the bands were continued on all four sides of the quarry, so that the lead fell into its place

196. EARLY ENGLISH QUARRY.

195. QUARRY PATTERNS (SHAW).

176. 14TH CENTURY QUARRY.

as interspace between two interlacing bands. It was better when there was no pretence of interlacing (below). Additional importance was sometimes given to the marginal band by tracing a pattern upon it, or, as on page 291, painting it in brown, and then picking out geometric tracery upon it. There came a time when marginal lines were omitted altogether. That was the usual, though not invariable, practice in the fifteenth century, by which time the draughtsman had apparently learnt to husband his inventive faculty. The continuous growth of the pattern, as well as the marginal acknowledgment of the lead lines, died out of fashion, and quarries were mostly painted sprig fashion. The character of these sprigs will be best judged from the specimens on page 289, some of the most interesting given in "Shaw's Book of Quarries." Quarry patterns do not, of course, occur in that profuse variety; it is seldom that more than two patterns are found in a single window, often there is only one. The range of design in quarries of this kind is limited only by the invention of the artist. It includes both floral and conventional ornament, animal and grotesque figures, emblems and heraldic badges, cyphers, monograms, mottoes, and so on. There is scope not only for meaning in design, but for the artist's humour;

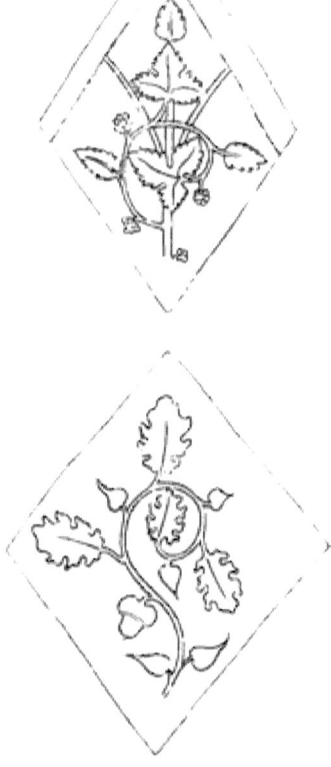

197. 14TH CENTURY QUARRIES.

S.G.

but, when all is said, the Late Gothic pattern windows, now given over entirely to quarry work, are of no great account as concerns their detail. The later quarry patterns are often pretty enough, sometimes amusing, but they go for very little in the decoration of a church. Plentiful as quarry work is everywhere, and characteristic as it is of Perpendicular glass, there is not much that shows an attempt to do anything serious with the quarry window. All that was done was to paint more or less delicate and dainty patterns upon the little lozenge panes. However, they were traced with a light hand and a sure one, and with a kind of spontaneity which gives them really what artistic charm they have.

198. 14TH CENTURY QUARRY.

The occasional endeavours to get stronger and bolder effects in quarry work were not very successful. At Evreux and at Rouen there are some late quarries painted more after the fashion of bold mosaic diaper: but the effect, though satisfactory enough, is not such as to convince one that that is the better way.

To heraldry, and especially to shields of arms surrounded by mantling (page 293), quarries form an excellent background, but only in the event of there being enough of them left free to show that it is a quarry window upon which the heraldry is imposed, or rather into which it is inlaid. Odds and ends of quarries want to be accounted for, as forming the continuation of the glass above and below. In the case of a window not a quarry window, it is a mistake to break up the background, as was sometimes done, into quarries, or rather into fragments of quarries. The object of the square or diamond shape is to break up a plain surface. If the ground is naturally broken up by figures, foliage, mantling, or what not, why introduce further quarry lines? They are not in themselves interesting. Their great value is in that they give scale to a window; but that is only on condition that they are seen in their entirety.

In Germany the place of quarries was supplied by roundels (page 292) unpainted. What applies to quarries applies in many respects to them; and they have a brilliancy which

199. ROUND GLASS, ROUNDELS, OR BULL'S-EYES

flat glass has not. They were usually enclosed in painted
borders of white and stain, and have a very delicate and pearly
effect; but where (as at S. Peter's, at Cologne) they occur in
great quantity as compared with coloured subjects, these appear
to be floating rather uncomfortably in their midst. The Italians,
who also used roundels in place of quarries, often let colour into
the interstices between them, and also little painted squares or

208. HERALDIC GLASS.

pateræ of white and stain. In the sham windows decorating the
Sistine Chapel at Rome, separating Botticelli's series of Popes,
the pointed spaces between the rounds are coloured diagonally
in successive rows of red, yellow, and green; but the result
is most pleasing where, as at Verona and elsewhere, the little
triangular spaces are neither of one tint nor yet symmetrically
arranged, but distributed in a quasi-accidental and unexpected
way. Sometimes it was the little patera that was in colour and
the rest white. In any case, the effect is refined, as it is at
Arezzo also, where the monotony of roundels, in sundry clerestory windows, is broken by figure medallions and other features

in white and colour. The adaptation of roundels to the circular shape is shown in the portion of a round window from Santa Maria Novella. What more remains to be said about roundels and quarry windows is reserved for the chapter on " Domestic Glass."

201. QUARRY FROM CHELTWOOD CHURCH.

202. WINDOW IN THE CERTOSA IN VAL D'EMA, FLORENCE.

CHAPTER XXIV.

DOMESTIC GLASS.

IT is customary to draw a distinction between "Ecclesiastical" and "Domestic" glass.

In mediæval days the Church was the patron of art; and, when kings and corporations commissioned stained glass windows, it was usually to present them to Mother Church. It is in churches, then, that the greater part of the old glass remains to us, iconoclastic mania notwithstanding; and it is only there that the course of glass painting can be traced. Once in a while, as at S. Mary's Hall, Coventry, one comes upon a great window designed to decorate a civic building; but the whiles are few and far between. When such windows do occur they prove not to differ widely from more familiar church work.

What, then, is the difference between the two kinds of glass? It is not that the one is ecclesiastical the other secular, the one religious the other profane art. "Sacred Art" is a term consecrated by use; but, strictly speaking, it is a meaningless combination of words, signifying, if it signify anything, that the speaker confounds the art of telling with the thing told. Art has no more a religion than it has a country. No doubt there clings always to the art of the devout believer some fervour of faith, as there may hang about the sceptic's doing a chill of doubt. The historian will enrich his glass with story, the preacher will convey in it a dogma. Poet or proser, philosopher or fool, may each in turn peep out of the window. Youth will everywhere betray its ardour, manhood its vigour, age its experience. A live man cannot help but put himself into his work. But none of that is art. His art is in the way he expresses himself, not in what he says; and there is no more religion in his glass painting than in his handwriting, though the graphologist may read in it his character.

The difference between church glass and domestic arises, speaking from the point of view of art, solely from architectural conditions. In so far as they are both glass, the same methods of glazing and painting apply to both. It is only in so far as the position and purpose of the two are different, that they call for different treatment in design. The treatment suitable to a great hall does not materially differ from that adapted to a church: the same breadth of design, the same largeness of execution, are required: what suits a cloister would suit a passage. When, however, it comes to the windows of dwelling-rooms, the scheme and execution appropriate even to the smallest chapels of a church, would most likely be out of place. The distinction is very much as that between wall decoration in fresco and cabinet paintings in oil- or water-colour.

In the house there is less need than in the church for severity, and more for liveliness, less occasion for breadth, and more for delicacy. The scale of the dwelling-room itself justifies, perhaps demands, a smaller treatment. Here, if anywhere, is opportunity for that preciousness of execution which, in work of more monumental character, it seems a pity to expend upon so frail a substance as glass—frailer than ever when it was the thin white glass employed for window panes. For, so far from the glazier of the sixteenth or seventeenth century imagining, as we mostly do, that it was any part of the purpose of domestic glass to shut out the view—less need in those days!—he employed in most cases a material which was not merely translucent but absolutely transparent.

This use of transparent glass marks a distinction, and forms something of a new departure. It was employed to some extent in Renaissance church work; but there it was more as a background to the stained glass window than as a part of it. Here the transparent glass is the window; and the design, whether in pot-metal or in enamel, shows more or less against the clear.

The relationship of certain seventeenth century windows at Antwerp to the Italian windows on pages 295, 299, 352, is obvious. They may be quite possibly founded upon them. There is the same arrangement of subjects in cartouches, set in geometric glazing of clear glass. But in the Italian windows one kind of glass is used throughout (the little pieces of thin pot-metal colour in the cartouches, and so on, scarcely count); and the proportion of the painted work to clear glass is so schemed that, although you may feel that the plain work wants just a touch of enrichment to bring it all together, you

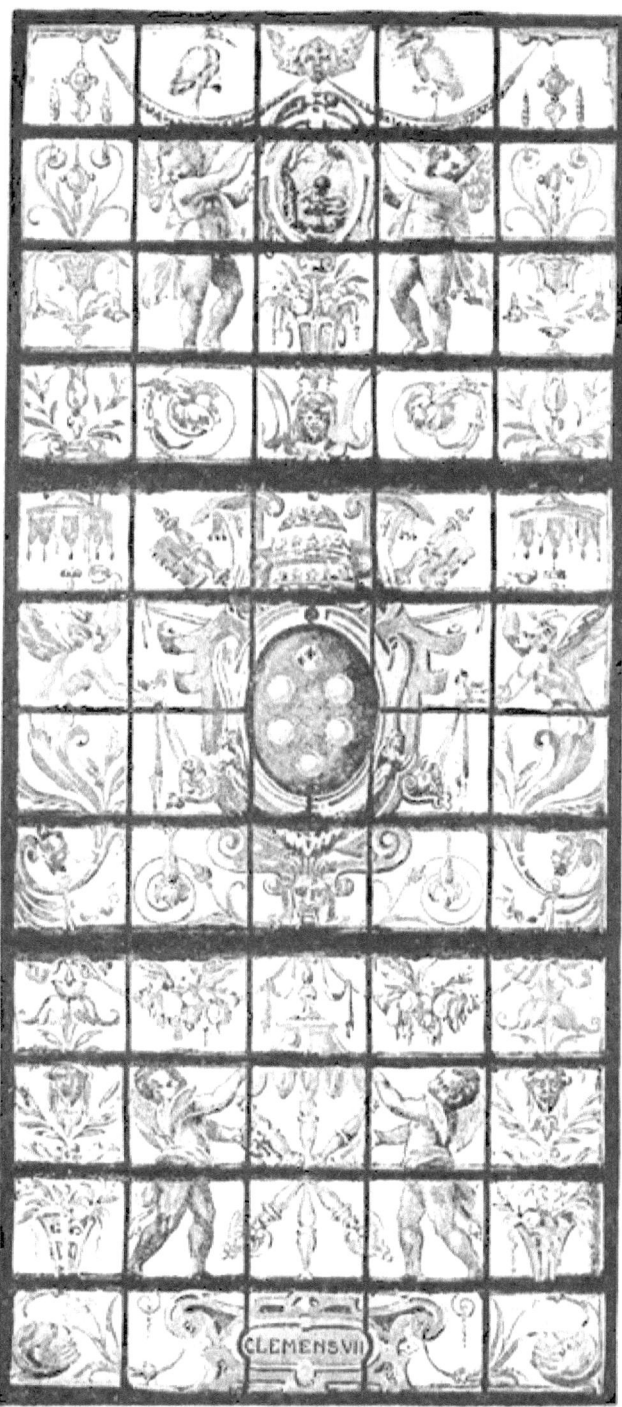

203. ITALIAN GRISAILLE, FLORENCE.

are not asked deliberately to imagine yourself to be looking through, beyond the painting, into space.

The detail in these windows from the Certosa in Val d'Ema, near Florence, is all outlined and painted in brown upon clear white glass, the flesh warmer in tint than the rest; the high lights are brushed out of a matt tint, and some pale stain is washed in. The artful thing about the design is, the cunning way in which the borders are planned, so as to avoid the absolute parallelism of marginal lines. For the rest the design is rather characteristically Late Renaissance, though the relation of border to cartouche, and of both together to clear glass, is better than usual. It will be noted that these are not strictly domestic windows; but they are designed to be seen about on a level with the eye, and from a distance of not more than ten feet, which is as far as the width of the cloister allows one to get away from them.

294. CERTOSA IN VAL D'EMA.

They fulfil, therefore, altogether very much the conditions which apply generally to domestic glass, and may be taken, if not as types of domestic work, at least as something on the way from the church to the house. This, though the common type of Italian Renaissance grisaille, was not invariable. At S. Frediano, Lucca, for example, there is a white window, which, except for a little medallion in its centre, might at a glance almost pass for thirteenth century work: the Cinque-Cento scroll is so rendered, with cross-hatched ground and all, as to suggest the early mediæval craftsman; it is centuries away from Da Udine in style.

The domestic quarry window differed, in mediæval work, in no respect from church work. In the sixteenth century it took rather a new form. It consisted no longer of a more or less diaper-like all-over pattern, but of a panel, designed to be glazed in quarries. Here, again, is an approximation to the seventeenth century practice of leading up pictures in rectangular panes, but only an approximation. There is this important difference, that the quarry window starts from the lead lines, and is religiously designed within them.

Thus to accept the simple square and obviously fit lines of quarry glazing, and to expend his art in painting upon them, simplifies the task of the glass painter; and he very frequently fell back upon that plan, more readily perhaps when he happened to know more about painting than about glazing. That was Da Udine's case, who is credited with the design of the windows in the Laurentian library at Florence, as of those at the Certosa in Val d'Ema. They bear a date some few years after his death: but they are so like what he certainly would have done that, directly or indirectly, the design is clearly due to him. The one illustrated on page 298 is quite one of the best of these windows; in the others the ornament is even less coherent. The characteristic arabesque is painted in brown enamel, with redder enamel for the flesh tints, some yellow stain, and a little blue enamel in the heraldic lozenge, all upon clear white glass. The effect is delicate and silvery and no appreciable amount of light is excluded (a point usually of some importance in domestic work; but, though the main forms are designed within the lead lines, one feels that these have not been considered enough, that the leads compete with the painting, and that the bars, in particular, which are far thicker than need be, and occur with unnecessary frequency (in fact, at every horizontal quarry joint but one), very seriously mar the effect of delicate painting. That is as much as to say that the design, graceful and fanciful as it is, does not fulfil the conditions of quarry glass.

It is not enough for complete success in this form of window that the quarry lines shall be the basis of the design; the painting also must be strong enough to hold its own against leads and bars. That is hardly the case with the exceptionally delicate ornament in the Dutch glass opposite. But here, notwithstanding that the scroll is slighter than the Italian work and more delicately painted, the central patch of enamel colour in the shield and mantling does, to some extent, focus the attention there, and so withdraw the eye from the lead lines. The window is not merely cleverly designed; it is a frank, straightforward, manly piece of work, marred only by the comparative heaviness of the leads. The truth is that a glass

205. DUTCH QUARRY WINDOW, S. K. MUSEUM

painter becomes so used to lead lines, and gets to take them so much for granted, that they do not offend him; and he is apt to forget how obtrusive they may appear in the eyes of the unaccustomed. Hence his sometimes seemingly brutal treatment of tenderly painted ornament.

Other good examples of Dutch domestic glass, not quite so good as this, but painted with admirable directness, are to be found at the *Musée des Antiquités* at Brussels. At the Louvre also the Dutch work is good. There are two lights there in which cartouches enclosing small oval subjects (fables) spread over the greater part of the quarry glazing, leaving only the lowermost of them comparatively empty. On these are painted butterflies, a dragon-fly, even a gad-fly, almost to the life. These flies upon the window pane, like the little miniature figures in the bottom corner quarries on page 301, are trivial enough in idea; but the idea is cleverly and daintily expressed; and one does not expect much else than triviality in seventeenth century design. Moreover, in the privacy of domestic life it is permitted to be trivial.

For dignity of treatment it would be difficult to match the specimen of Flemish glass shown on page 304, now at Warwick Castle. Like the Dutch and Italian work, it is painted on clear glass but without the prettiness of flesh tint, and the background to the ornament (it shows dull grey in the print) is brilliant yellow stain. This little light and its companion on page 98 are as large in style as they are beautiful in effect.

There is a gayer touch in the less seriously decorative panel of French work in the Louvre given on page 307. In that pot-metal is used for the dark ruby of the outer dress, and for the little bits of blue rather cunningly let into the spandrils of the arch. The fancifully designed canopy, the arabesque, and a portion of the drapery are in stain, all delicately painted upon clear glass, and glazed mainly on quarry lines—from which, however, the designer saw fit to depart. What he meant by the unfortunate circular lead line about the head is difficult to imagine. It can hardly be, like other erratic leading, the result of mending. No fracture could possibly have steered so carefully between the figure and the ornament. It looks almost as if at the last he had lost confidence in his technique, and, in trying vainly to avoid lead lines, had ended in giving them extraordinary emphasis.

In ultra-delicate domestic work the leads are more than

ever the difficulty. One is uncomfortably conscious of them in the wonderful series of windows—formerly at Ecouen, and now in the Château de Chantilly—in which is set forth in forty pictures the story of Cupid and Psyche. A specimen of these is given on page 218, thanks to the friendly permission of Monsieur Magne, who illustrates the whole of them in his admirable monograph of the Montmorency glass. The legend to the effect that Raffaelle designed and Palissy painted them, is past all possible belief; but they are very remarkable specimens of sixteenth century work, restored about the period of the First Empire, and mark somewhere about the high-water mark of French domestic picture glass.

A glance at these windows is enough to show that they were never schemed with any definite view to glazing. Rather it would appear that the pictures were first designed and then the leads introduced where best they could be disguised. But the disguise is everywhere transparent. Such gauzy painting is inadequate: it hides nothing. You see always the thick black lines of lead, cruel enough, but clinging in a cowardly way to the edges of weak forms, sneaking into shadows, and foolishly pretending to pass themselves off as the continuation of painted outlines not one-twentieth part so strong as they. The sparing use of glazing lines makes them all the more conspicuous. They must originally have asserted themselves even more than they do now: for the accidental lead lines introduced in reparation, however much they damage the pictures, do in a measure support the original glazing lines, and pull the windows together. The Chantilly glass goes to prove the impossibility of satisfactorily disposing of the leads in very small figure-subjects in grisaille. In work on a larger scale it wants only a man who knows his trade to manage it. Witness what was done in church work.

The propriety of executing figures in grisaille at all has been called in question by Viollet le Duc. "Every bit of white glass," he said, "should be diapered with pattern traced with a brush: and, since this treatment is not possible in flesh painting, flesh ought not to be painted." Moreover, he says that grisaille has always the appearance of vibrating, and the vibration fatigues the eye: therefore, he argues, it is labour lost to paint white figures. Far be it from an ornamentist to deny that a great deal too much importance is attached to figure work in decoration. But the amount of tracing necessary on

206. GRISAILLE, WARWICK CASTLE.

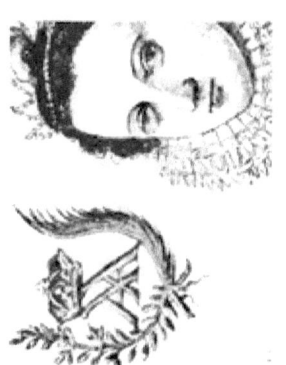

white glass is relative. In grisaille it is quite safe to leave some glass clear; and, if it is not worth while to paint figures, is it worth while to paint anything worth looking at, or worth painting?

The truth is, it wearies the sight to look at any glass for long at a stretch, and for a mere *coup d'œil* the most brutal workmanship would often do. But, if work is ever to be seen from near, the charm is gone when once you know how coarse it is. One tires of crude work, and delights more and more in what is delicate. Whoever has taken pleasure in such work as the windows at S. Alpin at Troyes would find it hard to renounce the figure in grisaille.

To return to the leading of grisaille. Of the two extremes, the bold, even the too bold, acknowledgment of the constructional lines of a window, is far preferable to the timid attempt to conceal them. The glaziers of the Renaissance eventually got over the difficulty by the simple plan of inserting into quarry windows (usually unpainted) or into pattern work of plain glass only, little panes of painted glass. In this way there are introduced into some windows at the Château de Chaumont some very beautiful little portrait medallions, outlined with a firmness and modelled with a delicacy which remind one of the drawings of Clouet. At the Germanic Museum at Nuremberg are some similar medallion heads, quite Holbein-ish in character. A later portrait panel, lacking the style and draughtsmanship of these, but very cleverly painted (by Linard Gontier they say), is reproduced on page 305. It represents, as the inscription and cypher go to show, Louis Treize and Anne of Austria, as bride and bridegroom. Its date, therefore, speaks for itself. Another little pane by Gontier, from the Hôtel des Arquebusiers at Troyes, now in the library there, is given on page 310. The characteristic ornamental work surrounding this, though not forming a consecutive frame to the picture, is of about the same period with it (1621). Its design consists of that modified form of Arab foliation (compare it with the detail on page 352), which was very much used in damascening and niello work; indeed, the French still call that kind of pattern "*nielle*." Here it is traced in a fine brown outline, and filled in partly with yellow stain and partly with blue enamel. The effect is pleasing.

It was in Switzerland that glass painting other than for churches was most extensively practised. The Council Chambers of Swiss towns, and the halls of trade and other

208 DOMESTIC GLASS, THE LOUVRE

209. PIERCED QUARRIES, WARWICK.

guilds, were enriched with bands of armorial glass across the windows; and throughout the sixteenth century it was the custom to present to neighbouring towns or friendly Corporations a painted window panel. Great part of these have been dispersed, and in Switzerland they are now perhaps rarer than in the museums of other countries. The Germanic Museum at Nuremberg and the Hôtel Clûny, at Paris, are rich in Swiss glass; and we have some at South Kensington. Superb examples, however, still remain in Switzerland—for example, in the Rathhaus at Lucerne—though they belong to a period as late as the first ten years of the seventeenth century.

The usual form of design consisted of a sort of florid canopy frame of moderate dimensions, enclosing a shield or shields of arms, supported by fantastically dressed men-at-arms. There was often great spirit in the swagger of these melodramatic swashbucklers, admirably expressive of the idea which underlies all heraldry: "I am somebody," they seem to say, "pray who are you?" It is a comparatively modest specimen of this class that is presented on page 90. In the windows of a private house it was frequently the master and mistress who supported the armorial shield, all in their Sunday best, and very proud of themselves too. Little Bible subjects were also painted, mainly in grisaille. It was for window panes that Holbein drew the Stations of the Cross, now among the chief treasures of the museum at Bâle. These also must be classed with domestic work. They may in some cases have been destined for a church; but they would much more appropriately decorate a private oratory.

These heraldic or pictorial panes go even beyond the delicacy of cabinet pictures, and are sometimes more on the scale of miniatures; but of such miniature painting the Swiss were masters. They carried craftmanship to its very furthest point, and among them traditions of good work lingered long after they were quite dead in France. Of English work there was not much; and of that the less said the better.

Far into the eighteenth century the Swiss still had a care for their window panes, and, when painting went out of fashion, engraved them with armorial or other devices. Precisely that kind of engraving was employed also upon polished mirrors, of which one finds examples in Italy.

Unpainted quarry windows in English houses were sometimes relieved, at the same time that ventilation was secured, by the occasional introduction (in the place of glass) of little fretted panels of pierced lead, as shown on page 308. Below is a diamond-shaped piercing of the Jacobean period.

220. QUARRY OF FRETTED LEAD.

211 DOMESTIC WINDOW PANE, TROYES

CHAPTER XXV.

THE USE OF THE CANOPY.

No one can have paid much attention to stained glass without observing the conspicuous part played in its design by the quasi-architectural canopy.

Inasmuch as it, in a sense, enshrines the figure, there exists some sort of symbolic reason for its use. But that is not enough to account for its all but universal employment. A more obvious excuse for it is, the purpose it fulfils in the construction of design. It is a means of accounting for the position of figures midway up the window, perhaps one above the other, and not standing upon the sill. It is at once framework and support to them, preventing them from seeming to float there in space.

Where the designer of the church designed also the glass for it, it was almost inevitable that he should plan it more or less upon architectural lines; and so we find that in windows known to have been designed by architects the canopy is very often the most conspicuous part of the design. But at all times the master-builder must have been a power, and at all times also even glaziers and glass painters must have been so intimately acquainted with forms of architecture, that it is not surprising they should have introduced them into their work.

The fact is, the designer happens upon something like a canopy almost without intending it, and, having arrived so far, perfects the resemblance to it. Suppose a window of four long lights, in each of which it is desired to introduce three figures. That means dividing it horizontally into three, which may be done by the use of bands of inscription, as at *a* in the diagram overleaf: there is no suggestion of architecture there. Supposing you wish to frame the window at the sides, so as to stop the picture, as at *b*, to the left of the diagram; you have still no very distinct suggestion of architecture. But if, the better to frame the picture, you add an extra band of colour, as shown at *c*, you arrive at once at something so like perspective as to indicate an architectural elevation. Indeed, that is precisely the form the canopy takes sometimes in Italian glass. Even when the cinque-centist framed his picture merely in lines he could hardly help giving them the appearance of mouldings, painting upon (as at Arezzo) egg-and-tongue or other familiar architectural enrichment in white and stain.

In the clerestory at Freiburg is a window in which the serried saints appear at first sight to be simply framed by lines of pale purple; but on examination these resolve themselves into a simple architectural elevation, with even a hint of unsuspected shadow in it. The date of that example is 1512; and canopies, not to go back to Græco-Roman decoration, begin with the beginning of Gothic. It is adduced, therefore, to show, not the origin of canopy work, but how inevitably something of the sort occurred.

212. DIAGRAM.

Its immediate source is clearly imitation. The thing is borrowed straight from architecture, and indicates, it may justly be said, if not a certain lack of inventive faculty on the part of the designer, at least some disinclination to take the pains to invent.

So in the thirteenth century we have funny little glass penthouses over the figures of saints, architectural in form but not in colour; in the fourteenth windows are crossed by rows of tall brassy disproportioned tabernacles, as yet flat fronted; in the fifteenth, white ghosts of masonry pretend to stand out over the figures; in the sixteenth, altar-like, or other more or less monumental, structures, are pictured with something like the solidity of stonework; and eventually the canopy is merged in painted glass architecture, which joins itself on as best it can to the actual masonry.

The forms of canopy typical of each period of architecture have been discussed in the several chapters on design, but something remains to be said upon canopy work in general, and upon particular instances of it.

The Early canopy goes for nothing as design. Its one merit is that it is inconspicuous. One could wish that the Decorated were equally so. There is, as a rule, no shutting your eyes to its mass of overpowering shrine work. When, by way of exception, it chances to be modest it is sometimes more interesting—as where it is scarcely more than a cusped arch, or where, as at Strasburg, it takes the form of an arcaded band across the window, in which are series of little demi-figures. At Cologne Cathedral also sundry saints are pigeon-holed in this way. *Apropos* of this, it should be mentioned that it invariably adds to the interest of a canopy, when, for example, the broad shaft of a Decorated canopy enniches angels and other figures, or when they are introduced among its pinnacles or in its base. The wide-spreading German canopy affords scope for variety of design not possible so long as the structure is confined within a single light. In some four-light windows at Erfurt (1349-1372) the broad shafts of the canopies, with saints in separate niches, occupy the whole width of the outer lights, leaving only two lights for the central picture. In a five-light window at Strasburg the canopy is five-arched, allowing separate arches in the outer lights for figures of saints, whilst the three central ones cover a single subject.

In canopies which include niches with separate subsidiary subjects, these are sometimes by way of prelude to the main story. In the cathedral at Berne is something of the kind. There, among the pinnacles of the canopy which crowns the subject of the Adoration, are seen the Kings setting out on their pilgrimage, journeying by night, having audience of Herod, and arriving finally at the city of Bethlehem.

In the great altar-like canopies of the Renaissance there is sometimes a gallery above, with angels or other figures, which give points of colour amidst the white. In any case, the canopy is usually more interesting when it is peopled.

The Perpendicular canopy is in effect much more pleasing than what had gone before, but it sins in its simulation of stonework. There also little figures in white and stain are very effectively introduced into the shafts and other parts of the construction, but more in the form of architectural sculpture. There are some very interesting instances of this at Fairford, though the canopies themselves are not otherwise peculiarly interesting.

The useful device of low, flat-topped canopies, adopted in the nave windows at Cologne Cathedral, seldom occurs out of Germany. It is there most successful. Indeed, these particular canopies are interesting examples of the interpenetration of architectural tracery as well as of its moderate and modest use.

Late German canopies are often much more leafy than French or English; they are less architectural—or rather, the architecture breaks out into more free and flowing growth. The charm of Late Gothic canopy work, as was said, lies in its colour, or in the absence of colour—in its silvery effect, that is to say. And one may safely add that quite the most satisfactory canopies, in whatever style, are those in which white largely prevails, modified by stain, but preserving its greyish character. In later Renaissance work white is still largely used: but it is made less brilliant by painted shadow, and so has less to excuse its architectural pretensions. At Milan there is a window in which what should be white is in various granular tints of brown.

The coloured canopy, to which the Italians adhered (as well as to the border enclosing it), does not frame them as the white glass does. The idea appears to be, on the contrary, that it should form part of the picture. Elsewhere than in Italy coloured canopies, other than yellow, are rare: but they occur. There are, for example, the hideous flesh-coloured constructions peculiar to Germany. At Troyes are some not unsatisfactory little canopies in green, and others in purple (1499). At Châlons-sur-Marne is an effective canopy (1526-1537) of golden arabesque on purple. At Freiburg (1525) is a steely-blue Renaissance canopy, from which depend festoons of white and greenish-yellow, against the ruby ground of the subject. And there are others satisfactory enough. But so invariably effective is the framework of white and stain, that to depart from it seems almost like giving up the very excuse for canopies.

The Late Gothic canopy work does most effectually frame the pictures, and gives light, of course, at the same time. It goes admirably with the colour scheme, which includes always a fair quantity of white, even in comparatively rich figure subjects. There is no denying, nor any desire to deny, its altogether admirable effect. If the effect were not otherwise to be obtained, the end would justify the means. But the effect is due simply to the setting of the subjects in a framework of white, not to the architectural character of the design. All that those Perpendicular canopies do could be done equally without architectural forms at all. Canopies make no more beautiful screens of silvery-white than, say, the Five Sisters at York. Intrinsically they are less interesting than pattern work. They give less scope for arranging subjects variously, just as one will: and they allow less range for the fancy of the artist. The most interesting canopies, and among the most effective, are those Early Renaissance picture frames (French, German, or Italian) which, whilst just sufficiently suggesting something near enough to architecture to be called canopies, are really little more than arabesque. One might almost say they are pleasing in proportion as they depart from the quasi-architectural formula.

The enormous value of the mass of white afforded by the canopy, as a setting for colour, has reconciled us too readily to its use. Why not this mass of white without pretended forms of masonry, without this paraphernalia of pinnacles? The architect alone, perhaps, in his heart likes canopy work, and would prefer it to any other kind of ornamental device. When he plans a window, or directs its planning, forms of architectural construction occur to him naturally. Supposing him to be an artist (as we have perhaps a right to expect him to be) he produces a fine thing; but were he to work upon more workmanlike lines, or, to speak quite precisely, more upon the lines of the worker in glass, how much better he would do —being an artist! In his reliance upon inappropriate structural forms, he makes the obvious mistake of depending upon the kind of thing with which he is most familiar, not the thing especially called for. Each particular craft has a technique of its own.

One other class of person also loves canopy work—the tradesman; but his affection for it is less disinterested, and more easily accounted for. The stock canopy (as every one knows who has been, as it were, behind the counter) is a famous device for cheapening production. The examples chosen for illustration throughout these pages do, on the whole, much more than justice to the periods which they were chosen to represent; but, taken altogether, they do not, even so, form a very effective plea for canopy work.

Were the canopy more defensible than it is in glass, it would still have monopolised far too large a place in the scheme of mediæval and Renaissance design. We owe largely to it, in connection with the gradually increasing claims of figure work, the all but extinction of pattern glass. Figure work is practically implied by the canopy. Occasionally, indeed, architecture has formed the whole *motif* of a window; but the case is so rare that it does not count. Once in a while there may be excuse, and even occasion, for almost any device.

There is no valid reason of art why figures and figure subjects should not be framed in ornament, designed indeed with reference to the architecture of the building, but not in the least in the likeness of architecture. This ornament might perfectly well be in white and stain. Ornamental setting in colour does occur in thirteenth century medallion windows, and again (though only by exception) in certain Early Renaissance glass; but by that time pictures, as a rule, absorbed all the interest of design. The instinct which makes us want to give even pictured personages some sort of roof above their heads is more natural than logical. Anyway, to make windows to look like niches in the wall, is an absurd ideal of design, and the nearer the glass painter gets to it the further he has gone off the track. If anything in the nature of a canopy be desirable, clearly it should be constructed on the lines, not of masonry, but of glazing.

CHAPTER XXVI.

A PLEA FOR ORNAMENT.

THERE is a direction in which glass has never been fully developed, that of purely ornamental design. This is the more to be deplored because that direction is the one in which was most scope for the peculiar depth and brilliancy of colour characteristic of mosaic glass. Ornament was used in the thirteenth century not only as a setting for figure medallions, but as of sufficient interest to form of itself most beautiful windows in grisaille. Presently the attractions of figure work put an end to that; and, furthermore, the preference for picture naturally led to the development of design in the direction of glass painting, which lent itself so much more readily than mosaic to pictorial expression. We owe to that, not only the perfection of glass painting, and its ultimate degradation, but the neglect of latent possibilities in more thoroughly mosaic glass, aye, in pure glazing.

Even in figure work, much might be done for clerestory and other distant work, at all events, in pure mosaic glass. Those who have not closely observed old glass have no conception of the amount of lead-work there is in the windows they admire, at the very moment that they deprecate leading, so little do these interfere with the design, when disposed with the cunning of a craftsman. One can imagine figures on a large scale boldly blocked out, with broad shadows, in which not only the shadows, but even the reflected lights in them, might be glazed in pot-metal, and from the floor of a big church the leads would be inappreciable. But, except in work upon an absolutely heroic scale, there would always be the difficulty of the flesh; the features would have to be painted; and glass pictures of this kind would needs be designed with a severe simplicity not calculated to satisfy the modern pictorial sense.

The advocates of painting complain that due consideration of the qualities of glass would limit the artist to the baldest kind of pictorial effect. Something certainly must be sacrificed to fit treatment of the material, or glass suffers, whatever picture may gain. That is what has happened. But if so much sacrifice is necessary to figure, why always adopt that form of design? Why not sometimes at least abandon subject, and seek what can best be done in glass, even though that be barbaric? It is not quite certain but that glass really lends itself only to a rather barbaric kind of design, or what we are barbarous enough to call barbaric. This is certain: the interest of figure work has put an end to ornamental glass. It has become almost an article of faith with us that, to the making of a window worth looking at, figure-design is indispensable. That should not be so. And, seeing that picture does not afford full scope for the qualities which glass-lovers most dearly love in glass, it seems rather cruel that picture should so largely preponderate in its design as to suppress the possibilities in the way of ornament. Why should it be so?

There are two very important reasons for the introduction of figure into glass, the one literary, the other artistic. In the first place, we love a story, that is no more than human; we want to know what it is all about, that is no more than rational; and figure subjects afford the most obvious means of satisfying those cravings of ours. But artists want these cravings satisfied by means of art. Some of them, perhaps, think more of the means employed than of the end achieved, and would have "art for art's sake." Theirs is a doctrine of very limited application. Sanity insists upon subordination of the means to end; and art is not an end in itself, nor is craftsmanship. It is not, therefore, for one moment suggested that story, sentiment, meaning, in windows, should be ruthlessly sacrificed to craftsmanship, even though expression implied the use of figure, which it does not. What is claimed, is merely this: that when you employ a material or a process some consideration is due to it.

Before undertaking to express an idea, it is always as well for the artist to consider how far its expression is consistent with art. If it can be expressed only at the cost of all that is best in art, it were better to adopt some other means of expression. If a particular craft is your one means of expression, and that particular thing cannot well be said in it, then say what can be said; it will be to much more purpose than saying even a better thing and saying it ill.

The better the thought, the greater the crime of saying it inadequately.

After all, the sentiment, or what not, which people ask for in glass, and which compels figure work, is not, in the majority of instances, by any means so important, even in their eyes, but that they would sacrifice it readily enough if they knew the price in art at which they would have to pay for it. Let patrons of stained glass, if they care for art, ponder this statement; it is not spoken in haste, but in conviction.

There is one reason of sentiment which would argue against great part of the use that is made of figure work, at all events in church glass, the doubt, namely, as to how far it is possible, in these days, to reconcile the devout with the decorative treatment of sacred subjects. We are all admiration when we gaze up at the splendid figure of Moses in the great transept window at Chartres. But it is the artist in us that is entranced, the lover of glass, and especially of colour; the artless worshipper might feel that the dignity of the Lawgiver would perhaps have been better expressed with less attention to decorative effect. We are not shocked at the archaic effigy, because we realize that reverence underlies its simplicity. In modern work it is otherwise. Artistic intention, admirable or not from the æsthetic point of view, is responsible for the introduction into our churches of delineations of all that Christians hold sacred so ridiculous, it is a wonder devout worshippers allow them to be there. The excuse for glass is its decorative effect. Its value is in its colour. A Saint in stained glass (to mention no higher Person) stands in a window for just so much colour: is not that rather a degradation of the saint?

In the second place, apart altogether from what has been called the literary interest (which no one will dispute) there is in figure work a charm, altogether artistic, in the very unexpectedness of the colour-patches you get in it, not accidental quite, but in many instances at least, inspired by accident. The besetting sin of ornament is obviousness; it has a way of distributing itself too symmetrically and evenly, of laying its secret bare to the most casual glance. We see at once there is nothing to find out in it, and our interest drops to zero.

In figure design, on the contrary, there are breaks even in the very best balanced scheme; there is always something unexpected, unforeseen, something to kindle interest; in fact, the difficulty is, there, to distribute the composition evenly enough. The question arises whether this sameness, and consequent tameness, of ornament, the way the points of intended interest recur with irritating frequency and regularity, resolving themselves into mere spots—whether this defect is inherent in ornament, and inseparable from it.

Proof that it is not is afforded by heraldry, distinctly a branch of ornamental design, in which, for precisely the same reasons as in figure work, we get just that inevitable deviation from system, and more especially from symmetry, which seems necessary to the salvation of ornament. Where by happy chance an ornamental window has been patched with glass not belonging to it, or where portions of it have been misplaced, we get similar relief from monotony. Here the unexpectedness of contrast, colour, and so on, is accidental: in heraldry it is, in the nature of things, unforeseen of the artist, and unavoidable. May not similar results be obtained of set purpose and design? Surely they may. Were it otherwise, it would be worth falling back now and then upon haphazard, and letting colour come as it might.

Happily there is no occasion for that feeble sort of fatalism. Given a colourist and a man with that sense of distribution (whether of line, mass, or colour) which makes the artist, what is to hinder him from deliberately planning so much of surprise as may be necessary to tickle the appetite for the ornamental? The ogre in the path is what we call economy. Because ornament can without doubt be more cheaply executed than figure work, it is taken for granted that it must be reserved by rights for cheap work. What else is there to recommend it? And, that being so, ornament being but padding, by all means, it is argued, let it be not only cheap but of the cheapest!

Design, moreover, if it be worth having at all, is costly, and there is clearly thrift in repeating the same pattern, and even one unit of it, over and over again. The practice of saving design in this way has become at last so much a matter of course, that no one thinks of designing an ornamental window, as a whole, without repetition of pattern—except the artist;

and with him it is a fond desire which he hopes perhaps some day to fulfil—at his own expense.

Under circumstances such as these, what wonder ornament is monotonous? It could not well be otherwise. But these conditions are not in the nature of things. Ornamental design has subsided because no one asks for, cares for, or encourages, ornament. It needs only to be in the hands of an artist—not necessarily a Holbein, but just a Rhodian potter, a Persian carpet weaver, a mediæval carver, or a nameless glazier—to be worthy of its modest place in art.

Considering the costliness of good figure work and the absolute worthlessness of bad, considering the way in which glass lends itself especially to ornament, considering how in ornament the qualities most necessary to decorative effect and most characteristic of the material can be obtained, surely the wiser policy would be to do what can so readily be done. When glass lends itself so kindly to ornament it seems a sin to neglect it. Is it quite past praying for, that there may still be a future for windows merely ornamental, which shall yet satisfy the sense of beauty?

BOOK III.

CHAPTER XXVII.

THE CHARACTERISTICS OF STYLE.

WHAT are the characteristics of the various styles in glass? How does one tell the period of a window? These are not questions that can be fully answered in the short space of a chapter, which is all that can here be devoted to it: but it may help those to whom a window tells nothing of its date, briefly to mention the characteristics according to which we class it as belonging to this period or that. With a view to conciseness and to convenience of reference it will be best to catalogue these characteristics rather than to describe them.

Any sub-division of glass into "styles" must be more or less arbitrary. One style merges into the other, and the characteristics of each overlap, so to speak. The most convenient lines of demarcation are the centuries; for, as it happens, the changes in manner do take place more or less towards the century end. The one broad distinction is between Gothic and Renaissance.

Gothic may best be divided into three periods—viz., Thirteenth century and before, Fourteenth century, and Fifteenth century and after.

Thirteenth century glass, commonly called "Early English," or, as the case may be, "Early French," may as well be taken to include, for our purpose, what little remains of twelfth century or Norman work. It includes naturally Early German work, which is Romanesque and not Gothic in character.

Fourteenth century glass belongs to the Middle or Transitional Gothic period. We call it "Decorated," for the inadequate reason that its detail is naturalistic.

Fifteenth century glass, with us "Perpendicular," in France

"Flamboyant," in Germany "Interpenetrated," may, for convenience' sake, be taken to include so much of Gothic as may be found lingering in the sixteenth century.

The *Sixteenth century* is more properly the period of the Renaissance. It is better not to apply to it the Italian term "cinque-cento," since the greater part of it is not of the purely Italian character which that would imply.

Seventeenth century glass is to be distinguished from that of the sixteenth mainly inasmuch as it shows more markedly that decadence which had already begun to set in before the year 1600. It may be conveniently described as Late Renaissance.

213. ST. REMI, REIMS.

Eighteenth century glass is not of sufficient account to be classed.

It will be seen that the dates above given do not quite coincide with those of Winston, who gives Early English to 1280, Decorated to 1380, and Perpendicular to 1530. There is here no thought of impugning his accuracy; but it seems more convenient not to distinguish a new style until the work begins markedly to differ from what had gone before, especially when the marked difference happens conveniently to coincide with the beginning of a new century; and Winston himself says of Perpendicular work (and implies as much of Decorated) that the style "can hardly be said to have become thoroughly established" until the beginning of the new century.

We have thus a century of Middle Gothic, the fourteenth century. What goes before is Early Gothic or Romanesque, as the case may be; what comes after is Late Gothic, cœval for a quarter of a century or more with the Renaissance.

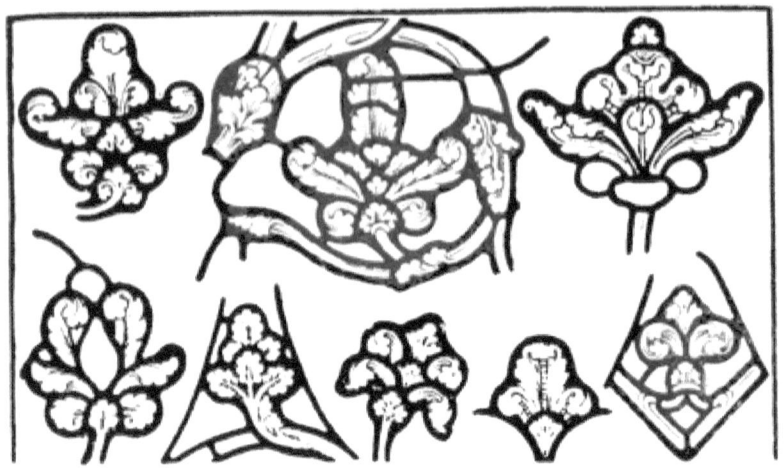

214. DETAIL FROM MEDALLION WINDOWS AT CANTERBURY.

EARLY GLASS.

The first thing which strikes one in Early Glass is either its deep rich, jewelled colour (Canterbury, Chartres), or its sober, silvery, greyness (Salisbury; Five Sisters, York). Exception to this alternative occurs mainly in very early ornamental glass (*circa*. 1300—S. Denis; S. Remi, Reims; Angers), in which white and colour are somewhat evenly mixed. Early figure work occurs also occasionally in colour on a white ground. The design of the richer class of windows consists largely of figure work. The design of "grisaille" windows consists mainly of ornamental pattern.

Composition.— Rich windows are of three kinds: medallion windows, rose windows, figure and canopy windows. Jesse windows form an exception. (Chapter XXIX.)

1. *Medallion Windows* are the most characteristic of the period (Chapter XII.). These contain figure subjects, on a quite small scale, within medallion shapes set in ornament (Canterbury, Chartres, etc.).

215. MOSAIC PANEL.

In the very earliest medallion windows (Angers, Poitiers) the ordered scheme of the medallioned window is sometimes interrupted by subjects not strictly enclosed in medallions. Or else, perhaps (Chartres), the subjects take the form of panels one above the other—they can scarcely be called medallions—with little or no ornament between.

After the first few years of the thirteenth century, however, the figure medallions (circles, quatrefoils, etc.) occur, as a rule, one above the other throughout the length of the light, with

216. DETAIL OF MEDALLION WINDOW, CHARTRES.

perhaps a boss of ornament between; the interstices being filled, in English glass with ornamental scroll work, in French with geometric diaper (opposite).

In the broad windows of Norman churches (pages 123, 124) the medallions are proportionately large, and are subdivided into four or five divisions, each of which is devoted to a separate picture. In our narrower lancet lights there is no occasion for that.

217. BARS IN MEDALLION WINDOWS.

The figures in medallion subjects are few and far apart, standing comparatively clear-cut against a plain background (page 325); compacter groups indicate a later period. Landscape is symbolised rather than represented by a conventional tree or so; a town by an arch or two, a battlemented wall, or the like.

Medallions are framed by lines of colour and beaded bands of white, but they do not, as a rule, separate themselves very markedly from their ornamental surroundings. The effect is one rather indeterminate glory of intense colour.

Except in quite the earliest medallion windows, the strong iron bars supporting the glass are, as a rule, bent (above), to follow the outline of the medallions. That was done in no other period.

2. *Rose Windows* occur mainly in French churches. They are a variation upon the medallion window. A great Rose window (Chartres, Bourges, etc.) may be regarded as a series of radiating medallion lights, with subjects relatively fewer in number, and a greater proportion of pattern work. Occasionally they consist of pattern work altogether. Smaller Roses (the only form of tracery met with in quite Early work) contain very often a central circular medallion subject, the cusps or foils round it being occupied with ornament, all in rich colour, even though the lights below it be in grisaille.

3. *Figure and Canopy Windows* (page 40) are more proper to the clerestory and triforium of a church, but they are not entirely confined to a far-off position.

With regard to them it should be mentioned that figures under canopies, sitting, or more often standing—one above the other in long, narrow lights—occur throughout the Gothic periods, and even in Renaissance glass. The characteristic thing about the Early ones is the stiffness and comparative grotesqueness of the figures and the modesty of the canopy. This last is of small dimensions. It may be merely a trefoiled arch (page 40). Usually it is more architectural (page 46), gabled, with a little roofing, and perhaps a small tower or two rising above, not beautiful. It is in fairly strong colours. It is so little conspicuous that it is not at first sight always distinguishable from the background to the figure. Occasionally the figure has no canopy at all. The saint stands front face, straight up in his niche, in a constrained and cramped position, occupying its full width, which is obviously insufficient. His feet rest in an impossible manner upon a label bearing his name: or, if that be inscribed upon a label in his hand, or on the background behind him, then he stands upon a little mound of green to represent the earth (page 40).

Figure and canopy alike are archaic in design, and rudely drawn. It is seldom that a figure subject on a smaller scale is introduced below the standing figure, as was frequently the case in later work. Groups of figures are characteristically confined to medallion windows.

The Border is a feature in Early glass. It is broad. In medallion windows it measures sometimes as much as one-fourth the width of the light. It takes up, that is to say, perhaps half the area of the window. It consists of foliated ornament similar in character to that between the medallions. Very broad borders occasionally include smaller figure medallions. In figure and canopy windows the borders are less, and simpler. Sometimes they consist merely of broad bands of colour interrupted by rosettes of other colours. Circumstances of proportion, and so on, influence the width of the border: but a broad border is characteristic of the Early period.

218. LE MANS.

259. CHARTRES.

In Rose windows the border is of less account, and is confined, as a rule, to the outer ring of lights, or, it may be, to their outer edge.

Detail.—Ornamental detail is severely conventional. In very Early work (page 327) it has rather the character of Romanesque ornament, with straplike stalks interlacing, often enriched by a beaded, zigzag, or other pattern, which may be either painted upon it or picked out of solid brown.

Early in the thirteenth century foliage assumes the simpler Gothic form, with cinque-foiled, or more often trefoiled, leafage (as here shown).

When it begins to be more naturalistic it is a sign of transition to the Decorated period. In Germany something of Romanesque flavour lingered far into the thirteenth century (page 330). There is properly no Early Gothic period there. Heraldry is modestly introduced into Early glass. The Donor is occasionally represented on quite a small scale in the lower part of a window, his offering in his hand; or he is content to be represented by a small shield of arms.

Colour.—The glass in Early windows is uneven in substance, and, consequently, in colour. This is very plainly seen in the "white" glass, which shades off, according to its thickness, from greenish or yellowish-white to bottle colour. The colour lies also sometimes in streaks of lighter and darker. This is especially so in red glass. The shades of colour most usually employed for backgrounds are blue and ruby. White occurs, but only occasionally.

The Early palette consists of:—

White, greenish, and rather clouded; red, rubylike, often streaky; blue, deep sapphire to palest grey-blue, oftenest deep; turquoise-blue, of quite different quality, inclining to green; yellow, fairly strong, but never hot; green, pure and emeraldlike, or deep and even low in tone,

260. AUXERRE.

221 PATCHWORK OF GRISAILLE, SALISBURY.

EARLY COLOUR AND GLAZING.

but only occasionally inclining to olive; purple-brown, reddish or brownish, not violet; flesh-tint, actually lighter and more pinkish shades of this same purple-brown. In very early work the flesh is inclined to be browner.

It must be remembered that, though the palette of the first glaziers was restricted, the proceeding of the glass-makers was so little scientific that they had no very great control over their manufacture. No two pots of glass, therefore, came out alike. Hence a great variety of shades of glass, though produced from a few simple recipes. They might by accident produce, once in a way, almost any colour. A pot of ruby sometimes turned out greenish-black. Still, the colours above mentioned predominate in Early work, and are clearly those aimed at.

Workmanship.—The glazing of an Early window is strictly a mosaic of small pieces of glass. Each separate colour in it is represented by a separate piece of glass, or several pieces.

222. S. KUNIBERT, COLOGNE.

The great white eyes, for example, of big clerestory figures are separate pieces of white glass, rimmed with lead, and held in place by connecting strips of lead, which give them often very much the appearance of spectacles (page 40). In work on a sufficiently large scale the hair of the head and beard are also glazed in white, or perhaps in some dark colour, distinct from the brownish-pink flesh tint peculiar to the period (same page). No large pieces of glass occur.

Upon examination the window proves to be netted over with lines of lead jointing, much of which is lost in the outlines of the design.

In large clerestory figures and the like, masses of one colour occur, but they are made up of innumerable little bits of glass, by no

223. S. KUNIBERT, COLOGNE.

means all of one shade of colour; whence the richness in tone.

Painting.—In Early glass painting plays a very subordinate part. Only one pigment is used, and that not by way of colour, but to paint out the light and define form.

Details of figure and ornament are traced in firm strong brush lines.

Lines mark the exaggerated expression of the face, the close folds of the spare drapery wrapped tightly round the figure, the serration of foliage, and so on (pages 33, 37, 324). Lines, in the form of sweeping brush strokes or cross-hatching, are used also to emphasise such shading (not very much) as may be indicated in

224. S. JEAN-AUX-BOIS.

thirteenth century work, or perhaps it should rather be said that the lines of shading are supplemented very often by a coat of thin brown paint, not always very easily detected on the deep coloured glass of the period.

White Windows, or "Grisaille."—Grisaille assumes in France the character of interlacing strapwork all in white. Sometimes this is quite without paint (page 25). Plain work of the kind occurs also with us; but it is dangerous to give a date to simple glazing. That at Salisbury (page 26) is probably not of the very earliest.

In France, as with us, such strapwork is associated with foliated detail, traced in strong outline upon the white glass and defined by a background of cross-hatched lines which go for a greyer tint (above).

After the beginning of the thirteenth century, this strapwork is sometimes in colour, or points of colour are introduced in the shape of rosettes, etc., and in the border (pages 137, 138).

In England there is from the first usually a certain amount of coloured glass in grisaille windows (pages 141, 332). Sometimes there is a considerable quantity of it (Five Sisters, York); but it never appears to be much. The effect is always characteristically grey and silvery.

So long as the painted foliage keeps closely within the formal

332

225. GRISAILLE, SALISBURY.

lines of strapwork, etc., it is, at all events in English glass, a sign of comparatively early thirteenth century work.

Later in the century the scroll winds rather more freely about the window (page 143).

The omission of the cross-hatched background and the more natural rendering of the foliation (page 386) announce the approach to the Decorated period.

Figure subjects in colour, planted, as it were, upon grisaille or quarry lights (Poitiers, Amiens), and grisaille borders to windows with figures in rich colour (Auxerre), are of exceptional occurrence.

Winston gives the year 1280 as the limit of the Early period, but there seems no absolute reason for drawing the line at that date. The use of stain, which was the beginning of a new departure in glass, does not pronounce itself before the fourteenth century. It seems, therefore, more convenient to include the last twenty years of the century in the first period, and to call it thirteenth century, accepting the more naturalistic type of foliage, when it occurs, as sign of transition; for, apart from that, the later thirteenth century work is not very markedly different from what was done before 1280.

FOURTEENTH CENTURY.

226. S. URBAIN, TROYES.

Decorated or Intermediate Gothic.—Decorated glass grows characteristically livelier in colour than Early glass; at first it becomes warmer, owing to the use of more yellow, then lighter, owing to the use of white. It does not divide itself so obviously into coloured and grisaille.

The figure subjects include, as time goes on, more and more white glass. The grisaille contains more colour.

Figures and figure subjects are now very commonly used in combination with grisaille ornament in the same window. That is a new and characteristic departure (page 159).

Composition.—Figure windows occur, indeed, with little or no ornament, in which case the subjects are piled one above the other, in panels rather than medallions, or under canopies. When the canopies are insignificant the result is one apparently compact mass of small figure work, as deep and rich perhaps in colour (S. Sebald's, Nuremberg) as an Early medallion window; but the colour is not so equally distributed; it occurs more in patches.

Decorated canopies, however, are usually, after the first few years, of sufficient size to assert themselves as very conspicuous patches of rather brassy yellow, which in a window of several lights (and windows now almost invariably consist of two or more lights) form a band (or if there are two or more tiers of canopies, a series of bands) across the window.

In the case of grisaille windows also, figures or figure subjects are introduced either in the form of shaped panels or under little canopies, and take the form of a band or bands of comparatively rich colour across a comparatively light window.

When these canopies are themselves pronounced, the window shows alternate bands of figures (rich), canopies (yellowish), and ornamental pattern (whitish). In any case these horizontal bands across the window mark departure from the earlier style.

Canopies.—Canopies occur now over subjects as well as single figures.

The canopy is designed in flat elevation. Any indication of perspective betokens the end of the period. It has broadish shafts, usually for the most part white, which terminate in pinnacles (page 155). It has seldom any architectural base: the figures stand upon grass or pavement. It has usually a three-cusped arch, and above that a pointed gable decorated with crockets and ending in a finial. Crockets and finial are usually in strong, brassy yellow. Above are pinnacles and shrine work in white and colour, including as a rule a fair amount of yellow.

It may rise to a great height, dwarfing the figure beneath it. This occurs very especially in German work.

Sometimes the most conspicuous thing in the window is

this disproportionate canopy. Its very disproportion is characteristic of the period.

In German work one great brassy canopy will frequently be found stretching right across the several lights of the window, over-arching a single subject. This triptich-like composition will occupy, perhaps, two-thirds of the height of the window. The background behind the pinnacles of this canopy may be either of one colour or of geometric diaper in mosaic (elsewhere characteristic of the Early period), finished off by a more or less arbitrary line—a cusped arch, for instance—above which is white glass. This kind of canopy has, by way of exception, an architectural base.

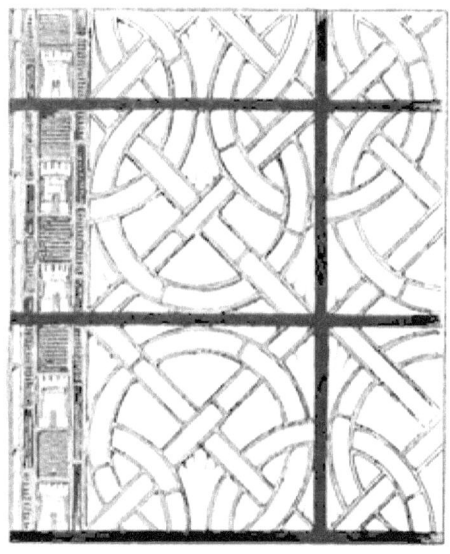

257. CHALONS.

Another German practice is to fill the window with huge circular subject medallions, occupying the entire width of the window, and intersected by the mullions.

Single-light windows have sometimes a central elongated medallion or panel subject (without canopy), above and below which is ornamental grisaille.

Borders.— All windows have, as a rule, borders; but they are narrower than in Early work.

Tracery lights, which now form a conspicuous part of the window, are, as a rule, also each separately bordered, often with a still narrower border in colour, or it may be only a line of colour.

Grisaille windows have usually coloured borders, foliaged or heraldic (as above). The border does not necessarily frame the light at its base; very often there is an inscription there. Between the coloured border and the stonework is still invariably a marginal line of white glass.

Sometimes, more especially in tracery, this white line is broad enough to have a pattern painted upon it, in which case there is no coloured border. Or this white border line may be enriched at intervals by rosettes or blocks of colour upon it. Or, again, it may be in part tinted with pale yellow stain.

Some such border is usually carried round each separate tracery light, with the result that Decorated tracery may usually be distinguished at a glance from later work by a certain lack of breadth about it.

There is no need to say more about Decorated tracery, seeing that the idea of this epitome is to enable

the amateur to form some opinion as to the period of a window, and not to prompt the designer. The geometric character of the stonework proclaims the period, and, unless there is something in the design of the glass to indicate a later date, it may be taken to belong to it. It cannot well be earlier if it fits.

Stain.—Yellow stain is proof positive that the glass is not much earlier than the fourteenth century, for it is only about that time that the process of staining white glass yellow was discovered. The occurrence therefore of white and colour upon the same piece of glass—*i.e.*, not glazed up with it, but stained upon it, is indicative of Middle or Late Gothic.

Stained yellow is always purer and clearer than pot-metal; when pale it inclines to lemon, when dark to orange. It is best described as golden. In comparison with it pot-metal yellow is brownish or brassy.

This yellow stain warms and brightens Decorated windows, especially those in grisaille. It naturally does away with a certain amount of glazing, for colour is now not entirely mosaic. Bands of yellow ornament in white windows, if stained, have lead on one side of them at most.

The hair of angels comes to be stained yellow upon white glass, which towards the fifteenth century takes the place of the flesh tint.

Figures.—Figures are still rather rudely drawn. They do not always fill out their niches, which, indeed, frequently overpower them. In attitude they pose and would be graceful. There is some swing about their posture, but it is often exaggerated. Drapery becomes more voluminous, fuller and freer, as shown opposite.

At the back of the figure hangs commonly a screen diapered damask-fashion—the diaper often picked out of solid paint.

Grisaille.—The distinguishing characteristics of Decorated grisaille are fully described in the chapter dealing with it. It has usually a coloured border. The foliated pattern no longer follows the lines of the white or coloured strapwork, but it does not interlace with the straps (pages 163, 333).

Coloured bosses adorn the centre of the grisaille panels. Frequently these take the form of heraldic shields, planted, as it were, upon the grisaille.

229. S. OUEN, ROUEN.

The practice of cross-hatching the background to grisaille foliage dies out in France and England. In Germany it survives throughout the period; or, it may be, the background is coated with solid paint, and the cross-hatching is in white lines scratched out of that.

Naturalism.—The foliation of the ornament is now everywhere naturalistic. That is the surest sign of the period, at first the only sign of change. In grisaille patterns and in coloured borders you can identify the rose, the vine, the oak, the ivy, the maple, and so on (pages 162, 166, 168).

In Germany, the design of ornamental windows consists often of naturalistic foliage in white and colour

15TH CENTURY GERMAN.

upon a coloured ground, the whole rich, but not so rich as Early glass (pages 171 et seq.). There also occur windows stronger in colour than ordinary grisaille, designed on lines more geometric than those of French or English glass of the period (page 170).

Colour.—Glass gets less streaky, evener, and sometimes lighter in tint, as time goes on. Flesh tint gets paler and pinker, and at last white; "white" glass gets more nearly white.

Much blue and ruby continue to be used; but more green is introduced, and more yellow, often the two in combination. In fact, there is a leaning towards combinations of green and yellow, rather than the red and blue so characteristic of Early glass. Green is frequently used for backgrounds. The pure bright emerald-like green gives way to greens inclining more to olive. In some German windows, green, yellow, and purple-brown predominate. Occasionally, in the latter part of the century, pale blue is modified by yellow stain upon it, which gives a greenish tint.

Painting.—Outline is still used; but it becomes more delicate. Shading is still smeared on with a brush. But in the latter half of the century it was the practice to stipple it, so as to soften the edges and give it a granular texture. This is not quite the same thing as the "stipple or matt shading" described on page 64, where the glass was entirely coated with a stippled tint and the lights brushed out.

Decorated glass is plentiful in England and Germany, not so abundant in France.

FIFTEENTH CENTURY.

Perpendicular Glass.—By the fifteenth century the glass painter had quite made up his mind in favour of more light. He makes use of glass in larger sheets, and of lighter and brighter colour. His white is especially purer than before, and he uses it in much greater quantities.

WELLS.

232 FIGURES, S. MARY'S, ROSS.

So decidedly is this so, that a typical fifteenth century window strikes you as a screen of silvery-white glass in which are set pictures or patches of more or less brilliant, rather than intensely deep, colour.

Design.—Design takes, for the most part, the form of figure and canopy windows, schemed somewhat on the same lines as in the Decorated period—the subjects, that is to say, cross the window in horizontal bands.

But there is so much white glass in the canopy work—it is practically all in white (as stone) touched with stain (as gilding)—and it so entirely surrounds the figure subjects, that you do not so much notice the horizontal bands (into which the subjects really fall when you begin to dissect the design) as the mass of white in which they are embedded.

Canopies.—The larger Perpendicular windows are now crossed by stone transoms, so that very long lights do not, as a rule, occur.

Each light has a canopy, without any enclosing border (233). The canopy stands, as it were, in the window opening, almost filling it, except that, above, behind the topmost pinnacles, are

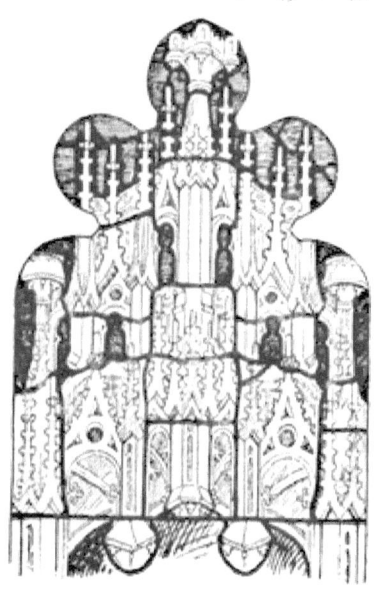

233. PERPENDICULAR CANOPY.

glimpses of red or blue background, not separated from the stonework by so much as a line of white, heretofore of almost invariable occurrence. The hood and base of canopy are shown in misunderstood perspective, indicating usually a three-sided projection (page 342).

Its shafts and base rest upon the ground, on which are painted grass and foliage, all in white and stain. When standing figures occupy the place of honour, the base may very likely include a small subject, illustrative of a scene in the life of the personage depicted above. Or the base may be a sort of pedestal (page 179).

The figures usually stand upon a chequered mosaic pavement in black and white, or white and stain, not very convincingly foreshortened (page 185).

In the canopy may be little windows of pot-metal colour, and in the base perhaps a spot or two of colour; but, whatever the amount of pot-metal (never much) or of stain (often a good deal), the effect is always silvery-white; and as time goes on the canopy becomes more solidly and massively white. The groining at the back of the niche just above the figures is a feature of the full-blown style. The vault is usually stained, less often glazed in pot-metal. There is more scope for this coloured groining in windows where the canopy runs through several lights. That is more common in France and Germany than with us. In English work each light has, as a rule, its own canopy.

In France, and more especially in Germany, the canopies are not seldom in yellow instead of white, golden in effect instead of silvery. Sometimes white and yellow canopies alternate (Nuremberg, Munich). The German canopy is often more florid, and less distinctly architectural than the English.

Perpendicular canopies are more in proportion to the figures under them than Decorated. Usually they are important enough to be a feature in the window, if not the feature. Sometimes, however, they are quite small and insignificant (East window, York), in which event the subjects appear more like a series of small panels, one above the other. In that case there is likely to be a large amount of white glass in the subjects themselves (pages 252, 339). Possibly the background is white. In any case, there is usually a fair share of white glass in the drapery of figures. The faces also are almost invariably white, often with stained hair; and this white flesh is characteristic of the period.

Until the turn of the century, landscape or architectural accessories are, to a large extent, in white and stain, against a blue or ruby ground.

Variety of colour in the background (or a further amount of white) is introduced by means of a screen of damask behind the figure, shoulder high, above which alone appears the usual blue or ruby background, diapered. The screen may be of any colour: purple-brown is not uncommon. When scale permits, the damask pattern is often glazed in colours, or in white and stain upon pot-metal yellow.

234. FIGURE AND CANOPY WINDOWS, BOURGES.

LATE GOTHIC STYLE.

225. FAIRFORD.

Heraldic shields are more conspicuous than ever in the design. Donors and their patron saints are often important personages in the foreground of the picture.

Tracery.—Tracery lights being now more of the same shape as the lights below, the glass is designed on much the same plan. That is to say, they also contain little figures under canopies. These are often entirely, or almost entirely, in white and stain, only here and there a point of colour showing in the background, more especially about their heads. Trefoiled, quatrefoiled, three-sided, or other openings not adapted to canopy work, have usually foliated ornament in white and stain, with border line of white and stain, the background painted in solid brown. Inscribed scrolls and emblematical devices in white and stain also occur in the smaller tracery lights.

Grisaille.—Grisaille takes almost invariably the form of quarries. The pattern of the quarries consists ordinarily of just a rosette or some such spot in the centre of the glass, delicately outlined and filled in with stain. A band of canopied figures sometimes crosses quarry windows, the pinnacles of the canopies breaking into the quarries above. Figures occur also often in white and stain, against a quarry ground, without canopy, standing perhaps on a bracket, or on a mere label or inscription band (York Minster). Occasionally we get subjects altogether in white and stain, without quarry glazing. In Germany unpainted roundels, or circular discs of white glass, take the place of quarries (page 292).

Detail of Ornament.—The detail of Perpendicular foliage is no longer very naturalistic; it has often the appearance of being embossed or otherwise elaborated. It is most commonly in white with yellow stalks.

Borders.—The border is no longer the rule, except in quarry windows. It is now very rarely used to frame canopies. Where it occurs it is usually in the form of a "block" border, differing only from that of the Decorated period by the character of the painted detail. Borders all in white and stain also occur.

The border does not follow the deeply cut foils of the window head. These are occupied each by its separate round of glass painted with a crown, star, lion's head, or other such device, in white and stain, against which the coloured border stops.

Stain.—Abundant use of beautiful golden stain is typical of the period. Stain is always varied, sometimes shading off by subtle degrees from palest lemon to deep orange. The deliberate use of two distinct tones of stain, as separate tints, say of a damask pattern, argues a near approach to the sixteenth century. So does the use of stain upon pot-metal yellow.

Other signs of the mature style are:—

1. The very careful choice of varied and unevenly coloured glass to suggest shading or local colour.
2. The use of curious pieces of accidentally varied ruby to represent marble, and the like.
3. The abrasion of white spots or other pattern on flashed blue (the abrasion of white from ruby begins with the second half of the century).
4. The introduction of distant landscape in perspective, and especially the representation of clouds in the sky, and other indications of attempted atmospheric effect.
5. The treatment of several lights as one picture space, without canopy.

Colour.—White glass is cooler and more silvery, more purely white. Red glass is less crimson, often approaching more to a scarlet colour. Blue glass becomes lighter, greyer; sometimes it is of steely quality, sometimes it approaches to pale purple. More varieties of purple-brown and purple are used. Purer pink occurs.

Drawing.—In the fifteenth century the archaic period of drawing is outgrown. Figures are often admirably drawn, more especially towards the end of the period, at which time the folds of drapery are made much of.

Painting.—Painting is much more delicate. The method adopted is that of stippling (page 64).

Figure and ornament alike are carefully shaded, quarry patterns and narrow painted borders excepted.

For a long while painters hesitated to obscure the glass much; they shaded very delicately, and used hatchings, and a

236 SCRAPS OF LATE GOTHIC DETAIL

LATE GOTHIC TECHNIQUE.

217. FAIRFORD.

sort of scribble of lines, to deepen the shadows. As a result the shading appears sometimes weak, but the glass is always brilliant.

With the progress of the century stronger stipple shading was used: more roundness and greater depth of shadow was thus achieved, at proportionate cost of silvery whiteness and brilliancy in the glass.

The characteristic of the later technique was that it depended less upon mosaic, and more upon paint.

Leads were not used unless they were constructionally unavoidable: and it was sought to avoid them. The nimbus, for example, was glazed in one piece with the head (page 189), stained perhaps, or with a pattern in stain upon it, to distinguish it from the face: or it showed white against the yellow hair.

From the lead-lines alone of an Early window, and of many a Decorated one, you could read the design quite plainly. The later the period the less that is so. By the end of the fifteenth century the lead-lines convey very often little or no idea of the picture, which they hold together but no longer outline. Canopies, for example, are sometimes leaded in square quarries, without regard to the drawing, except where that must be (page 342).

A pretty sure sign of period is afforded by the way the leads give, or do not give, the design. Exceptions are mentioned on page 73. Where leads seem to occur more or less as it happens, as though they might have been an afterthought, that is most positive proof of Late work.

SIXTEENTH CENTURY.

Renaissance glass does not, like Gothic, divide itself into periods. It was at its best when it was still in touch with mediaeval tradition.

The finest work in the new manner must be ascribed therefore

238. FRENCH RENAISSANCE, MOSAIC.

to the first half of the sixteenth century. After that its merits belong more to picture than to glass.

Apart from details of architecture, ornament (as above), costume and so on, which at once proclaim the style, it is difficult to distinguish between Gothic and Renaissance glass of the very early sixteenth century. The distinction does not in fact exist; for Gothic traditions survive even in work belonging, according to the evidence of its detail, to the Renaissance.

Design.—Design takes now mainly the pictorial direction. It spreads itself more invariably over the whole face of the window. The canopy, for example, is seldom confined to a single light.

Canopies.—The canopy scheme is at first not widely removed from Gothic precedent, although the detail may be pronouncedly Renaissance. It frames the subject as before; but it is less positively white. It is enriched with much more yellow stain; and the mass of white and stain is broken by festoons and wreaths of foliage, fruit, and flowers, medallions with coloured ground, ribbons, or other such features, in pot-metal colour. A simple François Ier canopy is given on page 349.

Sometimes these canopies consist rather of arabesque ornament than of anything that can properly be called architectural, in white and yellow (page 350), or perhaps all in yellow, upon a ground of pot-metal colour (page 205): that is to say, the setting out of the window and the technique employed are absolutely Gothic, and perhaps not even very late Gothic, whilst the detail is altogether Renaissance in design. This mosaic manner (as at Auch) bespeaks, of course, the early years of the Renaissance.

Another sure sign of lingering Gothic influence is where the round arch is fringed with cusping.

The more typically Renaissance form of design is where a huge monumental structure fills the greater part of the window, not canopying a subject, but having in front of it a figure group (Transept of S. Gudule, page 71). The foreground figures stand out in dark relief against the architecture and the sky beyond, seen through the central arch. Into this grey-blue merges very often a distant landscape, painted in great part upon the blue, and really seeming to recede into the distance. The effect of distance is largely obtained by contrast with the strong shadow of the soffits and sides of the arch seen in perspective.

We have here four characteristics of Renaissance glass:—
1. The monumental canopy with figures in front of it.
2. Strong contrast of light and shade.
3. Fairly accurate perspective in the architecture.
4. Something like atmospheric effect in the landscape, which is painted more or less upon the sky.

When in a canopy the shadowed portions of the architecture are glazed in deep-coloured glass (purple, as a rule), and not darkened by painting, it indicates the early part of the century. The canopy, instead of being arched, ends sometimes in a rich frieze and cornice (Church of Brou). When it is in two stages, enclosing two subjects, the lower one has naturally this horizontal entablature (Chapel of the Holy Sacrament, S. Gudule).

A less usual treatment is where the figures do not occupy the foreground, but are seen through the arch. The subject occupies, in fact, very much the position of a painted altar piece in a carved stone altar.

Foreground figures prove often to be donors and their patron saints. The head of the window above the great architectural canopy, as it is convenient to call it, is usually of plain white glass, glazed in rectangular or diamond quarries (page 71).

A coloured ground above a Renaissance canopy indicates Gothic tradition, and an Early period therefore (S. Jacques, Liege).

More to the latter half of the century belong the pictorial compositions in which architecture, more or less proper to the subject, fills great part of the window, the foremost arches adapting themselves, sometimes, to the stonework. In this case the architecture is in white glass, more or less obscured by painted shadow; and pot-metal colour occurs only in the figures, where it is perhaps quite rich, in occasional columns

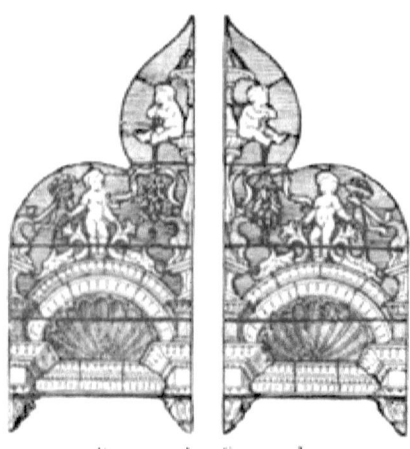

229. FRANÇOIS IER CANOPY, LYONS.

of coloured marble, and in a peep of pale-blue distance seen through some window or other opening (page 213).

The grey-blue distance has often figures as well as landscape and architecture painted upon it: to represent verdure it is stained green. Blue is more usual than white as a ground; but that also occurs, similarly painted. The not very usual landscape in white, with a blue sky above, in the windows of King's College Chapel, Cambridge, belongs to the early part of the century.

Tracery.—In small windows the subject, or its canopy, is often carried up into the tracery lights (page 368), or the architecture ends abruptly and horizontally at the springing of the arch, and the heads of the lights are treated as part of the tracery.

Tracery lights often contain figure subjects. Very commonly they are occupied by figures of angels robed in white and stain, or in rich colour, or with colour only in their wings, playing upon musical instruments, bearing emblems, scrolls, and so on, all on a coloured ground (page 280). There occur also, but less frequently, cherubic heads, portrait medallions, badges, twisted labels, or other devices, upon a ground of ruby, pale blue, purple, or purple-brown. A purple or purplish background is of the period.

Coloured grounds are used without borders. White grounds are usually diapered with clouds.

There is no very distinctive treatment of rose windows. They are filled as pictorially as they well can be. They contain, perhaps, a central subject and in the outer lights angels, cherubs, and the like, much as in other tracery lights.

Ornament.—The detail of their ornament is a ready means of distinguishing Renaissance windows. In place of Gothic leafage we have scrollwork of the marked arabesque or grotesque character derived from Italy. It needs no description.

SIXTEENTH CENTURY TECHNIQUE.

Screens and draperies have often patterns in white and stain on ruby and other coloured grounds, produced by abrading the red and painting and staining the white thus exposed. The process may be detected by the absence of intervening lead between the white or yellow and the deep ground.

Other damask patterns are stained on the coloured glass without abrasion, yellow on blue giving green, on purple olive, and so on.

Ornamental windows scarcely go beyond quarry work, with a border of white and stain. Except in quarry windows, borders are seldom used.

Grisaille windows scarcely occur. The little subjects in white and stain painted upon a single piece of glass, usually circular and framed in quarries or in a cartouche set in plain glazing (page 352), belong to a class by themselves.

Technique.—In many respects the technique of the Renaissance glass painter is only a carrying further of the later Gothic means. He uses more and more white glass, employing it also as a background; he uses more shades of coloured glass, especially pale blues, greens, and purples; he chooses his glass more carefully for specific purposes; he uses more coated glass, and abrades it; he makes greater use of stain, staining upon all manner of colours—ruby, blue, purple, green—and even painting in stain, and picking out high lights upon it in white. He paints delicate work more delicately. Flesh painting he carries to a very high point of perfection, more especially in the portraits of Donors. In strengthening his shadows he eventually gets them muddy. At first he used to hatch them to get additional strength; eventually he was not careful always so much as to stipple them. He uses often a warmer brown pigment for flesh painting, and by-and-by resorts to a quite reddish tint by way

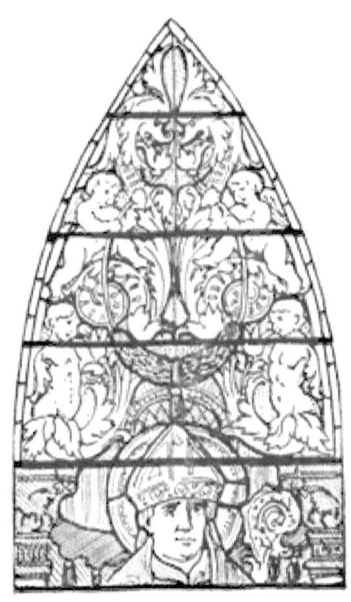

240. CHURCH OF S. PETER, COLOGNE.

S.G.

of local colour; he uses large pieces of glass when he can, and glazes his backgrounds and other large surfaces in rectangular panes. Above canopies he comes to use pure white glass, as if to suggest that the canopy is solid, and beyond only atmosphere.

The one quite new departure in sixteenth century technique was the use of enamel colour (see Chapter VIII.). That began to come into use towards the middle of the century. When you detect the least touch of enamel colour in a window, other than the pinkish flesh tint, you may suspect that it belongs to the second half of the century; when it seriously affects the design and colour of the window, you may be sure it does. But it is not until quite the end of the century that mosaic anywhere practically gives way to enamel painting.

The sixteenth century, therefore, includes, broadly speaking, all that is best in Renaissance glass and much that is already on the decline. There is a tide in the affairs of art; and after the full flood of the Renaissance, sweeping all before it, glazing and glass-painting sank to the very lowest ebb, out of sight in fact of craftsmanship. Only here and there, by way of rare exception, was good or interesting work any longer done,—as for example at Troyes, where good traditions, piously preserved in a family of exceptionally skilful glass painters, were followed long after they were elsewhere extinct.

241. S. JEAN, TROYES, 1675.

SEVENTEENTH CENTURY.

You may recognise seventeenth century work not so much by any new departure in design (except that it aims more and more at the effect of an oil picture, and that the portrait of the Donor and his family constitutes the picture) as by its departure from the old methods, the methods above described; by the introduction of pure white glass, glazed in geometric pattern, in the upper half of the window or, it may be, as a background; by the use of enamel paint instead of coloured glass; by the abuse of heavy shading (in the vain attempt to get chiaroscuro), and by a loss, consequently, of the old translucency and brilliancy; by the aggressiveness of the lead-lines (now that it is sought to do as much as possible without them); by the adoption of thin-coloured glass, toned by paint, instead of deep pot-metal; by the occurrence of whole panes of glass coated with solid paint; by the decay of the enamel; and by the general dilapidation of the window.

The unlearned must not be misled by the shabbiness of a window, by the breakages, the disfiguring leads which represent repair, the peeling off of the paint, and so on, into the supposition that these are signs

242. CERTOSA IN VAL D'EMA.

of antiquity. On the contrary, the very method of its making was the saving of Early glass, and Late work owes its vicissitudes largely to the mistaken process adopted in its execution, —by which you may know it.

It would be beyond the scope of a book about glass to go more thoroughly into the characteristics of style generally. Enough to indicate what more especially concerns the subject in hand.

Without some slight acquaintance with the course of art, it will perhaps be difficult to trace the development of glass design. Historical or antiquarian knowledge of any kind will make it more easy. Not merely the character of ornament or architecture, but the details of lettering, costume, heraldry, give evidence in abundance to those who can read it; but it is with art and craftsmanship that we have here to do.

The data given in this chapter and throughout are derived from the study of old work. Winston and other authorities have been referred to only to corroborate impressions gained by personal experience,—the experience only of a designer, a workman, a lover of glass, professing to no more learning than a student must in the course of study acquire. Nevertheless these few notes on what is characteristic in design and workmanship, may, it is hoped, be helpful to artists, craftsmen, students, and lovers of art, and perhaps sufficient for their guidance.

CHAPTER XXVIII.

STYLE IN MODERN GLASS (A POSTSCRIPT).

It is easy, and it is only too common a thing, for the designer to depend for inspiration over much upon old work ; but until he knows what has been done he is not fully equipped for his trade.

Moreover, a workman skilled only in his craft may be prolific in good work : one, on the other hand, learned only in archæology, is, in the nature of things, sterile. He may know as much about old glass as Winston, and fail as utterly even to direct design a-right as he did at Glasgow. The Munich windows there are glaring evidence as to what a learned antiquary and devoted glass-lover can countenance. Too surely the fire of archæological zeal warps a man's artistic judgment.

What, then, about historic style ? Are we to disregard it in our work ? That question may be answered by another : What about old work ? Old work, it is argued, should be our guide. Well, old work preaches no adherence to past styles. It went its own way, in delightful unconsciousness that the notion could ever occur to any one deliberately to go back to a manner long since out of vogue ; and when the idea of a Renaissance did occur to the artist, he very soon made it something quite different from the thing he set out to revive —if ever that was his deliberate intention.

It is too lightly assumed that " the styles " are there, ready made for us, and that all we have to do is to make our choice between them, and take the nearest to a fit we can find. So many of us only learn to copy, whereas the whole use of copying is to learn. Artists study style for information, not authority.

The truth is, no style of old glass is fashioned to our use. Early Gothic glass has most to teach us with regard to the mosaic treatment of the material, and perhaps also about breadth and simplicity of design ; but when it comes to figure drawing and painting, here is surely no model for a nineteenth century draughtsman. Renaissance work has most to teach in the way of painting and pictorial treatment: but it is not an exemplar of workmanlike and considerate handling of glass.

Because Early work was badly drawn, because Decorated was ill-proportioned, because Perpendicular was enshrined in stone-suggesting canopy work, because Renaissance was apt to depend too much upon finish, because seventeenth century work was overburdened with paint: must a man, therefore, according to the style of the building for which his work is destined, make it rude, misproportioned, stonelike, ultra-finished, or over-painted?

It happens that Early figure work in glass was mostly in deep rich colour. Are we to have no figures, therefore, in grisaille? It happens that later glass was, at its best, delicate and silvery in effect. Are we, therefore, to have no rich windows any more? Thirteenth century pictures were diminutive in scale. Are we to have no larger pictures ever? Sixteenth century subjects spread themselves over the whole window. Are we never to frame our glass pictures? And as to that frame, are we to choose once and for all the ornamental details of this period or that, or the formula of design adopted at a given time?

Whether in the matter of technique or treatment, of colour or design, no one style of old glass is enough for us. What does an historic style mean? Partly it means that during such and such years such and such forms were in fashion; partly it means that by that time technique had reached such and such a point, and no further. Must we rest there? If at a certain period in the history of design the scope of the glass painter was limited, his art rude, shall we limit ourselves in a like manner? If at another it was debased, ought we to degrade our design, just because the building into which our work is to go is of that date, or pretends to be? It was the merest accident that in the thirteenth century drawing was stiff and design more downright than refined, that the appliances of the glazier were simple, and the technique of the painter imperfect. It was an accident that silver stain was not discovered until towards the middle of the fourteenth century, that the idea of abrading colour-coated glass did not occur to any one until nearly a century later, that the use of the glass-cutter's diamond is a comparatively modern invention, and so on.

Out of the very scarcity of the craftsman's means good came: and there is a very necessary lesson to us in that; but to throw away what newer and more perfect means we have (all his knowledge is ours, if we will) is sheer perversity.

To affect a style is practically to adopt the faults and follies of the period. If you are bent upon making your glass look like sixteenth century work, you glaze it in squares, and introduce enamel. To treat it mosaically would be not to make it characteristic enough of the period for your pedant, notwithstanding that sixteenth century glass was, by exception, treated in a glazier-like fashion.

Should one, then, it may be asked, take the exception for model? The answer to that is: take the best, and only the best. It is no concern of the artist whether it be exceptional or of every-day occurrence; some kinds of excellence can never be common. Is it good? That is the question he has to ask himself.

With regard to the use of the forms peculiar to a style— Gothic Tracery or Renaissance Arabesque—that is very much a question of a man's temperament. Has he any sympathy with them? Does that seem to him the thing worth doing? If his personal bias be that way, who shall say him nay? Assume even that the conditions of the case demand Decorated or Italian detail, it does not follow that they demand precisely the treatment of such detail found in the fourteenth or the sixteenth century.

The style of a building is not to be ignored. To put, nowadays, in a thirteenth or fourteenth century church windows in the style of the fifteenth or sixteenth would be absurd; to put in a fifteenth or sixteenth century church windows in the style of the thirteenth or fourteenth, more foolish still. But it does not follow that in a church of any given century, the modern windows should be as nearly as possible what would have been done in that century.

No man in his senses, no artist at all events, ever denied that the designer of a stained glass window must take into consideration the architecture of the building of which his work is to form part. The only possible question is as to what consideration may be due to it.

The archæologist (and perhaps sometimes the architect) claims too much. Certainly he claims too much when he pretends that the designer of a window should confine himself to the imitation of what has already been done in glass belonging to the period of the building, or of the period which the building affects. Why should the modern designer submit to be shackled by obsolete traditions? What is his sin against art, that he should do this dreary penance, imposed by architectural or ecclesiastical authority? And what good is to come of it?

The unfortunate designer of modern glass is asked to conform both to the technique and to the design of glass such as was executed at the period to which belongs the building where his glass is to go, no matter how inadequate the one or the other, or both, may be. So far as technique is concerned, it can scarcely be questioned that the only rational thing to do, is to do the best that can be done under the circumstances.

That is equally the thing to aim at in design, simply one's level best. It seems strange that there should be two opinions on the subject. A building of some centuries past (or in that style) is to be filled with nineteenth century glass. Choose your artist: a man whose work has something in common with the sentiment of the period of the building, a man with education enough to appreciate the architecture and what it implies, with modesty enough to think of the decorative purpose of his work and not only of his cleverness; let such a man express himself in his own way, controlled only by the conditions of the case; and there would be little likelihood that his work would, in the result, shock either the feelings or the taste of any but a pedant—and if art is to conform to the taste of the pedant, well, it is time the artist shut up shop. Why will men of learning and research discount, nay, wipe out, the debt art owes to them, by claiming what is not their due?

Even though it were necessary or desirable that we should restrict ourselves to what might have been done in the thirteenth century or in the sixteenth, that would not argue that we must do only what was done. Surely we may be allowed to do what the men of those days might conceivably have done had they possessed our experience. Surely we need not go for inspiration to the glass of a period when glass was admittedly ill-understood, inadequate, poor, bad. It is quite certain that the thirteenth century workmen did not realise all that might be done in painted glass, quite certain that those of the seventeenth did not appreciate what might be done in mosaic glass. It would be sheer folly to paint no better than a thirteenth century glazier, because our window was destined for Salisbury Cathedral, to make no more use of the quality inherent in glass than was made by a painter of the seventeenth century, because it was designed for St. Paul's. Those who are really familiar with old work know that, even in periods of decline, work was sometimes done which showed no falling away from good tradition. You may find Renaissance glass almost as mosaic in treatment as thirteenth century work. But because that was comparatively rare, because the average work of the period was much less satisfactorily treated, modern Renaissance must, it is absurdly assumed, be on the same unsatisfactory lines.

Suppose we want modern Italian Renaissance, and, further, that we wish not only to retain the character of Renaissance detail but to get good glass, suppose also that we do not want forgery,—the thing to do would be, to inspire oneself at the very best sources of Italian ornament—carving, inlay, goldsmith's work, embroidery, no matter what (ornament is specifically mentioned because it is in ornament that the tyranny of style is most severely exercised), and to translate the forms thence borrowed into the best glass we can do. That, of course, is not quite so easy as appropriation, wholesale; it implies research, judgment, a thorough knowledge of glass; but it would certainly lead, in capable hands, to nobler work, and work which might yet be in the Italian spirit. The danger is that it would clash, not with Renaissance feeling, but with preconceived ideas as to what should be.

Our affectations of old style would be much more really like old work if they pretended less to be like it. Had the old men lived nowadays they would certainly have done differently from what they did.

An artist in glass cannot safely neglect to study old work, more especially in so far as it bears upon modern practice. It is for him to realise, for example, what artistic good there was in early archaic design, what qualities of colour and so on came of mosaic treatment, what delicacy is due to the liberty of the later Gothic glass painter, what fresh charm there was in the more pictorial manner of the Cinque-cento, and at what cost was this bought. Questions such as these are much more to the point than considerations of the date at which some new departure may have been made.

The several systems on which a window design was set out, the various methods of execution—mosaic and paint, pot-metal and enamel, smear-shading and stipple, cross-hatching and needlepoint, matting and diapering, staining and abrading—all these things he has to study, not as indices of period, but that he may realise the intrinsic use and value of each, that he may deduce from ancient practice and personal experience a method of his own.

Doubtful and curious points concern the antiquary not the artist. He had best keep to the broad highway of craftsmanship, not wander off into the byeways of archæology. Typical examples concern him more than rare specimens—examples which mark a stage in the progress of art, and about which there is no possibility of learned dispute. He wants to know what has been done in order to judge what may be done, and especially he wants to know the best that has been done.

The problem is how to produce the best glass we can in harmony with the architecture to which it belongs, but without especial regard to what happens to have been done during the period to which the architecture of the building belongs. We may even inspire ourselves at the sources of sixteenth century Italian art, and yet in nowise follow in the footsteps of the glass painters of the period, who were more or less off the track; we may set ourselves to do, not what they did (glass was not their strong point), but what they might have done. There, if you like, is an ideal worthy of the best of us.

If we pretend to be craftsmen we must do our work in the best way we know. If we are men, let us at least be ourselves. Let us work in the manner natural to us. If we undertake to decorate a building with a style of its own, let us acknowledge our obligation to it; let us be influenced by it so far as to make our work harmonious with it—harmonious, that is to say, in the eyes of an artist, not necessarily of a *savant*. Evidence of modernity is no sin, but a merit, in modern work. To see how a man adapted his design to circumstances not those of his own day, gives interest to work. We never wander so wide of the old mediæval spirit as when we pretend to be mediæval or play at Gothic. True style, as craftsmen know, consists in the character which comes of accepting quite frankly the conditions inherent in our work.

CHAPTER XXIX.

JESSE WINDOWS.

THE subjects depicted in stained glass tell the story of the Church, or preach its doctrine. Scenes from the Old Testament, from the Life of Christ, from the legends of the Saints, and so on, recur from the earliest Gothic times, and throughout the period of the Renaissance. These pictures accommodate themselves to the current plans of design, or the plan of design is chosen to suit them, as the case may be.

There is one subject, however, occurring from the first in glass, which does not fall into any of the usual schemes of design, and which, in fact, differs so entirely from any of them, that it forms a class of design apart. The subject, in fact, by way of exception to the rule, not merely affects but determines the decorative form of the window. This subject is the Descent of Christ—in short, the genealogical tree of the Saviour; and the window devoted to its delineation is called a Jesse window. Much freer and more varied scope for composition was offered by this piece of church heraldry than the ordinary medallion or figure and canopy window afforded, and the glazier turned it early to exceedingly decorative use. The tree is shown issuing, as it were, from the loins of Jesse. It bears his descendants, or rather a very arbitrary selection of them (it is as well not to inquire too strictly as to their legitimate right to be there), ending in the Virgin and the Saviour.

The earliest arrangement of a Jesse window is as follows: at the base is the recumbent figure of Jesse; the straight stem of the tree, proceeding from him, is almost entirely hidden by a string of figures, one above the other, occupying the centre part of the window, and represented, for the most part, as Kings; above them is the Virgin, also crowned; and in the arch of the window sits our Lord in Majesty, surrounded by seven doves, to signify the gifts of the Spirit. It is not perhaps quite clear upon what these figures sit. They hold on with both hands to branches of highly conventional Romanesque foliage, springing from the main stem, and occupying the space about the figures in very ornamental fashion. A series of half medallions on each side of this central design contain little figures of attendant prophets—in a sense, the spiritual ancestors of the Saviour. All this is in the deepest and richest mosaic colour, as in the beautiful bluish Jesse window at the West end of the cathedral at Chartres, which belongs to about the middle of the twelfth century. Very much the same kind of thing occurs at Le Mans and elsewhere.

Later the tree more often branched out into loops, forming oval or vesical-shaped spaces, in which the figures sat, as may be seen on page 362. The ground of the window is in that case blue, the background of the figure ruby. Had it been red the figures would probably have been upon blue. This particular instance, by the way, is said to be of the twelfth century, although the ornament has more the character of thirteenth century work. You see also the doves referred to encircling the figure sitting in Majesty, and the figures attendant upon the Virgin. Sometimes these are prophets, sometimes angels; sometimes they stand in little canopy niches, sometimes they are in the midst of the foliage. The fragment from Salisbury on page 117 formed most probably part of a Jesse window. The symbolic doves have often each a nimbus. A single dove represents, of course, the Holy Ghost.

A rather suggestive variation upon the orthodox Early scheme occurs in a window at Carcassonne. Each of the three lights is bordered with a rather geometric pattern. Within the border the central light is designed much on the usual lines : Jesse recumbent below, and above the figures of Kings, sitting each in his own little vesical-shaped space formed by the growth of the tree. In the side lights, however, the Prophets are provided with the very simplest canopies, one above the other.

An interesting arrangement is to be found in the clerestory of the cathedral at Tours, where the central light of a window has a Tree of Jesse, with the usual oval compartments, corresponding with hexagon-shaped medallions in the two sidelights, in which are depicted scenes presumably appropriate to the subject; it is difficult to make them out with any certainty.

Occasionally what seems at first sight a medallion window

243. PART OF EARLY JESSE WINDOW, MUSÉE DES ARTS DÉCORATIFS, PARIS.

resolves itself, as at S. Kunibert, Cologne, into a kind of genealogical tree, enclosing subjects illustrative of the descent of Christ. The rather unusual combination of medallion and vine shown below, also German, is of rather later date.

241. FREIBURG.

In the fourteenth century the tree naturally becomes a vine, usually in colour upon a blue or ruby ground, extending beyond the limits of a single light, and crossing not only the mullions, but the borders (which, by the way, often confuse the effect of a Decorated Jesse window). The vine extends also very often into the tracery, where sits the Virgin with the Infant Christ. The figure of our Lord is always, of course, the topmost feature of the tree— in the arms of the Virgin, in the lap of the Father, or sitting in Majesty. A variation upon ordinary practice occurs where the Father supports a crucifix. The figure of Jesse naturally, as at Shrewsbury (page 241), extends across several lights.

Occasionally a figure and canopy window proves to be also a Jesse window—a vine, that is to say, winds about the figures, and connects them with the figure of Jesse: but this combination of canopy work with tree work (as at Wells, some of the detail of which is given overleaf) is confused and confusing. A much happier combination of figures under canopies with tree work occurs in a sixteenth century window at S. Godard, Rouen, which has at the base a series of five figures, above whom spreads the tree, its roots appearing above the head of the central one, who proves to be Jesse.

By the fifteenth century the vine is rather more conventionally treated. It is usually in white and stain upon a coloured ground, or, if the leaves are green, the stems are white and stain. The figures also have more white in their drapery. In the earlier part of the century the main stem branches very often in an angular manner so as to form six-sided bowers for the figures, framing them, perhaps, in a different colour from the general groundwork of the window. Or the various lights of the window may have alternately a blue and a ruby ground. It is rarely that two figures are shown in the width of a single light, either in separate compartments or grouped in one.

Later the tree, oftenest in white and stain, branches more freely, not twisting itself any longer into set shapes or obvious compartments. The figures are, as it were, perched amongst its branches. In French and German work the tree, towards the sixteenth century, is not so necessarily a vine. It may take the form more of scrollwork, white or yellow, and the personages in its midst may be only demi-figures, issuing possibly from vase-like flowers or flower-like ornament.

That is so in a remarkably fine window in the clerestory of

245. PART OF A JESSE WINDOW, WELLS.

the cathedral at Troyes (three lights of which are shown on page 366), where the figures no longer occupy the centre of the lights, but are scattered about from side to side, balanced in a very satisfactory way by their names writ large upon the background. This characteristic lettering gives not only interesting masses of white or yellow on the ruby ground, but horizontal lines of great value to the composition. In the lower part of the window a separate screen of richest yellow marks off the figure of Jesse, and at the same time distinguishes the Donors, together with their family and their armorial bearings, from the merely scriptural part of the design. In earlier windows, it should have been stated, prominence is sometimes given to the really more important personages by drawing them to a much larger scale, or by showing them full-length when the others are only half-length, or by draping them all in white and stain, whilst the rest are in colours not so strongly relieved against the ground.

There are two other rather unusual Jesse windows at Troyes, both of Late Gothic period. The one is at S. Nizier: there the foliage is so rare as to give the effect almost of a leafless scroll. The other is at S. Nicholas: there the tree grows through into the tracery, where it appears no longer, as in the lights below, upon a deep blue ground, but upon yellow, the radiance, as it proves, from the group of the Trinity, into which the tree eventually blossoms.

Quite one of the most beautiful Jesse trees that exist is in a Late Gothic window at Alençon. It is unusual, probably unique in design. The figures, with the exception of Jesse, are confined to the upper lights and tracery, forming a double row towards the top of the window. This leaves a large amount of space for the tree, a fine, fat, Gothic scroll, foliated more after the manner of oak than acanthus leaves, all in rich greens (yellowish, apple, emerald-like) on a greyish-blue ground. It forms a splendid patch of cool colour, contrasting in the most beautiful way with the figures, draped mostly in purple, red, and yellow. The figures issue from great flower-like features as big as the width of the light allows, mostly of red, or purple, or white, with a calyx in green. The Virgin issues from a white flower suggestive of the lily. In the window shown on page 368 the tree blossoms also into a topmost lily supporting the Madonna. A characteristic feature about the Alençon

246. PART OF A JESSE WINDOW, CATHEDRAL, TROYES, 1499.

window is, the absence of symmetry in its scheme. Of the eight lights which go to make up its width, only three are devoted, below the springing of the great arch over it, to the Jesse tree. Three others contain a representation of the death of the Virgin, under a separate canopy, and in the two outermost lights are separate subjects on a smaller scale. This kind of eccentricity of composition is by no means unusual. A Jesse window very often occupies only one half or one quarter of a large Late Gothic window. And the strange thing is that the effect is invariably satisfactory, often delightful. You do not miss the symmetry, but enjoy the accidental variety of colour.

In sixteenth century work, and even before that, you meet with windows in which figures are in colours upon a white ground. In that case the tree is usually painted upon the white and stained. So it was in the beautiful Flemish window, parts of which are now dispersed over the East windows of S. George's, Hanover Square, calculated, there, rather to mystify the student of design. In it the grapes, it will be seen (page 216), are glazed in purple pot-metal colour. In the present condition of the window, now that the enamel-brown has partly peeled off, the grape bunches scarcely seem to belong to the rather ghostly vine behind them. That is a misfortune which not uncommonly happens where reliance has been placed upon delicate painting; but for all that this is noble glass, and the figures, as was also not uncommon at the period, are designed with great dignity.

There is distinction, again, in the drawing of the figures in the Jesse at S. Etienne, Beauvais, shown on page 368. That is a splendid specimen of characteristically Renaissance work. Jesse is honoured by a rich canopy of white and stain, which allows of a deep purple background separating him from his descendants. These appear as demi-figures, very richly robed, in strong relief against a pale purplish-blue ground of the atmospheric quality peculiar to the period. The vase-shaped flowers whence they issue are also in rich colour, dark against the ground, as are the variegated fruits and green leaves of the tree, but its branches are of silvery-white, suggesting of birch-bark. This tree-trunk is altogether too realistically treated for the ornamental leafage and still more arbitrary flowers growing from it; but it is a marvellously fine window, masterly

247 JESSE WINDOW, BEAUVAIS

in drawing and perfectly painted. And it owes positively nothing to age or accident. Indeed, the effect is somewhat diluted by restoration. Even on the reduced scale of the illustration given, you can detect in the head of the hatless figure to the right a touch of modern French character; and the fine colour of it all is fine in spite of the flatness of tint in the background, for which the nineteenth century must be held responsible.

Except for the confusion caused by the occasional introduction of canopies and borders, a Jesse window may be usually recognised at a glance. In the cathedral at Troyes, however, is what might be mistaken, at first sight, for a Jesse tree. But the recumbent figure is not that of Jesse, but of Christ. He lies, in fact, in the wine press, whence grows a vine bearing half effigies of the Twelve Apostles, and the patron saints of the Donor and his wife, who themselves had places in the lower portion of the sidelights, but the figure of the wife is now missing. The general design and effect of this window, and especially the seriousness of the ornamental portion of it, are such as almost to belie the period of its execution. It is an exceptionally fine window for the year 1625.

This same subject is anticipated in a sixteenth century window (1552) at Conches. There the Saviour treads the blue grapes, and a stream of blood-red wine issues from them. The frame of the press immediately behind him is designed to suggest the cross.

The Jesse window referred to in the north transept at Carcassonne is balanced by a window on the south, which is of peculiarly interesting design, not, to my knowledge, elsewhere to be found in glass, although it occurs in Early Italian painting. It represents the Tree of Life, of Knowledge of Good and Evil—which knowledge appears to be inscribed all over it and the window. It might almost be described as a tree of lettering, for it bears upon its branches (which are labels) and upon its fruit (which are heart-shaped tablets) voluminous inscriptions, not, in the present state of the glass, always easy to decipher, but most effectively decorative. On either side the window, by way of border to the outer lights, is a series of little figures, prophets, or whoever they may be, bearing other inscribed scrolls, mingling with the boughs of the tree, the leaves of which form, as it were, a kind of green and yellow fringe to the inscribed white branches. At the foot of the tree stand Adam and Eve, in the act of yielding to the temptation of the woman-headed serpent coiled round its trunk, and beyond are shown the Ark of Noah and the Ark of the Covenant. Amidst the upper branches is a crucifix, the narrow red cross so inconspicuous that the Christ seems almost to hang upon the tree, and at its summit is the emblem of the pelican, *Qui sanguine pascit alumnos*. This is altogether not only a striking, and, at the same time, most satisfactory window, but an admirable instance of the use of lettering in ornament. Lettering is very often introduced into Jesse windows, and forms sometimes a conspicuous feature in them; how much more use might be made of it is suggested by this Tree of Life.

CHAPTER XXX.

STORY WINDOWS.

THERE is something very interesting in the simple heartedness with which the mediæval artist would attack a subject quite impossible of artistic realisation, apart from his modest powers of draughtsmanship, or the limitations of glass.

The daring of the man may be taken as evidence of his sincerity. If he had not believed absolutely in the things he tried to pourtray, he could not have set them forth so simply as he did, not only in the quite archaic medallions of the twelfth and thirteenth centuries, but even in pictures conceived at the end of what we call the Middle Ages. It would be impossible nowadays to picture Paradise, as in the scene of the Temptation at Fairford (overleaf), with its bald architecture and little Gothic fountain, to say nothing of the serpent. But down to the sixteenth century no subject was impossible to the designer. Even the Creation did not deter him; on the contrary, it was a favourite subject in old glass, throughout the mediæval period (page 252): there is no shirking the difficulty of rendering the division of light from the darkness, or the separation of the waters from the dry land. Indeed, problems such as these are sometimes solved with very remarkable ingenuity, if not quite in a way to satisfy us: the Creator in the likeness of a Pope, triple crown and all, as at Châlons-sur-Marne, was pictured no doubt in all good faith and reverence.

Perhaps one of the most daring notions ever put into stained glass occurs in a window in All Saints' Church, North Street, York. The design illustrates an old Northumbrian legend called "The Pryck of Conscience," and boldly sets out to show—the fishes roaring, the sea a-fire, a bloody dew, and, as a climax, the general conflagration of the world. "Of heaven and hell I have no power to tell," wrote the "idle singer" (as he most wilfully miscalled himself) of this perhaps "empty day." It was left to the modern artist to discover that.

The subject most frequently affected by the designer of

the West window of a Gothic church was "The Last Judgment," in which appeared our Lord in Majesty, St. Michael weighing human souls, angels welcoming the righteous into heaven, and fiends carrying off the doomed to hell. These "Doom" windows, as they are also called, are not, to the modern mind, impressive— not, that is to say, as the pictures of reward and punishment hereafter they were meant to be. The scene strikes us invariably as grotesque rather than terrible, actual as it may have been to the simple artist, who meant to be a sober chronicler, and to the yet simpler worshippers to whom he addressed himself.

Apart from that, "Last Judgment" windows are among the most interesting in the church. The portion of the window, in particular, which is devoted to perdition is most attractive. Hell flames offered to the artist a splendid opportunity for colour, upon which he seized with delight. And the fiends he imagined! Doubtless those crude conceptions of his were very real to him, convincing and terror-striking. The grim humour which we see in them may be of our own imagining; but that the draughtsman enjoyed his creations no artist will doubt.

That is easy to understand. His subject allowed him freedom of imagination gave him scope for

98. THE TEMPTATION. FAIRFORD.

fancy, humour, colour; and all his faculties found outlet. No wonder his would-be fiends live beautiful in our recollection! In the midst of ruby flames dance devils, purple, black, and

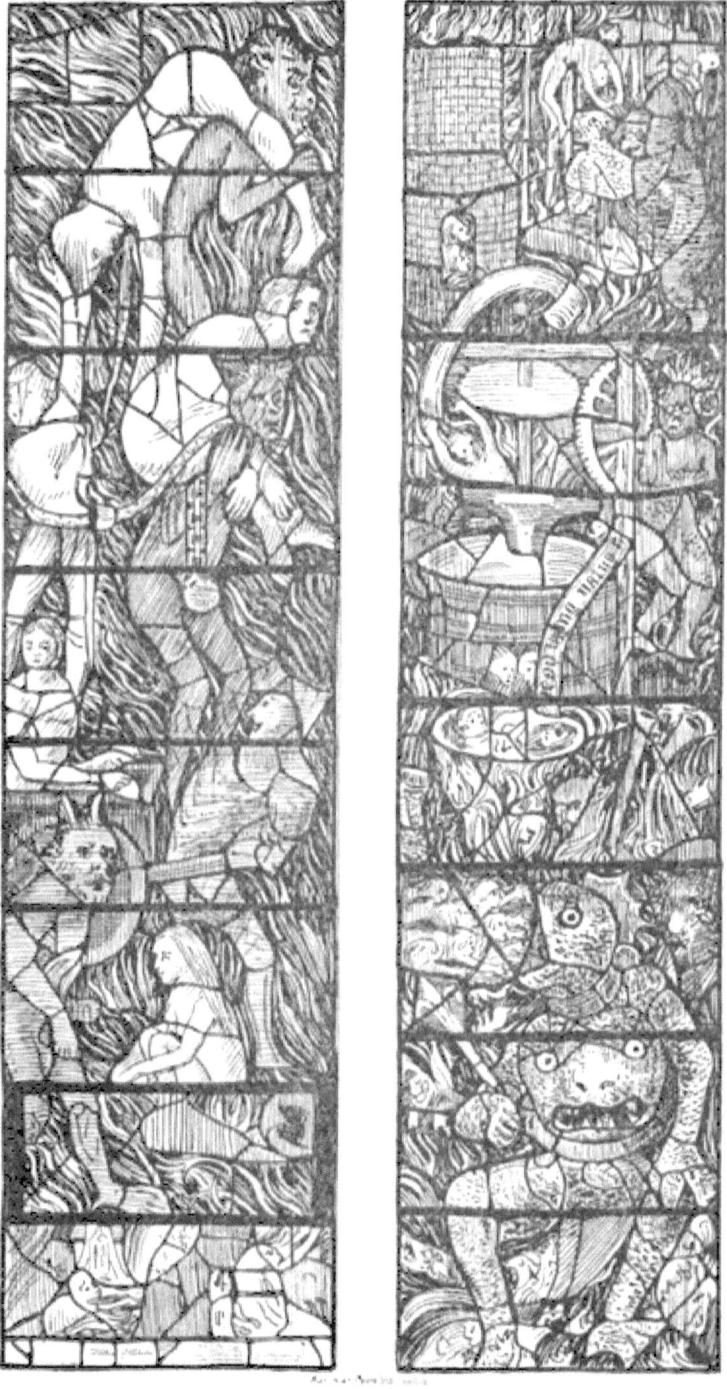

249 PART OF LAST JUDGMENT, FAIRFORD

brown, gnashing carnivorous teeth or yellow fangs, their beady, white eyes gleaming with cruelty. Devils there are apparently red-hot; others green and grey, with a beautiful but unholy kind of iridescence about them. As for the blue devils, they are beautiful enough to scare away from the beholder blue devils less tangible, which may have had possession of him. There is a great white devil in a window at Strasburg, who has escaped, it seems, from the Doom window near by, but not from the flames about him, a background of magnificent ruby. The drawing of a part of the Last Judgment from Fairford (page 373) gives only the grotesqueness of the scene, the quaintly conceived tortures of the damned; but that division of the glass is in reality a glory of gorgeous colour, to which one is irresistibly attracted. For that, as ever, the designer has reserved his richest and most glowing colour.

Some slight touch of human perversity perhaps inspires him also. At Fairford, at all events, he has put some of his best work, and especially some of his finest colour, into the figures of the Persecutors of the Church. Unfortunately, they are high up in the clerestory, and so do not get their share of attention; certainly they do not get the praise they deserve. Why, one is inclined to ask, this honour to the enemies of the Church on the part of the churchman? Was he at heart a heathen giving secret vent in art to feelings he dared not openly express? Not a bit of it! He was just a trifle tired of Angels, and Saints, and subjects according to convention; he was delighted at the chance of doing something not quite tame and same, and revelled in the opportunity when it occurred. In the tracery openings above the persecutors, where in the ordinary way would be angels, are lodged much more appropriate little fiends. They haunt the memory long after you have seen them, not as anything very terrific, but as bits of beautiful colour. The Devil overleaf, hovering in wait for the soul of the impenitent thief upon the cross, is not by any means a favourable specimen of the Fairford fiends.

Occasionally there is a grimness about the mediæval Devil which we feel to this day. In a window at S. Etienne, Beauvais, there is a quite unforgettable picture of a woman struggling in the clutches of the evil one. She is draped in green, the Devil is of greenish-white, the architecture is represented in a gloom of purple and dark blue; only a peep of pale sky is seen through the window. On the one hand, this is a delightful composition of decorative colour. On the other it is intensely dramatic. It sets one wondering who this may be, and what will be the outcome of it. The struggle is fearful, the fiend is quite frantic in action. One is so taken with the scene that one does not notice that his head is wanting, and has been replaced by one which does not even fit his shoulders. That the effect, for all that, is impressive, speaks volumes for the story-teller.

Alas, alas, the Devil is dead! His modern counterfeit is a fraud. You may see this at the church of S. Vincent, at Rouen, in one of the subjects representing the life of that saint, where he puts the devils to flight. The nearest of them is an evil-looking thing, ruby coloured, uncannily spotted, like some bright poisonous-looking fungus. The restorer has supplemented these retreating devils by a farther one painted on the grey-blue sky. The imp is grotesque enough, and very cleverly put in, but it plainly belongs no longer to the early sixteenth century. It suggests a theatrical "property," not the hobgoblin of old belief. That is just what the devilry in old glass never does.

250. FAIRFORD.

It must be owned that mediæval Angels charm us less. They are by comparison tame. Their colour is delicate and silvery, belike, but not seductive; their wings sit awkwardly upon them; they fulfil more or less trivial functions, bearing scrolls or emblems, shields of arms even. They are not in the least ethereal. They are too much on the model of man or woman. What possible business, for example, have they with legs and feet? Yet it is by the rarest chance that the body is, as it were, lost in a swirl of drapery, which, by disguising the lower limbs, makes the image by so much, if not the more angelic, at least the less obviously of the earth.

The glass hunter cannot but be amused every now and

again by odd anachronisms in mediæval and even later illustrations in glass. But wonder at them ceases when we remember how simple-minded was the craftsman of those days before archæology. If he wished to picture scenes of the long past—and he did—there was nothing for it but to show them as they occurred to his imagination—as happening, that is to say, in his own day; and that is practically what he did. He had perhaps a vague notion that a Roman soldier should wear a kilt; but in the main he was content that the onlookers at the Crucifixion should be costumed according to the period of William the Conqueror, or Maximilian, in which he himself happened to live. The practice had, at least, one advantage over our modern displays of probably very inaccurate learnedness, in that it brought the scene close home to the unlearned observer, and, as it were, linked the event with his own life. In short, there is more vitality in that rude story-telling than in the more elaborate histories, much less inaccurate in detail doubtless, to which to-day and henceforth artists are pledged.

There is no occasion to dwell upon the oddities of glass painting; they are those of mediæval art all through. If we take a certain incongruity for granted, the guilelessness of it only charms us. That same guilelessness enables the artist to make absolutely ornamental use of themes which to-day we might think it profane to make subservient to decorative effect. We never question his sincerity, though in the scene of the Creation, as at Erfurth, he made a pattern of the birds, pair and pair, each on its own tree. He can safely show the staff of S. Christopher, as at Freiburg, blossoming so freely as conveniently to fill the head-of the window and balance the Child upon his shoulder. According as it occurs to him, or as it suits his purpose, kings and bishops take part in the Crucifixion; S. Michael tramples upon a dragon big enough to swallow him at a mouthful; Abraham goes out, gorgeously arrayed in red and purple, to slaughter Isaac on a richly decorated altar, and a white ram, prancing among the green, calls his attention to itself as the more appropriate sacrifice; Adam and Eve are driven forth from Eden by a scarlet angel, draped in white, with wings as well as sword of flaming red. In this last case the peculiar colour has a significance. Elsewhere it implies the poverty of the glazier's palette, or indicates the sacrifice of natural to artistic effect. So it was that, till quite the end of the thirteenth century, we meet with positively blue beards, ruby cows, and trees of all the colours of the rainbow; and even at a much later date than that, primary-coloured cattle look over the manger at the Nativity, and Christ is shown entering Jerusalem on a bright blue donkey.

To the last the glass painter indulged in very interesting compound subjects—the Nativity, for example, with in the distance the Magi on their way; the Last Supper, and in the foreground, relieved against the tablecloth, Christ washing Peter's feet, the apostles grouped round so as to form part of each or either subject. Sometimes a series of events form a single picture, as where you have the Temptation, the Expulsion, Eve with her distaff, Adam with his spade, the childhood of Cain and Abel, and the first fratricide, all grouped in one comprehensive landscape.

Consecutive pictures, by the way, generally follow in horizontal not vertical series, beginning on your left as you face the window. There is no invariable rule; but in most cases the order of the subjects is from left to right, row after row, terminating at the top of the window.

From the beginning difficult doctrinal subjects are attempted, as well as histories and legends. In the sixteenth century the design is often an allegory, full of meaning, though the meaning of it all may not be very obvious. The Virtues, for example, no longer content to stand under canopies, systematically spearing each its contrasting Vice, harness themselves, as at S. Patrice, Rouen, to a processional car, in which are the Virgin, Christ upon the Cross, and sundry vases, preceded by the Patriarchs and other holy personages. Another interesting "morality," at S. Vincent, Rouen, is pictured in a medley of little figures each with descriptive label —" Richesse," for example, a lady in gorgeous golden array; "Pitie," a matron of sober aspect; "Les Riches Ingrass," a group of gay young men; "Le Riche" and "Le Poure," alike pursued by death. Another decorative device of the sixteenth century is the Virgin, lifesize, surrounded by her emblems and little white scrolls describing them—"Fons ortorum," "Sivit as Dei," and so on, in oddly spelt Latin. This occurs at Conches.

In Later Gothic, and of course in Renaissance glass, the

situation is, if not realised, at all events dramatically treated. One scarcely knows to which period to attribute the window at S. Patrice, Rouen, with scenes from the life of S. Louis, an admirably sober and serious piece of work. Conspicuous in it is the recurring mantle of the King, deep indigo coloured, embroidered with golden *fleurs-de-lys*, on an inky-blue ground. The whole effect is rich but strikingly low in tone. An exceptionally fine scene is that in which the King, in a golden boat with white sails, ermine diapered, a crown upon his head, kneels in prayer before a little crucifix, whilst his one companion lifts up his hands in terror: the man is clad in green; for the rest the colour is sombre, only the pale blue armour of the Saint, his dark blue cloak, for once undiapered—as if the artist felt that here the golden lilies would be out of place—and the leaden sea around: that extends to the very top of the picture, distant ships painted upon it to indicate that it is water. An inscription explains how :—

> "En revenant du pays de Syrie
> En mer fut tourmente . . . gde furie
> Mais en priant Jesu Christ il en fut delivré."

It must be allowed that the storm does not rage very terrifically; but the effect is not merely beautiful as colour but really descriptive, and something more.

It is only occasionally that this much of dramatic effect is produced; but touches of well-studied realism are common, as where, in the same church, at the martyrdom of a saint, the executioners who feed the fire shrink from the yellow flames and guard their eyes.

Decorative treatment goes almost without saying in the early sixteenth century. At S. Patrice, again, is a singularly fine instance of that. In the centre of the window, against a background of forest, with the distant hunt in full cry, S. Eustache stands entranced, his richly clad figure a focus of bright colour; facing him, in the one light, the legendary stag, enclosing between its antlers the vision of the crucifix, balanced, in the other, by the white horse of the convert: the note of white is repeated in the lithe hounds running through the three lights, and, with the silvery trunks of the trees, holds the composition together. This subject of the Conversion of S. Hubert was rather a favourite one in glass, and was usually well treated. The stag is invaluable. At Erfurth he stands against the green, a mass of yellow, with purple antlers, which form a vesica-shaped frame for the fabled vision.

The use of white, by the way, as a means of holding the window together is remarkable throughout Later glass, even apart from white canopy work. In the cathedral at Perugia there is a window in which a stream of white pavement flows, as it were, down through the groups of richly coloured figures, emphasising them, and at the same time connecting them with the canopy.

There is no end to the interest of subject in glass; but the subject would lead us too far astray from the purpose of this book. Enough has been said to indicate the kind of interest which each of us best finds for himself in glass hunting.

CHAPTER XXXI.

HOW TO SEE WINDOWS.

THE just appreciation of stained glass is more than difficult, and judgment with regard to it more than ordinarily fallible. It is too much to expect of a window that it should stand the test of a light for which it was not designed. The most conscientious artist can do no more than design it for the light by which he imagines it is most likely to be seen. There must inevitably be times of day, when the sun is in a position not favourable to it, and many days when the intensity of the light, even though it come from the right quarter, is not what he relied upon. It happens, of course, that glass is often seen under such conditions that the brilliancy of the windows on one side of the church is literally put out by a flood of light poured in upon them through the windows (brilliantly illuminated by it) on the opposite side. The best of critics could not appreciate the best of glass under circumstances like that.

Suppose the windows north and south of a church to be of equal merit, one's appreciation of them, at first sight, would depend upon the time of day; and the light which did most justice to the northern windows would do least to the southern, and *vice versâ*. Experience teaches a man to make allowances, but he can only judge what he has seen; and it is only with the light shining through a window that he can see its colour or judge of its effect.

The wonderful difference which the strength of the light makes in the appearance of a window, is nowhere quite so obvious as in the case of windows, not of glass, but of translucent alabaster—as, for example, at Orvieto, in the lower lights on either side of the nave, or, framed in black marble mullions, at the West end of the cathedral. The more or less square-shaped slabs of which they are formed are, in very many cases, made up of a number of pieces cemented together in lines which take very much the place of lead lines, and suggest, with the bars holding them in place, the practice of the glazier; but the effect is much less that of glass than of deepest amber in the unbroken panels, of gorgeous tortoise-shell in those that are patched and pieced together. These last are, if not the more beautiful, certainly the more interesting. The brown and gold and horny-white grow murkier when the light does not shine full upon the windows; but there is a mystery about the colour still, which makes up for the loss of brilliancy. If your mood is that way, you may find in the curious marbling of the stone strange pictures of cloudland and fantastic landscape. It is partly the shape, no doubt, of a circular slab high above the western door, which calls to mind the image of the moon with its mysterious mountains.

A more delicate, if not always so rich an effect, is to be seen in the great monolithic slabs which fill the five square-headed windows in the apse of the upper church at S. Miniato. Effect, did I say? Nay, rather effects, for they change with every gradation in the light. You may see at first little more than flat surfaces of pleasantly mottled white and purple-grey, translucent, but comparatively dull and dead. Then, as the sun creeps round the corner, a strange life comes into them. The white and palest greys begin to glow, and turn by slow degrees to pearly-pink, which kindles into gold, and deepens in the duskier parts to copper-red. The stronger markings of the stone now show out in unsuspected strength, and the lighter veins take on by contrast a greenish tint, so that the warm colour is subtly shot with its cool counterpart. If, when you first see the windows, the sun illumines them, the effect is less magical: you get your strongest impression first; but in the course of an hour or so a great change may take place—when, for example, towards noon the light passes away; but for a long while the stone remains luminous. Your eyes are open now, and in the delicate ashen-grey you see—or is it that you feel it to be there?—a tint of rose.

In proportion as it is less opaque than alabaster, glass is less perceptibly affected by changes of light; but, whether we perceive it or not, it owes all its effect to the light shining through it. The most fair-minded of us misjudge windows because we cannot see them often enough to be quite sure we have seen them at their best—that is to say, on the right day, and at the right time of day.

In comparing one window with another we are more than

ever likely to do injustice. Even if they happen to be both in the same church, the light most favourable to the one may, as just said, be quite the least favourable to the other. Each must in fairness be judged at its best; and it is no easy matter to compare to-day's impression with yesterday's, or it may be last week's—more especially when a newer impression of the same thing, staring you in the face, will stamp itself upon the vision. When years, instead of days, intervene, the justice of even the most retentive memory is open to gravest doubt.

Go to the church of S. Alpin, at Châlons, and in the morning you will find the East windows brilliantly rich: in the early afternoon, even of a bright day, they will be lacking in transparency, dull, ineffective. So at S. Sebald's, Nuremberg, the splendid fourteenth century glass on the north side of the choir proves absolutely obscure in the late afternoon. Grisaille, which was delicate under a moderately subdued light, will appear thin and flimsy with a strong sun behind it. It has happened to me to describe the same glass on one occasion as too heavily, on another as too thinly painted; and, again, to describe a window as warm in tone which memory (and my notes) had painted cool. On another occasion, well-remembered windows were not to be identified again. It seemed that in the course of a few intervening years they must have been restored out of all knowledge; a few hours later in the day there was no mistaking them, though they had, indeed, lost something by restoration.

When the most careful and deliberate notes tell such different, and indeed quite opposite, stories, notes made at times not far enough apart to allow for anything like a complete change of opinion on the part of the critic, it is clear that conditions of light go so far towards the effect of glass, that it is quite impossible to appraise it fairly the first time one sees it. The more momentary the impression on which one has to found an opinion, the more essential it is that we should choose the moment. The strongest light is by no means the most favourable to glass. In a glare of sunlight it is quite probable that some unhappy windows will have more light shining upon than comes through the glass. Happiest are the windows seen by "the subdued light of a rainy day." Occasionally a window, so deep that under ordinary conditions of light it is obscure, may need the strongest possible illumination ; but even in the case of very deep-toned windows—such, for example, as those in the transepts of the Duomo at Florence—the glass, as a whole, is best seen by a sober light. You get the maximum of colour effect with the minimum of hurt to any individual window, if there be any hurt at all. A really garish window may be beautiful as the light wanes. The great North Rose at Notre-Dame (Paris) is impressive at dusk.

Other conditions upon which the effect of glass largely depends are quite beyond our control. As a matter of fact, we rarely see it at its best. For one thing, we do not see it in sufficient quantity. We find it in here and there a window only, white light shining unmitigated from windows all round. Perhaps in the window itself there is a breakage, and a stream of light pours through it, spoiling, if not its beauty, all enjoyment of it. It is not generally understood how completely the effect of glass depends upon the absence of light other than that which comes through it. Every ray of light which penetrates into a building excepting through the stained glass does injury to the coloured window; more often than not, therefore, we see it under most adverse circumstances. It is worse than hearing a symphony only in snatches ; it is rather as if a more powerful orchestra were all the while drowning the sound. It takes an expert to appreciate glass when light is reflected upon it from all sides. The effect of some of the finest glass in Germany, as at Munich and Nuremberg, is seriously marred by a wicked German practice of filling only the lower half of the window with coloured glass and glazing the upper part in white rounds. That enables folk to read their Bibles, no doubt ; but the volume of crude white light above goes far to kill the colour of the glass. In such case it is not until you have shut off the offending light that it is possible to enjoy, or even to appreciate, the windows.

A comparatively dark church is essential to the perfect enjoyment of rich glass. The deep red light-absorbing sandstone of which Strasburg and Shrewsbury Cathedrals are built, adds immensely to the brilliancy of their beautiful glass.

White light is the most cruel, but not the only, offender. Old glass sometimes quarrels with old glass. An Early window is made to look heavy by a quantity of Late work about it, and a Late window pales in the presence of deep rich Early glass.

As for modern work, it is that which suffers most by comparison with old; but it arouses often a feeling of irritation in us which puts us out of the mood to enjoy.

Worst offence of all is that done in the name of restoration, where, inextricably mixed up with old work, is modern forgery; not clever enough to pass for old, but sufficiently like it to cast a doubt upon the genuine work, at the same time that it quite destroys its beauty.

Something of our appreciation depends upon the frame of mind in which we come to the windows. They may be one of the sights of the place; but the sight-seeing mood is not the one in which to appreciate. How often can the tourist sit down in a church with the feeling that he has all the day before him, and can give himself up to the enjoyment of the glass, wait till it has something to say to him? A man has not seen glass when he has walked round the church, with one eye upon it and the other on his watch, not even though he may have made a note or two concerning it. You must give yourself up to it, or it will never give up to you the secret of its charm.

CHAPTER XXXII.

WINDOWS WORTH SEEING.

THE course of the glass hunter seems never yet to have been clearly mapped out for him. Nor can he depend upon those who pretend to direct his steps. The enthusiastic description of the monograph proves in the event to have very likely no warrant of art; the paragraph in the guide-book is so cold as to excite no spark of curiosity about what may be worth every effort to see. Between the two a beginner stands uncertain which way to turn, and as often as not goes astray.

The question which perplexes him on the very outskirts of the subject is: Which are the windows to see? That depends. Some there are which every one who cares at all about glass should certainly see, some which the student who really wants to know should study, some which the artist should see, if merely for the satisfaction of his colour sense. To enumerate only a single class of these would be to write a catalogue; but catalogues are hard reading; the more interesting and more helpful course will be, to tell shortly of some of the windows best worth seeing, and why they should be seen. And if choice be made of instances typical enough to illustrate the history of glass, the list may serve as an itinerary to such as may think it worth while to study it, as it should be studied, not in books, but in churches.

Churches favourable to the study of Early glass in England are not very many. A series of thirteenth century windows is rare; and good examples, such as the fragments from the S. Chapelle, at South Kensington, are few and far between. The one fine series of medallion windows is at Canterbury Cathedral, in the round-headed lights of the choir. In the clerestory also is some figure work, on a larger scale, but less admirable of its kind. For good thirteenth century grisaille in any considerable quantity one must go to Salisbury, where, fortunately, the aisle windows are near enough to the eye to show the very characteristic patterns of the glass. To sit there in the nave and wait

251   GRISAILLE PATTERNS, SALISBURY.

until service is over, is no hardship even to the most ardent glass hunter. The silvery light from the windows facing him at the East end of the aisles is solace and delight enough. Yet more enchanting is the pale beauty of the Five slim Sisters, in the North transept of York Minster; that, however, is gained, to some extent, by the confusion of the pattern, which is not quite typically Early, but begins to show symptoms of a transition stage in design.

To appreciate at its full value the stronger colour of the Early mosaic glass one must cross the Channel. We have nothing in this country to compare in quantity, and therefore for effect, with the gorgeous glass illuminating the great French churches. Reims, for example, Bourges, Le Mans, are perfect treasure houses of jewelled light. But richer than all is Chartres. The windows there are less conveniently placed for study than at Le Mans, but they are grander, and more in number. At Reims the art is coarser, though the magnificence of certain red windows there lives in the memory. Emphatically Chartres is the place to know and appreciate thirteenth century glass. No other great church of the period retains so much of its original glazing; and since it is one of the largest, and the glass is very much of one period, it follows that no church contains so much Early glass. The impression it produces is the more pronounced that there is little else. Except for a modern window or two, one Late Gothic window, and some four or five lights of grisaille, which belong to the second period, the glass throughout this vast building is typically Early. It is well worth a pilgrimage to Chartres only to see it. You may wander about the church for hours at a time, unravelling the patterns of the windows, and puzzling out the subjects of the medallion pictures. To sit there in more restful mood upon some summer afternoon, when the light is softened by a gentle fall of rain, is to be thrilled by the beauty of it all. It is as though, in a dream, you found yourself in some huge cavern, lit only by the light of jewels, myriads of them gleaming darkly through the gloom. It is difficult to imagine anything more mysterious, solemn, or impressive. Yes, Chartres is the place in which to be penetrated by the spirit of Early mediaeval glass. There is a story told of a child sitting for the first time in his life in some French church, awed by the great Rose window facing him, when all at once the organ burst into music; and it seemed to him, he said, as if the window spoke. Words could not better express than that the powerful impression of Early mosaic glass, the solemnity of its beauty, the way it belongs to the grandeur of the great church, the something deep in us vibrating in answer to it.

Exceptionally interesting Early glass is to be found in the cathedral of Poitiers; but it is hurt by the white light from other windows. In the case of Early coloured windows it is more than ever true that their intensity can only be appreciated when all the light in the building comes through them. That intensity, as was said, is deepened where, as at Strassburg, the colour of the walls absorbs instead of reflecting light. There the red sandstone of which the church is built gives back so little light that, as you enter the door, you step from sunshine into twilight, in which the glass shines doubly glorious. Some of these (certain of the Kings, for example, on the north side of the nave, each with its huge nimbus eddying, as it were, ring by ring of colour, out to the margin of the niche) are of the thirteenth if not of the twelfth century: but they are typical of no period. The borders framing them are perhaps a century later than the figures. Indeed, the period of this glass is most perplexing to the student of style, until he realises that, after the great fire at the very end of the thirteenth century, remains of earlier glass, spared from the wreck, were incorporated with the newer work. And, not only this, but, what was rare in mediaeval days, the fourteenth century designer, in his endeavour to harmonise, as he most successfully did, the old work with the new, gave to his own work a character which was not of his period,—much to the mystification of the student, who too readily imagines that he cannot go far wrong in attributing to the glass in a church a date posterior to its construction.

The cathedral at Strassburg is rich also in distinctly Decorated glass, to all of which the tourist pays no heed. He goes there to see the clock. If he should have a quarter of an hour to spare before noon—at which hour the cock crows and the church is shut—he allows himself to be driven by the verger, with the rest of the crowd, into the transept, and penned up there until the silly performance begins. To hear folk talk of the thing afterwards at the *table d'hôte* you might fancy that Erwin Von Steinbach had built his masterpiece just to house this rickety piece of mock old mechanism.

Some of the most interesting glass of the Middle Gothic period is to be found in Germany, for tradition died hard there ; and, whilst thirteenth century glass was more often Romanesque than Gothic in character, that of the fourteenth often followed closely the traditions of earlier Gothic workmanship. The Germans excelled especially in foliage design, which they

252. 14TH CENTURY GERMAN GLASS.

treated in a manner of their own. It was neither very deep in colour nor grisaille, but midway between the two. The glass at Regensburg is an exceedingly good instance of this treatment : but instances of it are to be found also in the Museum at Munich, very conveniently placed for the purposes of study. The windows at Freiburg in the Black Forest should also be seen. But some of the very richest figure work of the period is to be found in the choir windows of S. Sebald's Church, at Nuremberg. Except for the simplicity of their lines these are not striking in design ; but the colour is perhaps deeper in tone than in the very richest of thirteenth century glass. The first impression is that the composition is entirely devoid of white glass ; but there proves to be a very small amount of hornytinted material which may be supposed to answer to that description. As the light fades towards evening these windows become dull and heavy : but on a bright day the intensity of their richness is unsurpassed. They have a quality which one associates rather with velvet than with glass.

Excellent Decorated glass, and a great quantity of it, is to be found at Evreux, and again at Troyes. The clerestory of the choir at Tours is most completely furnished with rich Early Decorated glass of transitional character—interesting on that account, and, at the same time, most beautiful to see. There is other Decorated work there with which it is convenient to compare it, together with earlier and later work more or less worth seeing. Again most interesting work, but not much of it, and that rather fragmentary, is to be found at the church of S. Radegonde, at Poitiers; but there was in France at about that time rather a lull in glass painting. In England, on the contrary, there is an abundance of it. There is good work in the choir of Wells Cathedral. Part of it is in a rather fragmentary condition, but it is all very much of a period: and there is enough of it to give a fair idea of what English Decorated glass is like. York Minster is rich in it. It is quite an object lesson in style to go straight from the contemplation of the Five Sisters, which belong to the latter part of the Early period of glass painting, into the neighbouring vestibule of the Chapter House, where the windows are of the early years of the Second Period, and thence to the Chapter House itself, where they are typically Decorated. The study of Decorated glass can be continued in the nave again, which is filled with it. Entering, then, the choir, you find mainly Perpendicular glass, much of it typical of English work of the Late Gothic period.

Other very beautiful Late Gothic work is to be found in some of the smaller churches of York, such as All Saints'. There is a window there made up of fragments of old glass, among which are some very delicately painted and really beautiful heads. This work is all characteristically English. English also is the glass in the Priory Church at Great Malvern. There is a vast quantity of it, too, which adds to its effect; but unfortunately, a great part of it now fills windows for which it was obviously not designed. This is the more unfortunate because, where it has not been disturbed, it shows unmistakable evidence of having been very carefully designed for its place. The tracery of the great East window is, for example, an admirable instance of the just balance between white and colour so characteristic of later Gothic glass. Again, the Creation window, amongst others, is a lesson in delicate glass painting.

Distinctly English in the delicacy of their painting are, again, the windows in the church of S. Mary, Ross. The far-famed windows of Fairford are, of course, not English. They were captured, the story goes, at sea, and brought to Gloucestershire, where a Perpendicular church was built to accommodate them. English antiquaries make claim that they are English, but internal evidence shows them to be Flemish or German. Considerable notoriety attaches to the Fairford windows owing to a theory which was at one time propounded to the effect that they were designed by Albert Dürer. The theory is now as dead as a back number, but the notoriety remains — and not undeservedly; for although this glass stands by no means alone, and is distinctly second to some contemporary work (such, for example, as that on the north side of the nave of Cologne Cathedral, which Dürer might conceivably have designed), it is remarkably fine; and it enjoys the comparatively rare distinction of practically filling the windows of the church. You not only, therefore, see the colour (which, rather than the painting, is its charm) at its best, but you have a complete scheme of decoration — Type answering to Anti-type, the Twelve Apostles corresponding to the Prophets, the Evangelists to the Four Fathers, and again

253. FAIRFORD.

the Saints opposed to the Persecutors of the Church. Most old glass owes something to the disintegration of its surface, and the consequent refraction of the light transmitted through it. In the Fairford glass the colours are more than usually mellow. The white, in particular, is stained to every variety of green and grey—the colour, as it proves, of the minute growth of lichen with which it is overgrown. It is said that, when the fury of iconoclasm was abroad, this glass was buried out of harm's way; which may possibly have hastened the decay of the glass, and so have given root-hold for the growth which now glorifies it.

It would not be easy to find finer instances of Late Gothic German work than the five great windows on the North side of Cologne Cathedral. There, too, one has only to turn right-about-face to compare early sixteenth century with nineteenth century German practice, and on precisely the same scale, too. Any one who could hesitate for an instant to choose between them, has everything yet to learn in regard both to glass and to colour. The garish modern transparencies show, by their obvious shortcomings, the consummate accomplishment of the later Gothic glass painters.

There is a very remarkable late Gothic Jesse window in the Lorenz Kirche at Nuremberg, and another almost equal to it in the cathedral at Ulm. The Tree of Jesse is very differently, but certainly not less beautifully, rendered in the fine West window at Alençon.

In most of the great French churches, and in many of the smaller ones, you find good fifteenth century work. At Bourges you have seven four-light windows and one larger one, all fairly typical. The best of them is in the chapel of Jacques Cœur, the Jack that built at Bourges quite one of the most remarkable of mediæval houses extant. But there is no one church which recurs before all others to the memory when one thinks of Late Gothic glass in France. One remembers more readily certain superlative instances, such as the flamboyant Rose window at the West end of S. Maclou, at Rouen, a wonder of rich colour, or the Western Rose in the cathedral there. The fact is, that the spirit of the Renaissance begins early in the sixteenth century to creep into French work; and, as glass-painting arrives at its perfection, it betrays very often signs of going over to the new manner. This is peculiarly the case in that part of France which lies just this side of the Alps; so much so, that a markedly mixed style is commonly accepted as "Burgundian." This is most apparent in the beautiful church of Brou, a marvel of fanciful Gothic, florid, of course, after the manner of the Early sixteenth century, extreme in its ornamentation, but, for all but the purist, extremely beautiful. The church itself is as rich as a jewel by Cellini, and infinitely more interesting; and the glass is worthy of its unique setting.

There is a very remarkable series of windows to see in the cathedral at Auch, all of a period, all by one man, filling all the eighteen windows of the choir ambulatory. Transition is everywhere apparent in them, though perhaps one would not have placed them quite so early as 1513, the date ascribed to them. A notable thing about the work is its scale, which is much larger than is usual in French glass of that period. Nowhere will you find windows more simply and largely designed or more broadly treated. Nowhere will you find big Renaissance canopies richer in colour or more interesting in design. The fifty or more rather fantastically associated Prophets, Patriarchs, Sibyls, and Apostles depicted, form, with the architecture about them and the tracery above, quite remarkable compositions of colour. And it is very evident that the colour of each window has been thought out as a whole. There is not one of these windows which is not worth seeing. They form collectively a most important link in the chain of style, without, however, belonging to any marked period. Indeed, they stand rather by themselves as examples of very Early Renaissance work, aiming at broad effects of strong colour (quite opposite from what one rather expects of sixteenth century French work), and reaching it. And though the artist works almost entirely in mosaic—using coloured glass, that is to say, instead of pigment—and depends less than usual upon painting, he yet lays his colour about the window in a remarkably painter-like way.

There are noteworthy windows at Châlons-sur-Marne, in the churches of SS. Madelaine and Joseph, which can be claimed neither as Gothic nor Renaissance, details of each period occurring side by side in the same window. At the church of S. Alpin at Châlons is a series of picture windows in grisaille, not often met with, and very well worth seeing.

Early sixteenth century glass is so abundant that it is hopeless to specify churches. Nowhere is the transition period better represented than at Rouen, and, for that matter, the Early Renaissance too. The church of S. Vincent contains no less than thirteen windows, with subjects biblical or allegorical, but always strikingly rich in colour. The choir is, you may say, an architectural frame to a series of glass pictures second to few of their period, and so nearly all of a period as to give one an excellent impression of it: the brilliancy of the colour, the silveriness of the white glass, and the delicacy of the landscape backgrounds is typical. Scarcely less interesting is the abundant glass in the church of S. Patrice, which carries us well into the middle of the sixteenth century and beyond; so that Rouen is an excellent place in which to study all but Early glass: there is not much of that to speak of there. Two exceptionally fine Renaissance windows are to be found in the church of S. Godard; and there are others well worth seeing whilst you are in Rouen, if not in every case worth going there to see, in the churches of S. Romain, S. Nicaise, S. Vivien, in addition to S. Ouen, S. Maclou, and the cathedral.

Yet finer Renaissance work is to be found at Beauvais—finer, that is to say, in design. One is reminded there sometimes of Raffaelle, who furnished designs for the tapestries for which the town was famous: these may very well have inspired the glass painters; but there is not at Beauvais the quantity of work which one finds at Rouen. The very perfection of workmanship is to be seen also in the windows at Montmorency and Ecouen (both within a very short distance of Paris): but, on the whole, this most interesting glass hardly comes up to what one might imagine it to be from the reproductions in M. Magne's most sumptuous monograph.

In a certain sense also the windows at Conches, in Normandy, are a disappointment. In a series of windows designed by Aldegrever one expects to find abundant ornament; and there is practically none. What little there is, is like enough to his work to be possibly by him; but one feels that Heinrich Aldegrever, if he had had his way, would have lavished upon them a wealth of ornamental detail, which would have made them much more certainly his than, as it is, internal evidence proves them to be. It would hardly have occurred to any one, apart from the name in one of the windows, to attribute them to this greatest ornamentist among the Little Masters. It is only the ornamentist who is disappointed, however, not the glass hunter. It is an experience to have visited a church like Conches, simple, well proportioned, dignified; where, as you enter from the West (and the few modern windows are hidden), you see one expanse of good glass, of a good period, not much hurt by restoration. The effect is singularly one. You come away not remembering so much the glass, or any particular window, as the satisfactory impression of it all—an impression which inclines you to put down the date of a pilgrimage to Conches as a red-letter day in your glass-hunting experiences.

There is magnificent Renaissance glass in Flanders, and especially at Liège, in which, for the most part, Gothic tradition lingers. Most beautiful is the great window in the South transept of the cathedral. The radiance of the scene in which the Coronation of the Virgin is laid, reminds one of nothing less than a gorgeous golden sunset, which grows more mellow towards evening when the light is low. In the choir of S. Jacques there are no less than five tall three-light windows, by no means so impressive as the glass at the cathedral, but probably only less worthy of study because they have suffered more restoration. The seven long two-light windows at S. Martin, though less well known, are at least as good as these. In most of them may be seen the decorative use of heraldry as a framework to figure subjects, characteristic of German and Flemish work. Very much of this character is the glass from Herkenrode, which now occupies the seven easternmost windows of the Lady Chapel in Lichfield Cathedral. They are pictorial, but the pictures are glass pictures, depending upon colour for their effect; and they are really admirable specimens of the more glass-like manner of the Early Flemish Renaissance. There is in the three windows at the East end of Hanover Square Church, London, some equally admirable glass, which must once have belonged to a fine Jesse window; but it has suffered too much in its adaptation to its present position to be of great interest to any but those who know something about glass.

All this work is in marked contrast to the not much later Flemish glass at Brussels—the two great transept windows, and those in the Chapel of the Holy Sacrament at S. Gudule, to which reference is made at length in Chapter VII. They are windows which must be seen. They are at once the types, and the best examples, of the glass painter's new departure in the direction of light and shade. On the other hand, the large East window at S. Margaret's, Westminster (Dutch, it is said, of about the same date), has not the charm of the period, and must not be taken to represent it fairly.

The brilliant achievements of William of Marseilles at Arezzo, and the extraordinarily rich windows in the Duomo at Florence, have been discussed at some length (pages 248, 268). They should be seen by any one pretending to some acquaintance with what has been done in glass. Other Florentine windows worthy of mention are, the Western Rose at S. Maria Novella, and the great round window over the West door at S. Croce, ascribed to Ghiberti. The transept window in SS. Giovanni e Paolo at Venice does not come up to its reputation. It is in a miserable condition, and as to its authorship (whence its reputation), you have only to compare it with the S. Augustine picture, which hangs close by, to see that it is not by the same hand. One of the multitudinous Vivarini may very likely have had a hand in it, but certainly not Bartolomeo. His manner, even in his pictures, was more restrained than that. There are a number of fine windows in the nave of Milan Cathedral, two at least in which the composition of red and blue is a joy to see. Earlier Italian glass is of less importance; the windows at Assisi, for example, are interesting rather than remarkable. They show a distinctly Italian rendering of Gothic, which is of course not quite Gothic; but to the designer they indicate trials in design, which might possibly with advantage be carried farther.

By far the most comprehensive series of Renaissance windows in this country is in King's College Chapel, Cambridge. In the matter of dignity and depth of colour, the small amount of rather earlier glass in the outer chapel holds its own; but the thing to see, of course, is the array of windows, twenty-three of them, all of great size, within the choir screen. It flatters national vanity, though it may not show great critical acumen, to ascribe them to English hands. Evidently many hands were employed, some much more expert than others. It seems there is documentary evidence to show that the contracts for them (1516-1526) were undertaken by Englishmen. Very possibly they were executed in England, and even, as it is said

254 RAISING OF LAZARUS, AREZZO

they were, in London. That they were not painted by the men who drew them, or even by painters in touch with the draughtsmen, is indicated by such accidents as the yellow-haired, white-faced negro, of pronounced African type, among the adoring Magi. It is as clear that the painter had never seen a black man as that the draughtsman had drawn his Gaspar from the life. Certain of the accessory scroll-bearing figures, which keep, as it were, ornamental guard between the pictures, might possibly have been designed by Holbein, who is reported to have had a hand in the scheme; but they are at least as likely to be the handiwork of men unknown to fame. But, no matter who designed the glass, it is on a grand scale, and largely designed. It is not, however, a model of the fit treatment of glass, though it belongs to the second quarter of the sixteenth century. For the designers have been more than half afraid to use leading enough to bind the glass well together, and have been at quite unnecessary pains to do without lead lines. The windows vary, too, in merit; and they bear evidence, if only in the repetition of sundry stock figures, of haste in production. Still, they have fine qualities of design and colour, and they are, on the whole, glasslike as well as delightful pictures. We have nothing to compare with them in their way.

To see how far pictorial glass painting can be carried, go to Holland. No degree of familiarity with old glass quite prepares one for the kind of thing which has made the humdrum market town of Gouda famous. Imagine a big, bare, empty church with some thirty or more huge windows, mostly of six lights, seldom less than five-and-twenty feet in height, all filled with great glass pictures, some of them filling the whole window, and designed to suggest that you see the scene through the window arch. They do not, of course, quite give that impression, but it is marvellous how near they go to doing it. No wonder the painters have won the applause due to their daring no less than to what they have done. Any one appreciating the qualities of glass, and realising what can best be done in it, is disposed at first to resent the popularity of this scene-painting in glass;—one measures a work naturally by the standard of its fame;—but a workman's very appreciation of technique must, in the end, commend to him this masterly glass painting. For the Crabeth Brothers, their pupils, and coadjutors, were not only artists of wonderful capacity, daring what only great artists can dare, but they had the fortune to live at a time when the traditions of their art had not yet been cast to the winds. Though working during the latter half of the sixteenth century, they were the direct descendants of the men who had raised glass painting to the point of perfection, and they inherited from their forbears much that they could not unlearn. Ambitious as they might be, and impatient of restraint, they could not quite emancipate themselves from the prejudices in which they were brought up. More than a spark of the old fire lay smouldering still in the kiln of the glass painter, and it flared up at Gouda, brilliantly illuminating the declining years of the century, and of the art which may be said to have flickered out after that.

This last expiring effort in glass painting counts for more, in that it is the doing not only of strong men but of men who knew their trade. It is extremely interesting to trace the work of the individual artists employed: which a little book published at Gouda, and translated into most amusing English, enables one to do. Dirk Crabeth's work is pre-eminent for dignity of design, his figures are well composed, and his colour is rich; although in the rendering of architectural interiors he falls into the mud, that is to say, into the prevailing Netherlandish opacity of paint. His brother Walter has not such a heavy hand: he excels in architectural distance, as Dirk does in landscape; and his work is generally bright and sparkling, not so strong as his brother's, but more delicate. Their pupils, too, do them credit, though they lack taste. Among the other more or less known artists who took part in the glass, Lambrecht van Ort distinguishes himself in canopy work, as a painter-architect might be expected to do; Adrian de Vrije and N. Johnson delight also in architecture, Wilhelmus Tibault and Cornelius Clok in landscape. Clok and Tibault compete in colour with the Crabeths, and go beyond them in originality.

Description of this unrivalled collection of later Dutch glass painting, except on the spot, is as hopeless as it would be dull. The windows must be seen. The men were artists and craftsmen, and their work is truly wonderful. Who shall attempt what these men failed to do? That is the moral of it.

The only other place where later glass is of sufficient worth to make it worth seeing, the only place where Seventeenth

century work arouses much interest, is Troyes. There is a quantity of it in the churches of S. Nizier, S. Pantaleon, and in the cathedral, attributed, for the most part, to Linard Gontier, who is certainly responsible for some of the best of it. But it is in the church of S. Martin-ès-Vignes, in the outskirts of the town, that it is to be appreciated *en masse*. There you may see some hundred and ten lights in all, executed during the first forty years of the seventeenth century. This is the place to study the decline and fall of glass painting—a melancholy sort of satisfaction. Here more thoroughly than ever must be realised how hopeless it is to evade in glass the glazier's part of the business: how powerless enamel is to produce effect; how weak, poor, lacking in limpidity and lustre, its colour is— and this even in the hands of an artist born, one may say, after his time. Gonthier was an incomparable glass painter. He could produce with a wash of pigment effects which lesser men could only get by laborious stippling and scratching; he could float enamel on to glass with a dexterity which enabled him to get something like colour in it; but he was not a colourist, nor yet, probably, a designer. The difference in the work attributed to him, and the style of his design (which is sometimes that of an earlier and better day) lead one rather to suppose that he adapted or adopted the designs of his predecessors as suited his convenience.

To see what glass painting came to in the eighteenth century you cannot do better than go to Oxford. You have there the design of no less a man than Sir Joshua Reynolds, painted by one of the best china painters of his day. None but a china painter, by the way, could be found to do it. It is not unfair, therefore, to compare this masterpiece of its poor period with the rude work of the fourteenth century, done by no one knows whom. And what do we find? Conspicuous before us is the great West window, which might as well have been painted on linen, so little of the translucency of glass is there left in it. It in no way lessens the credit of the great portrait painter that he knew nothing of the capacities of glass; that was not his *métier*. And there was no one to advise him wisely in the matter. But the result is disastrous. The beauty of his drawing—and there is charm at least in the figures of the Virtues—counts for little, as compared with the dulness of it all. It has neither the colour of mosaic glass nor the sparkle of grisaille. The white is obscured by masses of heavy paint, which, when the sun shines very brightly behind it, kindles at best into a foxy-brown; and even this is in danger of peeling off, and showing the poverty of the glass it was meant to enrich. Any pictorial effect it might have had is ruined by the leads and bars, which assert themselves in the most uncompromising manner. In short, the qualities of oil-painting aimed at are altogether missed, and the facilities which glass offered are not so much as sought.

It is no hardship to turn your back upon such poor stuff. And there, high up on the other side, are seven great Gothic windows. These are by no means of the best period. The design consists largely of canopy work, never profoundly interesting; the figures are, at the best, rudely drawn; some of them are even grotesquely awkward. Their heads are too large by half, their hands and feet flattened out in the familiar, childish, mediaeval way. In all the sixty-four figures there is not one that can be called beautiful. Yet for all that, there is a dignity in them which the graceful Virtues lack. They are designed, moreover, with a large sense of decoration. The balance of white and colour is just perfect, and the way the patches of deep colour are embedded, as it were, in grisaille, is skilful in the extreme. To compare them with the futile effort of the eighteenth century, opposite, is to apprehend what can be done in glass, and what cannot. The whole secret of the success of the mere craftsman where the great painter failed, is that he knew what to seek in glass,—colour, brilliancy, decorative breadth. He not only knew what to do, but how to do it; and he did it in the manliest and most straightforward way. Rude though the work, it fits its place, fulfils its function, adorns the architecture, gives grandeur to it. What more can you ask?

Domestic glass, such as that in which the Swiss excelled (window panes, many of them, rather than windows), is best studied in museums, whither most of it has drifted. There is no national collection without good examples. Better or more accessible it would be difficult to find than those in the quiet little museum at Lucerne—so quiet that, if you spend a morning there, studying them, you become yourself, by reason of your long stay, an object of interest. So little attention do these masterpieces in miniature glass painting attract, that the guardians do not expect any one to give them more than a passing glance; but they leave you, happily, quite free to pursue your harmless, if inexplicable, bent.

The list of windows worth seeing is by no means exhausted. In many a town, as at York, Tours, Troyes, Evreux, Bourges, Rouen, Nuremberg, Cologne, and in many a single church, you may find the whole course of glass painting, from the thirteenth to the sixteenth century, more or less completely illustrated; and, where that is so, of course one period throws light upon another. But the impression is always stronger when the century has left its mark upon the church.

Not until you have a clear idea of the characteristics of style, can you sort out for yourself the various specimens, which occur in anything but historic sequence in the churches where they are to be found. Having arrived at understanding enough to do that, you will need no further guidance, and may go a-hunting for yourself. To the glass hunter there are almost everywhere windows worth seeing.

CHAPTER XXXIII.

A WORD ON RESTORATION.

IF old windows have suffered at the hands of time, they have also gained, apart from sentiment, a tone and quality which the glass had not when it was new.

Their arch-enemy is the restorer, at whose hands they have suffered cruel and irreparable wrong. He is the thief who has robbed so much old glass of its glory, and a most impenitent one: there are times when any one who cares for glass could find it in his heart to wish he were crucified. So greedy is he of work, if not of gain, that restoration cannot safely be left even to the most learned of men; to him, perhaps, can it least of all be entrusted.

The twelfth century windows at S. Denis should be among the most interesting extant. They are ruined by restoration. The beauty which they may have had, which they must have had, is wiped out; and, for purposes of study, they are of use only to those who have opportunity and leisure to ferret out what is genuine amidst the sham. The S. Chapelle is cited as a triumph of restoration, an object lesson, in which we may see a thirteenth century chapel with its glass as it appeared when first it was built. If that is so, then time has indeed been kinder even than one had thought. No less an authority than Mr. Ruskin (in a letter to Mr. E. S. Dallas, published in the *Athenæum*) praises the new work there, and says he cannot distinguish it from the old. There is at least a window and a half (part of the East window, and the one to the left of that) in which, at all events, the old is easily distinguishable from the new. But if the new is not more obvious throughout, that is not because the new is so good, but because the old has been so restored that it is unrecognisable— as good as new, in fact, and no better. The old glass is so smartened up, so watered down with modern, that it gives one rather a poor idea of unspoiled thirteenth century work. A more adequate impression of what it must have been, may be gained from the few panels of it, comparatively unhurt by restoration, now in South Kensington Museum.

The story of destruction repeats itself wherever the restorer has had his way. Sometimes he has actually inserted new material if only the old was cracked, obscured, corroded; and has effaced the very qualities which come of age and accident. Sometimes he has indulged in a brand-new background. There, at least, it seemed to his ignorance, he might safely substitute nice, new, even-tinted, well-made glass for streaky, speckled, rough, mechanically imperfect material. Invariably he has thinned the effect of colour by diluting the old glass with new. Many quite poor new-looking windows, spick and span from the restorer (those, for example, at the East end of Milan Cathedral), turn out to contain a certain amount of old work, good perhaps, lost in garish modern manufacture. At Notre-Dame, at Paris, the considerable remains of Early and Early Decorated glass go for very little. One has to pick them out from among modern work designed to deceive. Certain windows at Mantes have suffered such thorough restoration that one begins to wonder if they are not altogether new; and you have precisely the same doubt at Limoges and at scores of other places. At Lyons an Early Rose has been made peculiarly hideous by restoration. Much of the harsh purple in Early French mosaic is surely due to the admixture of crude new glass. It is needless to multiply examples; they will occur to every one. All this old work swamped in modern imitation goes inevitably for nought. If the new is good it puzzles and perplexes one; if bad, one can see nothing else. What is crude kills what is subdued. It is as if one listened for a tender word at parting, and it was drowned in the screech of the steam-engine.

Early glass was so mechanically imperfect, and age has so roughened and pitted it, that its colour has, almost of necessity, a quality which new work has not; and one is disposed, perhaps too hastily, to ascribe all garish glass in old windows to the restorer. Many a time, however, the new work convicts itself. At Strasburg it is quite easily detected. You may check your judgment in this respect by surveying the windows from the rear. It is a very good plan to preface the study of old work by examining it from the churchyard, the street, the close, or in the case of a big church from its outer galleries.

The surface exposed to the weather, with the light upon it, explains often at a glance what would else be unaccountable. A vile habit of the restorer is to smudge over his glass with dirty paint, perhaps burnt in, perhaps merely in varnish colour; this he terms "antiquating."

The worse the new work added to the old, the more thoroughly it spoils it; the better the forgery, the more serious the doubt it throws upon what may be genuine. The modern ideal of restoration is thoroughly vicious. All that can be done is mending; and it should be an axiom with the repairer, that, where glass (however broken) can possibly be made safe by lead joints, no new piece of glass should ever be inserted in its place. Better any disfigurement by leads than the least adulteration of old work.

It is absurd to set good old work in the midst of inferior reproduction of it, as the common practice is, more especially in the case of Early work. Every bungler has thought himself equal to the task of restoring thirteenth century glass. It was rudely drawn and roughly painted. What could be easier than to repeat details of ornament, or even to make up bogus old subjects, and so complete the window? To paint figures anything like those in the picture windows of the sixteenth century was obviously not so easy, and the difficulty has acted as a deterrent. Where it has not, the discrepancy between old and new is usually unmistakable. Men like M. Capronnier, however, have sometimes put excellent workmanship into their restoration of Renaissance work, to be detected only by a certain air of modernity, which happily has crept into it, in spite of the restorer. But was it not he who flattened the grey-blue background to the transept windows at S. Gudule? The fine window at S. Gervais, Paris, with the Judgment of Solomon, has lost much of its charm in restoration. To compare it with the two lights in the window to the right of it, is to see how much of the quality of old glass has been restored away. That quality may be due in part to age and decay. What then? Beauty is beauty; and if it comes of decay (which we cannot hinder), let us at least enjoy the beauty of decay.

It has been proved at Strassburg that thirteenth or even twelfth century work may be quite harmoniously worked into fourteenth century windows. And even in the sixteenth century there were artists who managed to adapt quite Early mosaic glass to Renaissance windows, in which abundant stain, and even enamel, was used. The effect may be perplexing, but it does not deceive. Why will not a man frankly tell us what is new in his work? Then we could appreciate what he had done. But it is only once in a while that he takes you into his confidence. This happens, by way of exception, in a window at S. Mary's Redcliffe, Bristol, in the case of some figure work on quarry backgrounds, in which the new work is all of clear unpainted white or coloured glass, but so judiciously chosen that you do not at first perceive the patching. The effect is absolutely harmonious; and when you begin to study the glass, you do so without any fear that imposition is being practised upon you. Where the painting has in parts been made good, there is always that fear, as, for example, at S. Mary's Hall, Coventry: the windows have been restored with great taste: but one cannot always be quite sure as to what is modern.

The merest jumble of old glass, more especially if it be all of one period or quality, is far better than what is called restoration. Who does not call to mind window after window in which the glass is so mixed as to be quite meaningless, and is yet, for all that, beautiful? The Western Rose at Reims is an unintelligible jumble mainly of blue and green. It may not be design, but it is magnificent. Again, the Western lights at Auxerre, in great part patchwork, are simply glorious when the afternoon sun shines through.

At the East end of Winchester Cathedral is a seven-light window, reckoned by Winston to be one of the finest of a fine period. At the West end is an enormous window, which seems to be a mere medley of odds and ends. On examination you can trace in perhaps twelve out of forty-four lights of this last the outline of canopywork, and in two or three that of the figure under it; but for the rest, certainly in the two lower tiers (which are best seen), it is mere patchwork, including some quite crude blue, and a certain amount of common clear white sheet. The effect, when you examine it closely, is anything but pleasing. But as you stand near the choir screen on a not very bright morning, and look from one window to the other, the effect is just the opposite of what might have been expected. For the really fine East window has been restored; and, whether to preserve it or to bring old work and new into uniformity, it has been screened with sheets of perforated zinc! On the other hand, the really considerable amount of crude white and colour with which the West window has been botched is, so to speak, swallowed up in silvery radiance. Probably it helps even to give it quality; anyway, the effect is delightful. Indeed, it recalls the impression of the Five Sisters at York, or suggests some monster cobweb in which the light is caught. Beauty, forbid that any busybody should restore it! At Poitiers (S. Radegonde) is a grisaille window of the fourteenth century, all patched, defaced, undecipherable—mended only with thick bulbous bits of green-white glass—which is quite all one could desire in the way of decoration.

In very many churches there remain fragments of old glass in stray tracery openings, not enough to produce effect. The question has been what to do with them. A common practice is to use up such scraps in the form of bordering to common white quarry glass. That is

256. A RESTORATION AT ANGERS.

quite a futile thing to do. The effect of setting old glass amidst plain white is to put out its colour; and this, not only in the case of deep-coloured glass, but equally of Early grisaille; which when framed in clear glass, looks merely dirty. The most beautiful and sparkling of thirteenth century glass so framed would be degraded. At Angers are some windows consisting of a mosaic of scraps worked up into pattern (before the days of restoration as we know it); and the mere introduction amidst it of a strapwork of thin white sheet (above) is enough to take from it all charm of colour, all quality of old glass. Massed all together in one window, without such adulteration, the most miscellaneous collection of chips makes usually colour. In the

hands of a colourist it would be certain to do so. What if it
be confused? Mystery is, at all events, one element of charm,
and even of beauty.

It is not beyond the bounds of possibility to marry old work
with new; but the union is rarely happy. It wants, in the first
place, good modern glass. Further than that, it wants an
artist, and one who has more care for old work than for his
own. There is some satisfactory eking out old glass with new
at Evreux, where a number of small subjects, many of them

257. S. JEAN-AUX-BOIS.

old, are framed in grisaille, in great part new, in a very
ingenious way. At Munster is a window in which little tracery
lights (you can tell that by their shapes) are used as points of
interest in a modern composition—with a result, only less happy
than where, at S. Mary's Redcliffe, a window is made up almost
entirely of old glass, very much of one period, the more
fragmentary remains forming a sort of broken mosaic background to circular medallions, heads, and other important
pieces, arranged more or less pattern-wise upon it. Old glass
must needs be mended sometimes, patched perhaps; new may
have to be added to it; it has even to be adapted on occasion

to a new window, with or without the admixture of new; but none of this is restoration of the glass in the modern sense. That implies restoring it to what once it was—which is, on the face of it, absurd.

The effect of windows made up (as at S. Jean-aux-Bois, page 409) of segments of two or three old windows satisfies the artistic sense perfectly. What the restorer does is to take each pattern he finds in it for what he calls "authority," and to make two or three windows, all of which have much more the appearance of modern forgeries (which in great part they are) than of old work. The "antiquation" of the new glass in them deceives none but the most ignorant; but it does throw doubt upon the genuineness of the old work found in such very bad company.

If there remain enough old glass to make a window, let it be judiciously repaired; if there be not enough for that, let it be piously preserved, best of all, in a museum, where those who care for such scraps may see it: scattered about in stray windows in out-of-the-way churches they are practically unseen. Better than what is called restoration, the brutality of the mason who plasters up gaps in the clerestory windows of great churches with mortar, or the plumber's patch of zinc, which temporarily at least keeps out the weather and the crude white light, leaving us in full enjoyment of the colour and effect of old glass. How grateful we are when it is only cobbled, and not restored. Restoration is a word to make the artist shudder.

In a window at Auch, representing the Risen Christ, with, on the one side, the doubting Thomas, and on the other the Magdalene, the customary inscription, "Noli me tangere," is followed (in letters of precisely the same character) by the signature of the artist, Arnaut de Moles. It is the reverend Abbé responsible for the authorised description of the church, who suggests that it may have been with intention he signed his name just there. He has come off, as it happens, very much better at the hands of the restorer than most men. Had it been possible for him to foresee what nineteenth century "restoration" meant, well might he have written over his signature "Leave me alone"!

INDEX.

(The ordinary figures refer to the numbers of the illustrations, and those in black type to the pages of the book.)

ABRASION 60, 62
AIX-LA-CHAPELLE 14
ALABASTER windows 380, 381
ALENÇON 366
ANGELS 375
ANGERS 61, 62, 63, 256
  „ museum 168
  „ (S. Serge) 17, 85, 86
ANNEALING 63
ANTWERP 80, 82, 226, 227, 258
ARAB glass .. 19, 15, 16, 18, 19, 20, 21, 22, 23
ARCHITECTURE (due consideration of) 356
AREZZO 248, 41, 43, 181, 254
ASSISI 262, 53, 177, 187
AUCH 233, 280, 393, 410
AUGSBURG 118
AUXERRE 55, 75, 220

BACKGROUND 251
  „ (architectural) 209, 211
  „ (landscape) 209, 211
BARS .. 101, 113, 114, 122, 158, 267, 275
  „ (shaped) 68, 69
BEAUVAIS 374, 394, 247
BEVERLEY minster 74
BLACK PAINT (used for local colour) 89
BOLOGNA 264, 180
BONLIEU 11
BORDERS (Early) 114, 327
  „ (Decorated) .. 174—7, 335
  „ (Perpendicular) .. 190, 344
BOURGES 392, 70, 72, 234
  „ (S. Bonnet) 208, 157
BRABOURNE church 16
BRISTOL (S. Mary's) 407
BRITISH Museum 1

BROU 393
BRUSSELS (S. Gudule) 69, 79, 80, 233, 395, 42
BULL'S-eye windows 267

CAMBRIDGE (King's College) 216, 257, 396
CANOPIES (Early) 135, 313, 334
  „ (Decorated) 155, 197, 313
  „ (Italian) 264, 265
  „ (Perpendicular) 184 et seq., 340
  „ (Renaissance) 205, 221, 224, 225, 347
CANOPY (the beginning of the) .. 135
CANTERBURY 385, 23, 73, 79, 81, 214
CARCASSONNE 362, 369
CARTOUCHES 229
CHÂLONS 393, 12, 13, 98, 121, 122, 227
CHANTILLY 303, 160
CHARTRES 144, 387, 27, 71, 76, 103, 117, 216, 219
  „ (S. Pierre) 96, 115
CHETWODE church 201
CHOICE of glass 60, 101
CLERESTORY windows 283
CLOK (Cornelius) 399
COATED glass 49
COLOGNE 392, 147
  „ (S. Kunibert) .. 25, 28, 77, 222, 223
  „ (S. Peter) 240
COLOUR (Early) .. 122, 328, 330
  „ (Decorated) 338
  „ in quarry windows 287
  „ (Italian) 268, 270
  „ (Perpendicular) 346

CONCHES 394
CONFUSED effect 42, 134, 217
COSTA (Lorenzo) 264
COUTANCES 101
CRABETHS (the) 247, 399
CUTTING 8
" (economy of) 25

DA UDINE (Giovanni) 300
DECAY 219
DECLINE of glass painting 86
DECORATED borders 176, 335
" canopies .. 155, 313, 334
" colour 338
" composition 334
" figure design .. 157, 337
" grisaille 163, 337
" Jesse windows 363
" medallion windows .. 152
" quarries 290
" style .. .. .. 333—338
" tracery 278
DESIGN (banded) 160
" (Early) 36, 111, 112
" (effect of window shape upon) 113
" (essential conditions of) .. 96
" (Perpendicular).. .. 187, 340
DETAIL (ornamental) 328
DEVILS 374
DIAPER (geometric) 133
" (German) 171
" (painted or picked out) 35, 32, 33, 36, 49, 56
DONORS 221
" DOOM " windows 372
DRAMATIC effect 378
DRAWING 346

EARLY canopies 313
" colour 328, 330
" design 36, 111, 112
" English 327
" figures, their crudity 41
" glass (confusion in effect of) 42
" glazing 330
" grisaille .. .. 137 et seq., 408
" Jesse windows 362
" mosaic windows .. 32 et seq.
" ornament 40, 115, 130
" rose windows 273
" tracery 274

ECOUEN 394
ENAMEL 12 et seq., 77 et seq., 99, 232
" (influence of Byzantine) .. 17
" (objections to) 84
" (use of in ornament) 78
ENAMEL plus POT-METAL 79
ENGLISH (Early) 327
" (Perpendicular) 190
EVREUX 176, 177, 113, 118, 190, 191

FAIRFORD 374, 391, 34, 143, 144, 150, 173, 236, 237, 248, 249, 250, 253
FIFTEENTH century glass .. 322, 340
FIGURE-AND-CANOPY windows .. 326
FIGURE design 157, 337
FIGURES (Early) 41, 42
FIGURES and ornament .. 126, 319
FIVE Sisters (the) 146, 147
FLASHED glass 49, 50
FLESH tints 77, 106
FLORENCE 264, 270, 300, 179, 182, 183
" (Certosa in Val d'Ema) 202, 203, 204, 242
" (S. Maria Novella) 178, 199
FOURTEENTH century glass 322, 333
" " painting .. 47
FREIBURG 105, 126, 127, 244
FRENCH glass painting 75
" medallion windows .. 125

GEOMETRIC diaper (German) .. 171
" " (mosaic) .. 133
GERMAN foliated pattern windows 174
" geometric diaper 171
GLAZING 6, 15 et seq., 80, 82, 101, 229, 282, 168
" (Early) 330
" (economy in) 144
" (ingenuity in) 56
GLAZING plus PAINTING 43, 44, 53, 54
" in rectangular panes 80, 225
" shadows in pot-metal 72, 224
GONTIER (Linard) .. 80, 81, 229, 230
GOTHIC influence 203
" (Italian) 263
" landscape 253
" pattern windows 291
" tracery 280
GOUDA .. 223, 256, 258, 398, 401, 46, 161, 162, 165, 172, 176
GRISAILLE (Early) .. 137 et seq., 331, 408

INDEX.

GRISAILLE (Decorated) .. 163, 337
,, (Perpendicular) .. 192, 343
,, and colour .. 106, 120, 157

HERALDRY 198
HITCHIN church 21

INTERLACING 167
ITALIAN canopies 265
,, Gothic 263
,, glass.. 248, 260 et seq., 299

JESSE windows .. .. 360 et seq.
,, (Early) 362
,, (Decorated) 363
,, (Renaissance) 367
JEWELLERY (glass related to) .. 21
JOHNSON (N.) 399

KALEIDOSCOPIC effect 42
KING'S College, Cambridge.. .. 216, 257, 396
LANDSCAPE 209, 251, 256
LAST Judgment windows 372
LATE-GOTHIC pattern windows .. 291
,, ,, style 343
,, ,, technique 346
,, ,, tracery 280
,, ,, windows.. 178 et seq.
LATE-RENAISSANCE canopies .. 225
LEAD lines 38
,, outlines 23
LEADING (its influence on colour) 39
LEADS (contrivances for avoiding) 61, 62, 63, 97
,, (scheming of) 27, 28
LE MANS 20, 218
LICHFIELD 214, 395
LIÈGE 214, 395
LINCOLN .. 67, 93, 95, 185, 189, 192
LISIEUX 167
LOCAL schools 261
LONDON (S. George's, Hanover Square) 214, 159
LUCERNE 403
LYONS .. 26, 83, 84, 153, 188, 239

MALVERN 55, 37
MANY lights (windows of) 151 et seq.
MAP of a window 8
MARSEILLES (William of) 248
MATERIAL and design 107

MEDALLION windows 123 et seq..324, 325
,, ,, (Decorated) 152
,, ,, (French) .. 125
,, ,, of many lights 153
MEDIÆVAL artlessness 376
MENDING (judicious) 407
MIDDLE-GOTHIC glass .. .. 162 et seq.
MILAN 263
MISUSE of shading 68
MONTMORENCY 394, 40, 158
MOSAIC 5, 6
,, (marble and glass) 29
,, diaper 133
MULLIONS 151, 195, 197, 198, 240, 272
MUNICH museum .. 124, 128, 129, 131

NATURALISM 337
NEEDLE-POINT work .. .. 87 et seq.
NETHERLANDISH glass 73, 302
NEW departures 109
NIMBUS (the) 208
NORBURY 114
NUREMBERG 224, 125
,, (S. Lorenz) 164
,, (S. Sebald).. 163

OBSCURATION 68, 79, 82
OLD work (the spirit of) 358
ORNAMENT (a plea for) .. 317 et seq.
,, (Early).. .. 40, 115, 130
,, (Decorated).. 160
,, (Perpendicular).. .. 343
,, (possibilities in).. .. 321
,, (Renaissance) 349
ORVIETO 380, 19
OXFORD (All Souls' College).. 35, 141
,, (New College) 179, 401, 48, 109, 137

PAINT (brushing out) 64
,, (early use of) 33
,, (first use of) 11
PAINT as local colour 57
PAINTED mosaic glass .. 43 et seq.
PAINTER as glass designer (the) 69
PAINTING 6, 44, 45, 47, 53, 59 et seq., 64, 68, 85, 89, 103, 105, 190, 211, 247, 263, 331, 338, 346
PAINTING out .. 11, 34, 35, 44, 45, 278
PALETTE (the early) 328
PARIS (Louvre) 208
,, (Musée des Arts Décoratifs), 243

PARIS (S. Eustache) 223
  ,,   (S. Gervais) 166
PATTERN windows (German) .. 174
  ,,   ,,   (Late Gothic) 291
PECKITT 233
PERPENDICULAR 340
  ,,   (English) .. 188, 190
  ,,   (German) 188
PERPENDICULAR borders 344
  ,,   canopies .. 184, 340
  ,,   colour 346
  ,,   design 187, 340
  ,,   detail 343
  ,,   drawing 346
  ,,   grisaille 343
  ,,   ornament 343
  ,,   style 340
  ,,   tracery 278, 279, 343
PICKING out 35, 103
PICTORIAL *versus* DECORATIVE .. 238
PICTURE (achievement in) 250
  ,, (the ideal glass) 246
PICTURES (a medley of) 195
PICTURE-WINDOWS .. .. 236 *et seq*.
PISA 263
PLAIN glazing .. 226, 166, 167
  ,,   ,, and painted grisaille 139
POICTIERS 388, 24, 58, 59, 60
POSSIBILITIES in the way of ornament 321
POT-METAL 5
PRATO 184

QUARRIES .. 146, 168, 192, 283 *et seq*.
QUARRY-LIKE patterns 169
QUARRY windows (colour in) .. 287

REGENSBURG .. 389, 123, 128, 131, 252
REIMS 92, 99
  ,, (S. Remi) .. 118, 22, 65, 66, 213
RENAISSANCE canopies .. 205, 347
  ,,   ,,   (Late) .. 225
RENAISSANCE Jesse windows .. 367
  ,,   landscape 255
  ,,   ornament.. 349
  ,,   tracery .. 280-282, 349
RESOURCES of the glass painter, 95 *et seq*.
RESTORATION .. .. .. 404 *et seq*.
REYNOLDS (Sir Joshua) .. 401, 402
ROSE windows .. .. 272 *et seq*. 326
  ,,   ,, (Early) 273

ROSS (S. Mary) 55, 145, 232
ROUEN 392, 394, 45, 119, 238
  ,, (S Godard).. 154
  ,, (S. Ouen) 29, 229
  ,, (S. Patrice).. .. 377, 378, 155
  ,, (S. Vincent) 375, 377, 44, 156, 175
ROUNDELS .. 293, 199

S. DENIS 404
S. JEAN-AUX-BOIS 87, 88, 100, 224, 257
S. MINIATO 381
SALISBURY 385, 15, 30, 64, 97, 102, 221, 225, 251
SCRAPS 409
SENS 90
SEVENTEENTH century glass 233, 323
  ,,   ,,   style .. 352
SHADING (misuse of) 68, 70, 73, 79, 80, 247
  ,, (the beginning of) .. 13, 45
SHREWSBURY 38, 39, 57, 139, 142, 152, 171, 174
SILVER stain 52
SINGLE-FIGURE windows .. 118, 197
SIXTEENTH century glass .. 323, 347
  ,,   ,,   style 348
  ,,   ,,   technique .. 350
  ,,   ,,   windows 201 *et seq*.
SOISSONS 89, 91
SOUTH KENSINGTON Museum .. 205
STAIN 50, 52, 60, 61, 62, 105, 182, 336, 344
STANTON S. John 120
STORIED windows 195, 209, 371 *et seq*.
STRASBURG 388, 134
STYLE .. 111, 112, 156, 177, 178, 323
  ,, (Early) 324
  ,, (Decorated) 335, 338
  ,, (Late Gothic) 343
  ,, (Perpendicular) 340
  ,, (16th century) 348
  ,, (17th century) 352
  ,, (the characteristics of) 322 *et seq*.
  ,, in modern glass .. 354 *et seq*.
SUBJECTS not within mullions .. 198
SUBJECT-WINDOWS 197
SWISS glass 87, 94, 308

THIRTEENTH century glass .. 322
  ,,   ,,   ornament .. 130
TIBALDI (Pellegrino) 264

Tibault (Wilhelmus) 399	Van Linge 233
Time of day to see windows (the) 382	Van Orley (Bernard) .. 69, 222, 245
Tours 362, 389	Van Ort (Lambrecht) 399
Tracery (Early) 274	Van Thulden 233
,, (Decorated) 278	Verona (S. Anastasia) 199
,, (Gothic) 280	Warwick Castle 54, 206, 209
,, (Perpendicular) 343	Water Perry 94
,, (Renaissance) .. 280-2, 349	Wells 390, 136, 231, 245
Tracery lights .. .. 272 *et seq.*	White and colour (combination of) 193
Transition 165, 178, 181, 333	White as a frame for colour 192, 315
,, from Gothic to Renaissance .. 65, 202, 204	White-line work 91
,, from plain glazing to painted grisaille .. 139	Winchester 407
Tree of Life (the) 370	Window plane (the) 242
Triforium windows 284	Window shape (effect of, upon design) 113, 211, 212, 240
Troyes .. 32, 366, 401, 112, 148, 149, 151, 228, 246	Windows (how to see) 380 *et seq.*
,, (museum) 211	Wine press (the) 368
,, (private collection) 207	Workmanlikeness 244
,, (S. Jean) 241	Workmanship (Early) 330
,, (S. Martin ès Vignes) 230, 47, 169, 170, 255	Yellow stain 52
,, (S. Urbain) 31, 108, 114, 226	York 147, 192, 277, 387, 146
	,, (All Saints) 371, 36

Note.—*The name of a town without mention of a church may be taken to mean that the glass is in the cathedral or principal church.*

THE END.

BRADBURY, AGNEW, & CO. LD., PRINTERS, LONDON AND TONBRIDGE.

www.ingramcontent.com/pod-product-compliance
Lightning Source LLC
Chambersburg PA
CBHW022059300426
44117CB00007B/517